DATE DUE			

Felix Frankfurter
A TRIBUTE

Felix Frankfurter
A TRIBUTE

Edited by

Wallace Mendelson
University of Texas

REYNAL & COMPANY
New York 1964

One could read everything that he has written—a formidable task from several points of view—and still have little more than an inkling, if that, of why this man has evoked in so many such passionate devotion and exercised for half a century so profound an influence. I can think of no one in our times remotely comparable to him. . . .

DEAN ACHESON

Contents

Contents

Felix Frankfurter
A TRIBUTE

Introduction

Democracy is a device that insures we shall be
governed no better than we deserve.
                                        —BERNARD SHAW

Behold, I do not give lectures or a little charity,
When I give I give myself.
                                        —WALT WHITMAN

The most important thing about a man is his philosophy—especially if the man is Felix Frankfurter. The professor who left
Harvard for the bench in 1939 was generally considered a liberal (in some quarters even a radical). Since then he has been
deemed a voice of conservatism. If in fact the apparent change
occurred, its impact upon history must have been profound. For
during most of his years as judge four of his colleagues were
dedicated liberals: Justices Black and Douglas at first with their
brothers Murphy and Rutledge, later with Warren and Brennan.
Added to theirs, Mr. Justice Frankfurter's vote would have
meant a libertarian majority, and presumably a death sentence for
most cold-war security, and related, measures.

In fact, however—unless I am steeped in error—F.F.'s basic
outlook did not change. In private life he was, and is, one of the
great liberals of our day. But it is crucial in his philosophy that

1

a judge's private convictions are one thing, his duty on the bench quite another. This was the teaching of Holmes. By failing to heed it, the proprietarians among the "nine old men" destroyed the old Court—just as the libertarians might have destroyed the new one, if they had had enough votes to do so. Whether as professor or judge, whether with respect to liberty or property, F.F. is skeptical of government by the judiciary. The judge's job, as he understands it, is to decide "cases" and "controversies," not to create a brave new world—the legislative function having been given to others. For him, even in the realm of civil liberty the essence of government by the people is government by the people—not a nursemaid who lets the children play if they behave.

> As society becomes more and more complicated and individual experience correspondingly narrower, tolerance and humility in passing judgment on the experience and beliefs expressed by those entrusted with the duty of legislating emerge as the decisive factors in . . . adjudication.

It is not that F.F. loves liberty less, but that he loves democracy—*in all its aspects*—more. The difficulty is that both individual freedom and majority rule are indispensable in the democratic dream. Yet neither can fully prevail without destroying the other. To reconcile them is the basic problem of free government. Chief Justice Stone put it briefly:

> There must be reasonable accommodation between the competing demand of freedom of speech and religion on the one hand, and other interests of society which have some claims upon legislative protection. To maintain the balance between them is essential to the well-ordered functioning of government under a constitution. Neither is absolute, and neither can constitutionally be made the implement for the destruction of the other. That is where the judicial function comes in.

Mr. Justice Frankfurter cannot believe or pretend that reconciliation is achieved via wordplay with clichés like "liberty of contract" or "freedom of speech." The single-value, conditioned reflex gives him no respite from the painful process of judgment. The bent of his mind is inductive; he is a seeker, not a professor, of truth. And so, recognizing that First Amendment freedoms merit special respect, he cannot dismiss the fruits of popular government with a presumption of invalidity. In short, he starts with problems, not with answers. For he knows with Holmes that his own "certitude is not the test of certainty"— that when legislatures disagree with him they may be right. It follows that judicial intrusion upon the extrajudicial processes of government is permissible only in accordance with that ancient tradition of restraint which all American judges have professed—when their varying "preferred place" values were not at stake.

It is ironical that he is now condemned by some for the very quality that won him a seat on the bench: respect for the legislative way of life. It is even more ironical that for essentially the same approach which earned Holmes a liberal reputation, Frankfurter is now deemed by some a conservative. What has changed, of course, is the relative liberalism of Court and legislature. But in F.F.'s view the people's representatives are due the same deference, be they liberal or conservative. Obviously he sees as an abiding democratic principle what some find merely a gambit in the great game of power politics.

One need not insist that the Justice has never fallen short of his own goal. For surely his defections are few, and it may be that—except for Learned Hand—he has left more choices to the people than has any other great modern judge. Plainly he finds the crux of the democratic process not so much in its immediate legislative product as in the educative and tension-relieving role of the process itself. A generation ago he wrote:

3

> In a democracy, politics is a process of popular education—the task of adjusting the conflicting interests of diverse groups . . . and bending the hostility and suspicion and ignorance engendered by group interests . . . toward mutual understanding.

To frustrate these pragmatic political accommodations by judicial absolutes is to impede our chief device for maintaining peace among men who are deeply divided—sometimes even in their conceptions of right and wrong. Moreover, "holding democracy in judicial tutelage is not the most promising way to foster disciplined responsibility in a free people."

Obviously F.F. cannot accept what Barbara Ward Jackson calls the "Marxian miasma": the belief that the greater the centralization of authority, the more infallible it becomes. For him, the basic principle of American government is still the dispersion of power. That is why, as Professor Jaffe has observed, he "is forever disposing of issues by assigning their disposition to some other sphere of competence." It was in this spirit that Mr. Justice Brandeis said, "The most important thing we do is not doing." Some call this abdication (when their "preferred" values are at stake). So be it then: "abdication" in favor of "the exhilarating adventure of a free people determining its own destiny."

Plainly F.F. has always been uneasy with judicial supremacy —whether with respect to personal interests called property or those called liberty. Of course the people may go wrong (whatever that means ultimately). Yet in his view, "to fail and learn by failure is one of the sacred rights of a democracy."

Here, for me, is the crux of the matter. Behind all the subtle complexity of his jurisprudence—as suggested in some of the essays that follow—lies a patient confidence in the people. Every element of his being rejects what Professor Berman calls the "underlying assumption" of Soviet law: that "the citizen is not a mature, independent adult . . . but an immature, dependent child or youth. . . ." And so from first to last, Felix Frankfurter has been wary of judicial efforts to impose JUSTICE on the people—to force upon them "better" government than they are able at the moment to give themselves. It is his deepest conviction that no five men, or nine, are wise enough or good enough to wield such power over an entire nation. Morris Cohen put it bluntly: If judges are to govern, they ought to be elected.

How could F.F. not trust men in general when he has such capacity for discovering and cherishing the unique endowments of every individual within his ken—from chauffeur to statesman, from housemaid to philosopher? Indeed, perhaps his greatest talent is the talent for bringing out the best in others (which is not to say that he has never inspired the worst). If, as some believe, he has too much confidence in government by the people, the "fault" may be a function of his own amazing success in human relationships. Yet F.F.'s devotion to popular government is not naïve. He knows the wisdom of Santayana's observation that "If a noble and civilized democracy is to subsist, the common citizen must be something of a saint and something of a hero. We see, therefore, how justly flattering and profound, and at the same time how ominous, was Montesquieu's saying that the principle of democracy is virtue."

For those who have not more directly experienced it, this volume may give a hint of F.F.'s capacity for friendship and the impact of his personality. In a limited way, I am a unique witness on this point—for only I know with what acknowledgments of gratitude and indebtedness so many undertook to contribute their essays. Surely Reinhold Niebuhr spoke for many when he said that F.F. is "the most vital and creative person I have ever known." And from another segment of the intellectual world Archibald MacLeish has said that "Posterity may or may not take our word for it that Felix Frankfurter had more influence on more lives than any man in his generation."

WALLACE MENDELSON

Presentation of
American Bar Association Medal

Annual Dinner, August 15, 1963

Citation

Mr. Justice Frankfurter: Immigrant to these shores as a boy, educated in our public schools and institutions of higher learning, you were marked for distinction from an early day; master of spoken and written English; devoted to the ideals of democracy, public service and the reign of law; student, scholar and teacher of law; analyst and master of our polity and of its roots in the history of the common law; student of our constitutional system, federalism and the role of the courts; writer of perception and precision on the law and kindred subjects; outstanding member of our profession, which has been called "the highest political class and most cultivated portion of society," and Justice of the Supreme Court of the United States.

We of the American Bar Association, in recognition of your contributions as a teacher, scholar, public servant, lawyer and judge, confer upon you the highest accolade within our power. We wish you happiness in the years to come. May you reflect with satisfaction on your full life and tasks well done in the highest traditions of the Bench and Bar.

Acceptance by Mr. Justice Frankfurter

"We live by symbols."

With such boring frequency am I wont to quote this phrase which Mr. Justice Holmes was fond of using that at length Mrs. Frankfurter was driven to reply, "I wish Holmes had never said that." Yet a good epigram, unlike a good treatise, cannot be bettered. I use it unashamedly again tonight. For the academic procession which marked these proceedings is for me a deeply significant symbol—a symbol of the long and honored tradition of the bar that the law is a learned profession.

My regret that I am unable personally to share this occasion with you is mitigated only by the fact that my place is taken by Mr. Phil C. Neal, my friend since his student days at the Harvard Law School, now the Dean of the Law School here at the University of Chicago, worthy successor to many distinguished predecessors. I have asked Mr. Neal to express my profound appreciation to President Smith, to the Board of Governors of the American Bar Association, and to all who are present here tonight, for the honor conferred upon me. I am enduringly grateful for this stamp of approval which you place upon my life's devotion to the various roles in which I have tried to serve our mistress, the law. If you will forgive the presumption of a self-appraisal, I cannot but feel that the surest claim I have to this distinction is the intensity with which I have attempted, throughout my years at the bar, the podium and the bench, to share in the work of preserving the aspiration of lawyers to learning—the aspiration to meet those high standards which the traditions and demanding methods of the common law impose upon the legal profession.

I am not unmindful that it has been said, indeed, I sometimes confused the podium and the bench—interrupting with abrupt cross-questioning the prepared speeches of lawyers who argued before the Court, a few of whom, it seemed to me, had in the press of business made their whole preparation by memorizing their briefs on the Washington plane. I have never resented this criticism, partly because it was true, partly because I have felt that, however different the functions which they serve, the law's own peculiar methods of searching inquiry were by no means different for the judge, the professor, the lawyer, the legal scholar, the student of the law. In my first conference as a member of the Court, I remember that that great Chief Justice, Charles Evans Hughes, in replying to some remarks of mine, several times called me "Professor Frankfurter." Catching himself at last, he began apologetically to retract the term. I stopped him, saying, "Please, Mr. Chief Justice, don't apologize. I know of no more honorable title than that of Professor." Yet I may say that the title which Mr. Justice Brandeis reminded us was the rightful one of the lawyer—Counselor at Law—is not less honorable.

Judge, scholar, counselor at law, student (and we are none of these things who are not students), all are pledged to a common service as instruments of our civilization. Dean Pound has most compactly described the service: "Civilization involves subjection of force to reason, and the agency of this subjection is law." If law is to have a strength adequate to the task, the widest learning—constant cultivation of the legal mind by exposure to every subject of human investigation—is requisite. Thus only

can those through whose decisions the law emerges escape shal-
lowness, oversimplification, too quick acceptance of uncritical
formulas which, by plating the mind against self-examination,
impair its capacity for reasoned judgment.

Elihu Root put the same thought somewhat differently when
he spoke of the public service of the profession of the law. By
this he meant to express not only the obvious fact that lawyers
tend to dominate our American public life, but also that, as
lawyers, they are under solemn obligation to bring to the gov-
ernance of that public life the reasoned, disciplined, surface-
dissolving inquiry which is the method of the law in its finest
tradition.

Mr. Root was one of the first three recipients of the American Bar Association Medal. You may imagine with what humble
pride I recall that the others were Mr. Justice Holmes and my
beloved Professor Samuel Williston, that artist of the classroom
whose great writings went abroad and took the whole profession to school. The early award of the Medal to three such
men has enhanced even the great worth that it derives naturally
from the Association which bestows it.

Thank you for it—for this symbol of our common dedication
in the law.

The Humanity of this Man

Dr. Henry A. Murray,
Professor Emeritus, Harvard University

For a long-standing friend and venerator of Mr. Justice Frankfurter, an invitation to join the advocates and witnesses here
assembled to testify as to his character and accomplishments is
cause for jubilation in the marrow. But then, for a long-standing
friend and venerator of this enthralling man, what a cruel thing
it is to be informed that one must limit what one has to say to a
mean square foot of print! With hordes of lively images of
meetings with this horn of plenty and scads of partial aperçus
and waves of unabated gratitude and wonder mounting in my
mind and crowding forward to the gates of utterance, I would
rather be called upon to offer a thumbnail sketch of the history
of the United States than to choose out of this mob of memories one incident, one deed, one critical reaction, which, di-
gested into words, would adequately convey the pervasive spirit
of this man's variegated life. Among his numerous close friends
are poets and storytellers whose gifts entitle them to try to con-
cretize the general by portraying the wide wonder of his nature

in a single episode. But certainly to this endeavor a psychologist, dealer in abstractions, must close the valves of his ambition. And furthermore, since the law has been the sun around which this learned man's planetary system of ideas has perpetually revolved, and since my ignorance of the law has never been relieved, my status has always been that of an outsider to the dominant establishment. As a result—and here at the outset this should be made plain—I have nothing in my mind, nothing at all to tell, about Mr. Justice Frankfurter. My part, perforce, will be confined to the submission of one metaphorical hypothesis about the nature of F.F., more or less on the assumption that F.F. contains the Justice, and not that the Justice contains him.

The hypothesis is simply this: that someplace in the soul of F.F.—not far from center, I would guess—is a compass of sensitive vitality whose magnetic needle can be counted on to point with unexcelled precision to indubitable human worth in whatever man or woman this may happen to reside; and in addition, that it is largely by this compass that he has, subconsciously and consciously, steered his course since boyhood, in moving as he often did—with a surplus of unembarrassed outbound energy at the instant disposal of a sharply focusing intelligence—from one human environment or social circle to another.

A subhypothesis is that this compass, this herotropic compass, if you please—in-built by the industry of an elect minority of genes and subsequently perfected by a procession of experiences in the world—played an indispensable part in the education of F.F. Indeed, the precocious development of his intellect and personality up to the age of thirty, let us say—when he and Mr. Justice Holmes became fast friends—might well be cited as a spectacular illustration of the efficacy of the "habitual vision of greatness," as Whitehead put it, in promoting and molding the formative processes that mark the progress of a genuine education. What I am stressing here as relevant to the unusual career in learning of this marvelously mature and mellow man is the great extent to which it was encouraged by the sight, rather than by the vision, of a plurality of ideals rather than of one, and of ideals that were not solely in his mind and divorced from all impurities, but out there, embodied in the character, deeds, and sayings of numerous remarkable human beings, who, defective as they may have been and been perceived by him to be in some respects, were nonetheless, to use his words, "men of stature and depth and quality in great things." And what is most noteworthy is that these cynosures were men whose hearts and minds he captured, sometimes at first sight, and thenceforth grappled to his soul with hoops of steel.

Some have tried and some will try again to tell us how it was that this enchanter—this ebullient and disciplined, gay and fiercely serious, tough and tender, idealizing realist, merger of rationality and passion, with no passports from his background —could, as Holmes bore witness, walk deep into the heart of the citadel of so many fastidious older men. Eventually someone may be granted a full revelation of this mystery. It is my part to suggest but two determinants of the quickness and deepness of these affinitive encounters, the first being that herotropic compass in F.F.'s soul with its finely discriminating needle of admiration which would never respond to anything trivial or commonplace, but only to evidences of authentic human excellence. And second, in conjunction with that compass, we should not fail to emphasize the mastery of language which enabled F.F. to translate messages from his magnetic needle into apt and pithy words, to be delivered with exuberance, or with gentle subtlety and tact, or sometimes by innuendo, at exactly the right moment. In various insightful and felicitous reactions of this nature, untainted by candied compliments or any gross and global stereotypes of flattery, as well as in F.F.'s telling eyes and laughter, the older man could plainly apperceive with what immediacy some valid portion of the best in him had been delightedly discovered and bountifully appreciated without a trace of insincerity or envy. This, in most instances, I would guess, has been the initiating open-sesame to the shared awareness of affinity at the core of being and so to the weaving of the bonds of friendship between the older and the younger man. Whether this surmise is strictly true or not, F.F. is certainly one of this era's greatest recognizers and admirers of what is unequivocally most lovable and valuable in human nature; and this is no mere pinch of honor, for (to extract a sentence from a trenchant paragraph by Thomas Mann) "admiration is the best thing we have; yes, if I were asked what emotion, what reaction to the phenomena of this world, to life and art, I considered the finest, happiest, most constructive, most indispensable, I should answer unhesitatingly: admiration."

During F.F.'s renowned years of teaching at the Harvard Law School, his compass was pointing not so exclusively to achieved stature in certain older men but more often than before to women and to younger men, especially to indications in his students of intellectual promise combined with idealism, rectitude, and zest. Within a few years the dependability of that compass had become an acknowledged fact in Washington, and F.F. was not infrequently called in to serve as a kind of one-man selection board for this or that position in the government. (With a percentage of bull's-eyes that is quite enough, I must admit, to disjoint the nose of a professional psychologist.) By this time, as we well know, F.F. was a firmly stationed cynosure himself, a courageous, unpretentious, charismatic "older brother figure" (rather than a "father figure") for an ever expanding circle of talented young men in league with a better future for their country, young men who had come "to believe in great things" because this great apple of their collective eye believed with fervor in great things.

FELIX FRANKFURTER—*A Tribute*

What is most astonishing, possibly unparalleled, about F.F.'s galaxy of exceptional "best friends" of all ages, sorts, and statuses is that for years the number of them has been beyond reckoning, even by him perhaps, but at any rate, in striking contradiction to the estimate of the mostly introverted Henry Adams: "One friend in a lifetime is much; two are many; three are hardly possible." What has made the difference? Has F.F.'s interest in human beings, his quest for mettle and fraternity, been more avid and untiring? his magnetic needle more acute? so accurate that subsequent disillusionments were rare? Or have his bestowals been more spontaneous and copious? his demands less selfish? Or has he been more tolerant and forgiving? less vulnerable to the ravages of wounded vanity? Has a greater capacity for caring made him more devoted, more assiduous in keeping up the circulation, the flow of animated commerce, in the once-established cords of fellowship? Or has his psychical metabolism been proceeding all these years at a continuously higher rate, uninterrupted by reductions of available energy, catnaps of attention, or sluggish meanderings of fantasy, with the result that he has lived more than two average human days in every one of his, and so had all the time he needed to be both great in the circumference of his generosity and great in his profession? Or, as a last question, was the degree of intimacy which Henry Adams had in mind reserved by F.F. for his love's center, his beautiful wife, Marion, whose mysterious inwardness of spirit provided the balancing complementary pole to his expansive openness? The scope of my role does not include consideration of the partial answers to such questions, which are contained in certain perceptive essays by members of his inner circle: the vivid portrayal, for example, of F.F. as "The Loving Spirit" in that memorable little masterpiece by Dean Acheson in the *Harvard Law Review*, 1962, 76, pages 14–16. Pertinent to my theme, however, are a few additional comments to be made relative to F.F.'s practice of the fine art of fructifying conversation.

A distinctive feature of F.F.'s style of discourse is the agile and unerring way he has of entering the realm of his interlocutor's experience and competence and finding within that realm fertile areas of mutual concern. He never crams his own preoccupations, pressing as they may be, into indifferent or unknowledgeable ears. To be sure, he is a teeming hive of hardly containable mentations, pretty nearly always on the point of bursting, but it is dialogues, not monologues, that he relishes—especially the give-and-take of timely information and evaluative judgments, of seminal ideas and illustrative anecdotes, as well as brisk dialectic duels, and mixed with any one of these, salty epigrams, witty repartee, outbursts of laughter, and here and there a dash of badinage. And since for him it is no whit more blessed to give out a gem of thought than to receive one (seizing it for later usage with an explosion of appreciation), he is a sharp and hopeful, sometimes even patient, listener, alert as a prospector to the faintest glint of precious ore. And whenever he intuits the existence of some shy, concealed facility, he smokes it out, or creates an atmosphere so conducive to its exercise that it emerges and flowers in his presence. In short, he is not only the discoverer, recognizer, and appreciator but also the educer, generator, and nurturer of veritable human assets. The answer, then, to those who contend that most of his swans are geese is simply that in *his* contagious presence all of them (but one) *are* swans, geese though some of them may be in the company of others. And then, in this connection, who has tallied up the perennial parade of geese whose brains, hearts, and probity have been weighed and found wanting in the scales of this veteran connoisseur of character?

There are certain signal moments in the course of our habitually prosaic lives when a plenitude of feeling, be it sorrowful or joyful, gives rise to a felt need for equivalent words as vehicles of expression and communication; but all too often the need is distressfully defeated by the ineptness of our fumblings for articulate creation. We are simply unable to represent either the particularities of the evoking situation or the distinctive nature and degree of our emotion in a form that, at the least, will satisfy us or, at the most, will save the integrity of that experience from the oblivious drift of time. Privately paralyzed and frustrated at such a moment by our own ineptitude, some of us, whether seized by grief, despair, love, compassion, or exultation, are prone to turn for sustenance to cherished passages from literature, perhaps most often to the poets of Biblical and of later days. But when the given emotion or given sentiment is shared by a large number of our fellow beings and the occasion is public—a festival, anniversary, or memorial service—and no traditionally prescribed readings, sacred or secular, are appropriate or sufficient, we have nothing to depend on except the possibility that the timely genius of some living man, an alchemist of language, will prove equal to the office of giving consummate utterance to what is resident in each of us. Now, in line with my thesis at this point is my impression that over the last three decades, at those times when it could be confidently predicted that the demands of the assembled company for a suitable and eloquent expression of their thoughts and feelings would be most exacting, their intolerance of the slightest grating touch of grandiosity, bathos, or banality most acute, it was F.F. who was elected more often than any of his countrymen to perform this magic for them all. Surely he has had no rivals, or but very few, when what was most profoundly wanted by those forgathered in the name of an eminent and revered man was a candid and inspiring celebration of just those extraordinary virtues and achievements which most deserved commemoration.

In tributes and testimonies of this sort, on the level of distinction sustained by those that have been published in *Of Law and Men*, F.F. has offered for the envisagement of younger men, now and in the future, various casts of greatness illustrating particular aspects or varieties of the incessantly perpetuated and forever evolving ancient and ageless myth of the hero. In short, throughout the era when our most gifted and seductive dramatists, novelists, and poets have been conspiring to convince us that life is meaningless and man is of no account—hollow, powerless, contemptible, and absurd, dead to this world and to its future—F.F. has been incessantly extolling and exemplifying the exact opposite, and thereby, in consonant deeds and words, has proffered for our appraisal what might well turn out to be the very antidote and remedy for the duress and desperation that is now at large.

And so to end with a summary of my thesis regarding one constituent of F.F.'s multifeatured personality as manifested outside the sphere of law: The needle of his compass has never pointed steadily to anything in the sky, to anything transcendent or to any absolute, or to anything in the natural environment, or to anything in the distant past or distant future. For him, the magnetism has resided in the stuff of the ideal incarnate in human character, in the very best that operates in man, especially when stretched and tested in face-to-face engagements here and now. For man is the maker of all deities, inventor of all abstractions, builder of all laws, and from first to last, the measure of all things, the very meaning of the earth. And so to man let us restore the flown-away values and ideals, in order that these essences and powers may participate in his existence and the quality of human life—the intensity and warmth, the breadth, depth, and elevation of each occasion—may be most creatively enhanced.

A Man for All Seasons

Sir Howard Beale, *Australian Ambassador to the United States of America*

Early in 1962, before Mr. Justice Frankfurter resigned from the Court, my wife and I persuaded him to go with us to New York to see Robert Bolt's play about Sir Thomas More, *A Man for All Seasons*.

It is a superb play: beautifully written; poignant, but with much humour; dramatically satisfying; and uplifted by Paul Scofield's fine acting in the role of More. I can still see the Justice, sitting between us in the darkened stalls, leaning forward to catch and savour the choice words and luminous phrases that came across the footlights.

One passage in the play I remember especially, and it was, appropriately enough, about the law. At this particular point More is Lord Chancellor—the head of the judiciary and a most powerful person—and his daughter, Alice, and her prospective husband, Roper, are protesting because More will make no move to arrest one Rich, who, although pretending to be a friend, is preparing to change sides and become a dangerous enemy.

18

ALICE   While you talk, he's gone!

MORE   And go he should if he was the Devil himself until he
         broke the law!

ROPER   So now you'd give the Devil benefit of law!

MORE   Yes, what would you do? Cut a great road through the
         law to get after the Devil?

ROPER   I'd cut down every law in England to do that!

MORE   Oh? And when the last law was down, and the Devil
         turned round on you—where would you hide, Roper,
         the laws all being flat? This country's planted thick
         with laws from coast to coast—man's laws, not God's
         —and if you cut them down—and you're just the man
         to do it—d'you really think you could stand upright
         in the winds that would blow then?"

At the end of this passage the Justice could not contain himself. "That's the point," he kept whispering to us in the dark,
"that's it, that's it!"

On the trip up to New York we had a drawing room on the
train. With the idea of conserving his energies a little, we suggested that he should lie down on the settee and sleep while we
sat in the chairs. We should have known better. After much
argument he did at last consent to occupy the settee, but that
was about all. Throughout almost all the journey he talked: a
sparkling stream of comment, quotation, reminiscence, argument, mischief, wit, and wisdom. Occasionally he would lie
back and shut his eyes; but then he would be up again, stabbing
the air in our direction with his finger, developing some new
line of thought, or giving some new twist or illustration to what
he had been saying. We certainly covered the water front that
afternoon.

There are many who have known the Justice much longer
than I have, for we did not meet until early in 1958. Before that

he was only a name to me. But it was a famous one: the champion of Sacco and Vanzetti in the twenties; professor of law at the celebrated Harvard Law School; adviser to President Roosevelt in the days of the New Deal; the friend of my Prime Minister and my Chief Justice; the author of various books and articles which came my way; and the Frankfurter J. whose judgments I had occasion to read from time to time.

So as soon as I arrived in this country I called on him, and we seem to have been engaged in a sort of semicontinuous dialogue ever since. Sometimes it has been in his chambers at the Supreme Court; sometimes at the embassy; or in his chaotic study at the old house in Georgetown, where Matilda and Ellen were constantly feeding us with their own cunning and delectable versions of kidneys sauté or fricasseed tripe, for which they soon discovered I had an indecent weakness.

One of the things that strikes one most about the Justice is the enormous range of his knowledge and interests. Not just his great legal erudition, which is to be expected, but many other things as well: the classics; music; his insight into American political and social history, and into British (and, surprisingly enough, Australian) parliamentary and political affairs; what Gladstone said on such-and-such an occasion, and so on. He remembers everything. One time I told him an anecdote about John Stuart Mill. He listened to the story, laughed at the right place, and then said, "It wasn't John Stuart Mill, it was Herbert Spencer."

And then there is his modesty—I almost said his damnable modesty. Most men, as they grow older and have increasing achievements to their credit, become at least a bit egotistical (some of us, alas, do this before we are old and without any particular achievements to our credit at all); but not so the Justice. From his manner you would never know that he is a great jurist, respected throughout the English-speaking world; that he has been the friend and confidant of Presidents and statesmen; and that eminent men from many countries consider it an honour to visit him. He has what Shakespeare, in the words of Henry V before Harfleur, called "modest stillness and humility" (but without the stillness, of course).

Perhaps best of all, there is his wonderful generosity of spirit: outgoing, considerate and—yes—loving. Watch him with children, or listen to what those who have worked for him say about him, and see their faces light up when they speak of him. He can be critical and even caustic at times, but he can never be mean.

But he can be grave and very severe. For instance, where matters of public duty and high principle are concerned, he makes no concessions whatever. I do not doubt that this is why he is held in such high regard by so many who have never met him. Much of his life has been lived in the public eye—in his various crusades, at Harvard, in government, by his writings, and on the bench—and the things he has said and the causes he has fought for have by no means always been popular. Yet from the beginning the American people have known—have felt it in their bones, so to speak—that he, their servant, was always *true*.

Bolt took the title of his play from a contemporary description of More written by one Robert Whittington for Tudor schoolboys of the day:

> More is a man of an angel's wit and singular learning; I know not his fellow. For where is the man of that gentleness, lowliness, and affability? And, as time requireth, a man of marvellous mirth and pastimes; and sometimes of as sad gravity: a man for all seasons.

This was written more than four hundred and thirty years ago, and things change, so we are told. But what I have been trying to say is that Felix Frankfurter, too, is "a man for all seasons."

Felix Frankfurter at Oxford

Isaiah Berlin, *Oxford University*

I first met Felix Frankfurter in, I think, the first or second week of the autumn term of 1934 at Oxford in the rooms of Roy Harrod in Christ Church. I called on him one afternoon in October, in order to return a book. I was followed into the room by Sylvester Gates, then a lawyer in London, whom I knew; he was accompanied by a small, neat, dapper figure, who was introduced as Professor Frankfurter. His name, I am ashamed to say, was then scarcely familiar to me: I vaguely connected it with the New Deal and Mr. Roosevelt, but in no clear fashion; but this may merely be evidence of my own provincialism and lack of acquaintance with world affairs. I do not know whether the impending arrival of Felix Frankfurter as visiting Eastman Professor had caused a stir in the Law Faculty at Oxford, but I can testify to the fact that his visit was otherwise unheralded. Visits by eminent professors from foreign universities were not unusual at Oxford, then as now; and no matter how distinguished, such visitors were not, and are not, lionized; indeed, at times too little notice is taken of them. (Whatever the sociological explanation of this phenomenon, it is one that brings relief to

22

some and much chagrin and disappointment to others.) At any rate, when I was introduced to Professor Frankfurter, I wondered about his identity and attributes. I knew Gates to be a man of exceptionally fastidious taste—indeed, one of the cleverest, most intellectual, and civilized men I had ever met; he had brought a friend—a professor of law, doubtless distinguished in his own field, and that was all. Within five minutes, however, a conversation sprang up, about politics, personalities, Mr. Stimson (whom the professor evidently knew well), Sir John Simon, Sacco and Vanzetti, the Manchurian invasion, President Lowell and his behaviour to Professor Harold Laski, to all of which the unknown professor contributed with such vivacity, and so extraordinary and attractive a mixture of knowledge and fancy, that although I had not intended to stay, I listened (although I am, by nature, liable to interrupt) in a state of complete and silent fascination. After an hour or so an urgent appointment did finally force me to leave, without giving me an opportunity of enquiring about who this remarkable personage might be. A few days later he dined at All Souls, which was my own college. His host on this occasion was, I think, Geoffrey Dawson, the editor of *The Times*, and one of the most influential political figures in England in his day. By this time I had discovered the identity of the remarkable stranger, nor was there, at All Souls, any way of avoiding this knowledge: Dawson and his circle (he had invited guests and got his friends to do so also) looked on Frankfurter, as I perceived, less as an academic figure than as a man of influence in Washington, an intimate friend and adviser of the President of the United States, and a man whom it was for obvious public reasons evidently desirable to cultivate. He responded to this treatment with the greatest naturalness and lack of self-consciousness. I do not suppose that he disliked being made an object of such attention—it was not surprising at All Souls, which, at that time particularly, was a meeting place of a good many persons prominent in public life, among whom there were some very powerful men, but he did not display the slightest sign of grandeur, did not pontificate, did not speak in that measured and important fashion which often characterizes the speech of one eminent person conscious of discussing affairs of state with other, equally weighty figures. He talked copiously, with an overflowing gaiety and spontaneity which conveyed the impression of great natural sweetness; his manner contrasted almost too sharply with the reserve, solemnity and, in places, vanity and self-importance of some of the highly placed persons who seated themselves round him and engaged his attention. He spoke easily, made his points sharply, stuck to all his guns, large and small, and showed no tendency to retreat from views and political verdicts some of which were plainly too radical for the more conservative of the public personages present; they were hailed with the greatest approval by the majority of our generation of fellows— then very young—who formed the outer circle of Frankfurter's audience, and were divided from most of their elders by irreconcilable differences of view on most of the political and social issues of that day—Manchuria, the "Bankers' Ramp," Fascism, Hitler, unemployment, slumps, collective security (Abyssinia and Spain were still to come). After something like two hours of talk on grave issues, Frankfurter cast a sharp look round the room and decided to make a break for freedom. Fidgeting visibly, he rose from his chair and made as if towards the table on which decanters of whisky and brandy and small chemist's bottles of seltzer water stood in rows. But long before he reached it—he was evidently in no need of artificial stimulation —he almost literally buttonholed a junior fellow who looked lively and sympathetic, and engaged him in frivolous conversation of some sort. Dawson, Simon, Lionel Curtis, and other mandarins tried to bring him back to great Anglo-American issues. In vain. He would not be detached from this junior fellow—I think it was Penderell Moon—who was afterwards to play so original, fearless, and admirable a part in India, and insisted on involving himself in some purely intellectual controversy that was clearly of no interest to the statesmen. Presently he drifted over into the corner of the room where the junior fellows were talking among themselves. Here he behaved with so gay, childlike, and innocent a warmth of feeling, and talked with such enjoyment of, it seemed, everything, that the young men were charmed and exhilarated, and stayed up talking with him until the early hours of the morning. Whenever I met him at dinner elsewhere in Oxford, I observed the same phenomenon: a certain amount of firm cultivation of him by those who felt it their right and duty to be talking to him as a representative of influential American circles in the law or government; the same polite but unenthusiastic response by the Eastman Professor; apparent unawareness on his part that some people were much more important than others; of affectionate familiarity in his dealings with everyone, which lightened the atmosphere in the most portentous milieux and delighted those who were young and observant. Oxford in the twenties and early thirties was stiffer, more class-conscious, hierarchical, and self-centred than it is now (it may, of course, be only because I was young that I think so—but there is, I believe, a good deal of objective evidence for this too), and Felix Frankfurter had an uncommon capacity for melting reserve, breaking through inhibitions, and generally emancipating those with whom he came into contact. Only the genuinely self-important and pompous resented this, and they did so most deeply. I heard Maynard Keynes, who was himself a famous and merciless persecutor of pretentiousness and humbug, and a considerable expert on the subject, accord recognition to Frankfurter as a master of this craft: indeed, he said that he placed him first among Americans of his acquaintance in this respect, although he supposed that Holmes had been even more formidable and less inclined to mercy. Indeed, Frankfurter had his blind spots. He was a genuine Anglomaniac: the English, whatever he thought of their public policies, individually could do little wrong in his eyes. It needed a great deal of stupidity, wickedness, or personal nastiness or rudeness on an Englishman's part to arouse unfriendly sentiment in Felix Frankfurter's breast. In general, he liked whatever could be liked, omnivorously, and he greatly disliked having to dislike. Everything delighted him: the relations of one ex-military fellow of a college to another; C. K. Ogden's attitude to London restaurants; unequal success in the wooing of their academic hosts achieved by various German exiles then in England and the socially ludicrous consequences of this; Salvemini's deflation of the late Professor Harold Laski's rhetorical homage to Burke; his own progress in London and Oxford. His sense of the ridiculous was simple but acute, his enjoyment of incongruities irrepressible. He was not what is known as a good listener: he was too busy; like a bee, carrying pollen from an unbelievable number of flowers (and what seemed to some mere weeds), he distributed it and caused plants which had never been seen to do so to burst into sudden bloom. The short memoranda, several lines long, scribbled in pencil, and often accompanied by cuttings or offprints, stirred pools that had not been known to move before; this social gift he displayed to the point of genius. But to return to Oxford. Those who were sensitive to status, and suffered from fears that their own might not be adequately recognized, and dreaded irreverence in all its forms, complained of the Eastman Professor's unseasonable frivolity, his lack of taste, his noisy laughter, his childishness, his Americanisms, his immature enthusiasm, his insensitivity to the unique qualities of Europe in general, and Oxford in particular—a lack of *gravitas*, a deliberate defiance of the genius of the place—and so on. These strictures were certainly groundless: our guest did not practice irreverence for its own sake. He admired Oxford, if anything, too deeply and devotedly, and with a sensibility that exceeded that of his critics. He understood what there was to understand. If he struck sharp notes occasionally, he did so intentionally, and they were not discordant in the ears of most of those who turned out, in the next quarter of a century, to be the bearers of the central traditions of Oxford, and of much of the intellectual life of England both before and after the Second World War. I do not know what impact he made on Oxford lawyers or the undergraduates who went to his lectures. So far as I and my friends were concerned, his genius resided in the golden shower of intellectual and emotional generosity that was poured forth before his friends, and liberated some among them who needed the unlocking of their chains. Whenever, during his first and subsequent visits, I met him at dinner in colleges or private houses, the same phenomenon was always to be observed: he was the centre, the life and soul of a circle of eager and delighted human beings, exuberant, endlessly appreciative, delighting in every manifestation of intelligence, imagination, or life. He was (to use the phrase of a man he did not like) life-enhancing in the highest degree. No wonder that even the most frozen monsters in our midst responded to him and, in spite of themselves, found themselves on terms of both respect and affection with him. Only the vainest, and those most "alienated" (a term then not in common use) from their fellow men, remained unaffected by his peculiar type of vitality or positively resented it. Attitudes towards him seemed to me a simple but not inadequate criterion of whether one was in favour of the forces of life or against them. I do not intend this as a moral judgment, or a judgment of value at all: there are moral, aesthetic, and intellectual qualities of the rarest value which seem incompatible with a positive attitude to life; I mean this distinction only as a statement of fact.

FELIX FRANKFURTER—*A Tribute*

He came to us twice again, once on a purely private visit, once to receive an honorary degree, and the welcome in each case from his friends and the friends of his friends was justifiably rapturous. I recollect no particularly memorable observations or epigrams by him, or about him, then or at any time, but two occasions stand out in my recollection as characteristic. One was a dinner party in Christ Church. I cannot now recollect who was host—perhaps it was again Sir Roy Harrod. All that I recollect is that a charade was acted by some of us after dinner, and such was the degree of vitality infused by the guest of honour that the acting (if I remember rightly, it had something to do with a jealous eighteenth-century French marquis and his peccant wife) became passionately expressive. I shall not reveal the identities of the actors; they have all attained to celebrity since. Felix applauded the performance and egged the actors on until the realism of the actors reached a maximum degree of intensity. I do not think I shall ever forget the expressions on the faces, the gestures, the inflections of voices on this extraordinary occasion. For Oxford dons—the most self-conscious, inhibited human beings in an already intensely self-conscious and inhibited society—to have broken out of their prisons to such a degree was something that only the most potent force could achieve—an elixir powerful enough to break through the most sacred spells. This liberating power seems to me evident in all Felix's dealings, from the most intimate to the most public, ever since the beginning of his career. Oxford, made by nature and art to be the greatest possible obstacle to this force, proved it indeed to be literally irresistible.

The second occasion is one that he mentions himself in his reminiscences: a dinner party held by him and his wife[1] at Eastman House, then situated in Parks Road, attended among others by Sylvester Gates, Freddie and Renée Ayer, Goronwy Rees, Maurice Bowra, and one or two others, including, I think,

28

the famous expatriate Guy Burgess,[2] who was then staying in Oxford, and was pursuing a profession about which we were not clear—I think he published a city letter of financial advice, or something of the kind—at any rate, he was excellent company and, in those days, a friend of mine and of several of the others present. It is alway difficult to convey to others what it is about a particular occasion—particularly a private one—that makes it delightful or memorable. Nothing conveys less to the reader or (rightly) nauseates him more than such passages as "How we laughed! Tears rolled down our cheeks," or "His irresistible manner and his inimitable wit drew gusts of merry laughter from us all! How happy we were then, so young, so gay, such high spirits! How little did we see the shadows gathering over us all! How sad to reflect on the subsequent fate of X.Y.Z.! What a summer it was, etc." The evening, terminated, as Felix himself reports a little inaccurately, in a bet between Freddie Ayer and Sylvester Gates about whether the sentence of the philosopher Ludwig Wittgenstein "Whereof one may not speak, thereon one must preserve silence [*Wovon Man nicht sprechen kann, darüber muss Man schweigen*]" occurs once or twice in his *Tractatus Logico-Philosophicus*. Freddie said that he could only have said it once. He was then sent in a taxi to consult the text in his own flat in the High Street, and came back to report that Wittgenstein had indeed, as Gates maintained, said it twice, once in the introduction and once in the main body of the text, and paid ten shillings' forfeit. Why was this so memorable? Only because the mixture of intellectual gaiety and general happiness generated at this and other dinner parties was too uncommon in so artificial an establishment as the University of Oxford—where self-consciousness is the inevitable concomitant of the occupations of its inhabitants—not to stand out as a peak of human feeling and of academic emancipation. Courage, candour, honesty, intelligence, love of intelligence in others, interest in ideas, lack of pretention, vitality, gaiety, a very sharp sense of the ridiculous, warmth of heart, generosity intellectual as well as emotional—dislike for the pompous, the bogus, the self-important, the *bien-pensant*, for conformity and cowardice, especially in high places, where it is perhaps inevitable—where was such another combination to be found? And then the touching and enjoyable Anglomania—the childlike passion for England, English institutions, Englishmen —for all that was sane, refined, not shoddy, civilized, moderate, peaceful, the opposite of brutal, decent—for the liberal and constitutional traditions that before 1914 were so dear to the hearts and imaginations especially of those brought up in Eastern or Central Europe, more particularly to members of oppressed minorities, who felt the lack of it to an agonizing degree, and looked to England and sometimes to America—those great citadels of the opposite qualities—for all that ensured the dignity and liberty of human beings. That which has sometimes been taken for snobbery in Felix Frankfurter—a profound possible misreading of his character—was, in fact, precisely this. His feeling for England was subjected to strain during the troubles in Palestine: he was a stouthearted Zionist, and his conversations in Oxford on this topic with the late Reginald Coupland—the principal author of the Royal Commission's report, which to this day is the best account of the Palestine issue of its time— are still unrecorded. Coupland frequently remarked that Frankfurter had taught him more on this subject than the officials instructed to brief him and had doubtless made enemies by the courage and candour of his views. His part in this, like his contributions to the law, his influence on the policies of the New Deal, his work in United States government departments before he became professor, his advocacy of Sacco and Vanzetti, his public life and influence in general, may be worthier of comment and commendation than the personal qualities upon which I have dwelt here. But it is these last, and not the attributes which made him important to the leading political men in England by whom he was assiduously entertained, that made their deepest impact upon the academic community in Oxford—the subject to which I had elected to confine myself.

No one had ever captivated so many unlikely and resistant members of an apparently forbidding fortress so swiftly. Obituaries often refer to the deceased's "genius for friendship." Not the dubious quality indicated by this cliché, but an unrivalled power of liberation of human beings imprisoned beneath an icy crust of custom or gloom or social terrors—this seems to me to be Felix Frankfurter's rarest single personal gift. It was this that penetrated our defences—ramparts that have kept out and needlessly frustrated many a good and interested and intelligent and well-intentioned man.

Felix Frankfurter

Jean Monnet, *Economist*

I am honored to be able to say that for many years Mr. Justice Frankfurter has been my very good friend.

When he retired from the Supreme Court, many of those who paid tributes to him claimed that over the years he had changed from a liberal into a traditionalist. This was not so. It is the times that have changed, not he. Throughout the years that I have known him, his fundamental beliefs have remained firm.

His conception of the role of the Justice is deceptively simple, but it is very profound. He has always believed that the duty of a judge in a democratic society is to interpret the law without partiality or prejudice, because the law is the expression of the people's will. Whatever his own feelings, they must not deter him; nor must the pressure of political expediency stand in the way of justice and democracy. Only thus, through the supremacy of laws and institutions, can civilized society be built, developed, and freedom preserved.

It would be a mistake to believe that great men of law are men without passions and allegiances, emotionless and aloof. The secret of Felix Frankfurter's greatness lies in the depth of his passion for liberty. This is no cold and abstract virtue.

He once declared:

I do take law very seriously, deeply seriously, because fragile as reason is and limited as law is as the expression of the
institutionalized medium of reason, that's all we have standing
between us and the tyranny of mere will and the cruelty of unbridled, undisciplined feeling.

It is a measure of Felix Frankfurter's stature that this incisive
master of words and ideas, this brilliant and colorful contro-
versialist, should thus have conceived his own role as Justice
in terms of self-abnegation.

In a letter to me, Felix Frankfurter once wrote: "I try never
to forget Justice Holmes's admonition that 'the mode by which
the inevitable comes to pass is effort.'" He was referring to the
effort to unite Europe—to create for nations laws and institutions
such as unite individuals in civilized society. But his words
apply equally to his own devoted efforts as Justice. They never
faltered, and I know with what heart searching and regret he
laid down his office. In his judgments and speeches he has built
a monument which deserves to stand among the classics of
American democracy.

We in Europe are engaged in building a democratic United
States to take its place with the United States of America as
an equal partner for freedom and peace. Often in the past, in
times of trouble or success, I have been encouraged and inspired
by my friend Felix Frankfurter—by his firmness, his deep
optimism, his trenchant common sense.

In a speech he made shortly before his retirement he affirmed
once more his deepest faith, reminding his hearers that the
United States "has been built on trial and error, distrusting
all absolutes." It was in the same spirit that he had written in
one of his most famous judgments: "The mark of a truly civilized man is confidence in the strength and security derived
from the enquiring mind." Such a man is Felix Frankfurter.

Trips to Felix

Garson Kanin, *Playwright*

I never knew Professor Frankfurter of the Harvard Law School, and Associate Justice Frankfurter of the Supreme Court of the United States was a figure as awesome as his title, but Felix is my friend. He laughs at my jokes, even when they are feeble, disapproves of my far-out neckties and notions, chats with me on the telephone until our wives make us stop, answers every letter, and shares my problems. That he is some thirty years my senior has only now occurred to me. Felix is everyone's contemporary.

To most men whose lives are bound up with the law, the theatre world in which I live and work is a rocket ship journey away, but Felix has made himself part of it, as he has with so many worlds within the world. For years I gave him a subscription to *Variety*, which he read completely and with enormous interest. Why should motion picture grosses in Dayton, Ohio, interest him? Simply because everything does. Everything, that is to say, which concerns activity, aspiration, and creativity.

His subject is human beings; not in the abstract, nor in the mass, but one by one. Each individual who comes within his

ken is a creature to be studied, observed, and above all, understood. In Felix's life there are no strangers. Upon being introduced to someone, he makes the comfortable assumption at once
that he and they are, and have been for some time, members
of the same nonexclusive organization.

Ruth Gordon, as my wife-to-be, brought him into my life.
(What a dowry!) She and I were a wartime romance and had
tacit marriage plans. When, where, and how remained unan-
swered questions until a series of coincidences brought us both
to Washington, D.C., for the same two-week period—she,
playing in Chekhov's *The Three Sisters* at the National Theatre; I, on an army assignment to the OSS. The fates appeared
to have spoken. We decided to wait no longer. Felix approved.
Moreover, he volunteered to perform the ceremony. The day
before it was to take place, he phoned to convey some dismay-
ing news. He had learned that, although an Associate Justice
of the Supreme Court of the United States, he was not em-
powered to officiate at a marriage.

"But why not?" I asked.

"Because," replied Felix, "it's not a federal offense."

Across the years I have had the good fortune of spending
many hours with him. Because my memory is poor, and because
I wished to preserve the essence of these rare times, I have
habitually written down the gist of our meetings.

Let my part of this collection, then, be a sampling of some
of these notes.

Newman and the "ands." In the midst of our discussion tonight
about style in writing, R. asked F.F. whom he most admired
as a user of the English language. F.F. replied that although it
was difficult to single one out, John Henry Newman came to
his mind. When R. asked why, F.F. went to his bookshelves,
took down a volume, leafed through it swiftly, found a passage,

and read it aloud, with relish. He pointed out the way in which Newman had used the word "and" as a serial connection. Most English teachers, he said, working by the rule book, would have thought all those "ands" unnecessary, and would have suggested commas instead. "All right," said F.F., "let's see." He read again, eliminating the "ands," showing how the force had been weakened. The repeated use of the little word had given a mounting poetic feeling to an otherwise bland section. The English lesson ended. I noted that the demonstration had excited him.

F.F. said today that he knows of no attitude more rare than that of disliking a man and, at the same time, admiring his work.

Data. The basis of knowledge and wisdom, says F.F. "You've got to take it in," he cries. "You've got to look for it and find it and take it in. You can't get it by sucking your fingertips."

Discussing ———, F.F. says, "He has brains, but no sense."

He says, "The mode by which the inevitable is reached is effort."

I could have kicked him today. He was talking about C. C. Burlingham, one of his special heroes. "He is a man of great age, as you know," said F.F., "and he gave me the most valuable advice I have ever had on the subject. Long ago he said to me, 'You'll do well and live long if you take care to remember that the forties are not the thirties; that the fifties are not the forties; that the sixties are not the fifties, and so on and so on. Do you see? One thing more: form the habit of lying down for an hour before dinner every evening.'"

I look at the old F.F., spry as a puppy, and say, "Well, it certainly has worked for you, hasn't it?"

"Me?" says F.F. "I've never done any of it. I haven't the time!"

He says, "My views on capital punishment are well known. I am unalterably opposed to it. However, I would like to reserve its use for a single crime: that of picking up a brand-new book and cracking its binding when opening it."

Holmes. He talks of the early Justice Holmes. "In those days," F.F. reminds us, "the Court did not sit in the Supreme Court building, but in the Capitol. Holmes would walk home—in all sorts of weather. He did this until he was well into his eighties. He used to stop and pay a short call every evening on Henry Adams, who lived on the site of the present Hay-Adams Hotel. Holmes recalled that as time went by he found himself stopping in only every other day, then only once a week, then once a month, until he stopped going entirely. He explained why. 'I find that my energies are too depleted by Henry Adams' sterile skepticism.'"

F.D.R. He tells of visiting F.D.R. in 1933. It was on the eve of F.F.'s departure for Oxford. F.D.R. said, "Well, I probably won't be seeing you for a year now, so before you go, have you any word of advice?"

"Yes, Mr. President," said F.F. "It's this. If you don't develop an opposition pretty soon, I advise you to go out and buy one."

Scholarship. He talks this morning of his first American days, of landing at Ellis Island at the age of twelve, never having heard or seen a word of English. He began to go to school. He recalls a teacher—Miss Hogan, who used to chastise offending pupils with a simple uppercut. She ordered his classmates to refuse to listen to him if he spoke German, and thus he began to learn English. He found his way to the reading room at Cooper Union, not in search of education, but of warmth. The Frankfurters inhabited a cold-water flat, and Cooper Union was heated. It was here that he formed his still firm habit of devouring newspapers and periodicals of all kinds. He went on to high school and began to work toward one of the scholarships for the Horace Mann School, which were being offered by Joseph Pulitzer. When the term ended, the principal sent for F.F. and informed him that, although his marks had been exceptional, he had just missed winning one of the scholarships. There had been an unusually large number of outstanding pupils that year. The principal went on to explain that since F.F's record was so good, they could offer him an education at the Horace Mann School at half tuition. F.F. points out that this was a considerable concession—the tuition for the year being two hundred and fifty dollars. The training at Horace Mann was outstanding, and the graduates favored in job opportunities. It became a family problem. His father was barely managing to make ends meet, and the decision was finally made not to take on the added burden. After all, he could go to C.C.N.Y. for nothing, and that is what he did. He looks out of the window and there are tears in his eyes as he goes on.

"Think of it," he says, "if I'd won one of those damned scholarships I would not have had this grand life I have had. I wouldn't have gone to the Harvard Law School. Horace Mann people went to Columbia. And that's where I'd have been when Henry Stimson asked the Dean of the Harvard Law School to recommend some bright young talent, since he couldn't afford to pay them much. And the Dean sent me down to work for Henry Stimson—the beginning of everything for me. Why, if I hadn't gone to Washington at that time, I wouldn't have met and married Marion. . . . Working for Stimson, I was paid seven hundred and fifty dollars a year. In money, that is. I was paid much more than that in life."

Movie. At four o'clock this afternoon we took him to the Trans-Lux Theatre to see *Anatomy of a Murder*. He had read the book, and since Joseph Welch (who appears in the film) is his former student, he had a special interest. He sat through it all at the edge of his seat, riveted. During the trial scenes he continually whispered comment, most of which was too technical for me. At the climax, a dramatic surprise, F.F. jumped out of his seat, pointed at the screen, looked at us, and shouted, "You see, he broke the first rule of cross-examination! Never ask a question to which you do not know the correct answer."

Fanny. He tells us tonight of how Justice Holmes and his wife reacted when he announced that he was going to marry Miss Marion Denman. He had, on an earlier occasion, brought Miss Denman to call. She had made a most favorable impression upon them, especially upon Justice Holmes, who had a singular appreciation of beautiful women. The first meeting was gay. Holmes told a slightly risqué story. F.F. reminded him, teasingly, that Miss Denman was a minister's daughter, whereupon Holmes threw out his arms, lifted his head to the ceiling, and cried, "Blessed be the Lord, for I have done some little harm today!"

Some weeks later, when F.F. announced to the Justice that he was going to marry Miss Denman, Holmes jumped up and shouted for Fanny. "Dickie!" he called. "Dickie bird!" (F.F. gets up at this point to give a brilliant imitation of Mrs. Holmes coming into the room. She was old and infirm and moved without lifting her feet from the floor.) As she came in, Holmes said to F.F., "Tell her! Tell her!"

"I'm going to marry Miss Denman," said F.F.

Fanny said nothing, but turned and slid out of the room. He and Holmes thought this behavior odd. Somewhat embarrassed, they went on talking about other things. All at once,

Fanny returned. She held out her fists and asked F.F., "Which do you think she would like? This?" She opened one fist, revealing a piece of jade. "Or this?" She opened her other fist, which contained a piece of amber. F.F. pointed to the amber and said, "This, I think." Fanny handed it to him, turned, shuffled out of the room, and was seen no more that day.

Nervous. F.F. kept using the word "nervous" today, and I began to think that it meant something different from what it does to me. I asked, "When you say a person is nervous—what do you mean, exactly?" He thought for a moment. "Why, a nervous person," he replied, "is a person who makes other people nervous!"

Courtesy. He gets on the subject of courtesy and stays on it too long for me. Finally I say to him, somewhat impatiently, "Oh, what the hell's so important about courtesy?" He fixes me with one of those cool looks and says, "Courtesy, my boy, is the lubricant of life."

Reference. He is constantly diving into reference works. One afternoon I chide him about this and, hugging a volume of the Britannica to his breast, he says, "All right, some people, like you, make things up and others, like me, have to *look* things up. What about it?"

Shrewd. A language discussion today begins with the use of the word "shrewd." "Lincoln," says F.F., "was a shrewd man. He was shrewd politically."

"Are you criticizing him?" I ask.

"Of course not. When I say 'shrewd,' I mean that he was *shrewd*." F.F. frowns in thought and says, "I remember once describing Jesus Christ as shrewd. Marion raised hell with me about it. Yes. We had a bitter disagreement. Oh, well. That was twenty-five years ago. More."

"I think Marion was right," I venture. "The word 'shrew' is certainly not complimentary in any sense."

F.F. bristles. "But what's that to do with 'shrewd'?"

"Two forms of the same word, no?"

"Of course not," he insists, and we are off into the dictionaries. Small ones, large ones, and the tremendous Oxford with its cross references. He finds an essay on the word "shrew" and reads it aloud. He is astonished to find that a man can be a shrew, and that it has to do with small animals, ferrets of some kind. Now it leads to the word "shrewd," a form of the word "shrew." He looks at me. "Imagine you being right," he says.

We get on to other words. He says there are some he cannot bear. He calls them "tired words," used so much that they have lost their meaning. He explains that he is constantly at his clerks to avoid these in preparing briefs. He laughs as he relates that it has become a custom for his departing clerks to leave a memorandum for the incoming clerks about: ". . . all my eccentricities, and idiosyncrasies, and peculiarities, and each clerk finds new ones, and by now I suppose it must be an enormous, fat file, because there have been about forty clerks, and each one has doubtless discovered *something!*"

He is troubled by "lawyers' language," as when they speak of "the thrust of an argument." He dislikes the words "seminal" and "impact." Worst of all—"semantic." The other day a counsel answering a challenge from the bench said, "Oh, well, that's just a matter of semantics." F.F. snapped down, "Of course. All our work, our whole life, is a matter of semantics, because words are the tools with which we work, the material out of which laws are made, out of which the Constitution was

41

written. Everything depends on our understanding of them. So it's useless to say, 'Oh, well, that's just a matter of semantics.' "

The illness. He tells us that on November 24, 1958, his physician, Dr. Walter Bloedorn, was doing a routine checkup. F.F. had been having some unimportant pains, but had done nothing about them, since he knew that this examination was forthcoming. When it ended, the doctor said, "Well, I'm afraid we're going to have to go right over to the hospital."

F.F. said, "I see. Do you suppose I'll have to be there for a while?"

"Yes," the doctor replied, "I expect you're going to have to be there for *quite* a while. . . . I'll get an ambulance."

"Is that absolutely necessary?" asked F.F. "I have my Tom downstairs. Couldn't he take us over?"

"All right," said the doctor.

They got into the car and drove to the hospital, where they met with Dr. George Kelser, who advised a confirmation of the tests. F.F. said to Dr. Bloedorn, "I'll ask only one favor. That you go over and explain this situation to Marion, so that she doesn't have to get it on the telephone or in the wrong way." The doctor agreed. F.F. said, "Look here. I want to ask you fellows something and I'll be guided by your opinion and advice in the matter. Do you think I should sit down right now and write out my resignation from the Court?"

Dr. Kelser said, "No, no."

Dr. Bloedorn said, "No, there's no need for you to do that."

F.F. said to Dr. Kelser, "Now it would be impossible for you, Doctor, ever to know anyone more ignorant of the structure and function of the human body than I. I don't understand anything about what's happening. I'll do exactly what you tell me. I'm placing myself in your hands because I simply don't know.

But let me ask you, am I now, as a result of this, permanently damaged?" He laughed as he added, "Is there, in fact, going to be a crack in the golden bowl?" Dr. Kelser smiled and said, "Oh, dear me, no. It's nothing like that at all." He went on to explain the coronary occlusion, the reasons for the bed rest, and for the various medications, explaining that nature was going to create a new channel to take the place of the one which had been dammed. This might take some time, but when it had been accomplished, he would be as good as he was before, perhaps better.

Recalling it now, F.F. is gay and says it all worked out precisely as they had said. "I'm planning to live as long as Charlie Burlingham." He chuckles. His friend C. C. Burlingham lived to be one hundred and one years old.

Shaw. F.F. tells about an encounter with George Bernard Shaw. A dinner at Lady Astor's, followed by a debate. F.F. says, "I can't report it honestly without seeming immodest, but I must tell you that I made mincemeat of him." He smiles. "Of course, he made the mistake of choosing the wrong subject—the American Constitution."

He quotes A. E. Russell as saying, "I believe that experts should be on tap, but never on top."

The hospital. He is sitting up, gay and larky, the center of his small, new world of doctors, nurses, orderlies, and other lives.

He tells us that he is writing two books.

"How?" I ask.

"In my head, of course," he replies.

F.F. asked Dr. Kelser, "Now what lesson can I draw from this occurrence?" The doctor replied, "None. There's nothing that you did or didn't do on the day it happened, or on the day before, that brought it on. It would have happened anyway. Maybe earlier, or later, or while you were asleep. But you had nothing to do with it." F.F. was astonished. "Do you mean to say that nature is as capricious as that?"

Dr. Kelser: "Yes, Mr. Justice, just as capricious as that."

Hackett. F.F. looks at me tragically and says, "You know that since I saw you last I've suffered a severe blow. A severe blow." Something about his fixed expression conveys that he is about to pop a joke, so I play straight for him and say, with mock solemnity, "Oh, yes, I know."

His voice cracks as he adds, "I've lost my beloved friend Francis Hackett." It is not a joke, after all. F.F. is shattered. He insists that Hackett died of a broken heart, of a massive frustration involving his play *Anne Boleyn*. A rich American dilettante had promised to produce it in America, and the Hacketts, in need of money, counted heavily upon it. F.F. says, quaking, "That man—that louseboob—broke every single promise he made, and betrayed my friend." He is far more disturbed by Mrs. Hackett's difficulties than he is by his own. Felix.

Audree. He has turned this hospital room into his sort of laboratory, where he studies men and women. He looks out of the window as he says, "I have had a serious experience here." I assume that he is speaking of his attack, but it turns out otherwise. "You saw that nurse who went out a while ago? The tall, pretty, blond one? Audree? We've been spending many hours here together, and I've had an opportunity to find out a great deal about her life. She is a devout Catholic. Look here. I have spent a good deal of energy attempting to avoid prejudice. But the dogma of the Catholic Church or of any other denomination, for that matter, has always put me off. Now this girl, this

44

Audree—I have never known generosity of such quality, nor such rare kindness. Oh, yes, far, far beyond duty. Overwhelming courtesy. And I have been asking questions, delving into the matter, trying to discover the wellspring of such superior behavior." He sits up and leans forward. "Do you know what it turns out to be? Can you guess? Simply this—a practical application of her Catholicism. I've never known anyone who practiced a religion, whose everyday life is based upon a religion as much as this girl's is." He leans back and smiles, as he continues. "I told Dean about this. Remember he's the son of an Episcopal bishop, and Dean said, 'Well, that's a damned sight more than can be said for you and me, Felix.' "

Eichmann. I say to F.F., "Ruth came down today because she especially wanted to see you, but I came to ask an important question." He looks at me, ready. I have often seen that open, poised expression on his face, watching him on the bench. "The Eichmann execution," I say. He nods immediately. I continue. "I know that you are opposed to capital punishment, yet you supported the legality of Eichmann's capture in Argentina, and of the trial itself. Now. Does your stand on capital punishment obtain in this case?"

F.F. begins slowly. "I don't know what my views would have been or what position I would have taken had I been called upon to decide whether or not to prosecute this man. The idea of a death sentence in this case is meaningless, because one does not, cannot, mete out punishment for a crime such as his. There is no punishment imaginable which would be commensurate with the crime committed."

I remind F.F. that a delegation of forty or fifty Israeli scholars, scientists, artists, and intellectuals, led by Martin Buber, called on the President of Israel in an attempt to get him to stay the execution. F.F. jumps at this and asks, "Really? Are you sure? Did that happen? I had not heard." He is pleased by the news, even though the appeal was unsuccessful. It seems to him important that such an effort was made.

The attack. Later, at the house, Marion tells what happened this time. She blames it on "that damned wheel chair." She means the chair in which he works in his chambers in the Supreme Court building. It has ball-bearing casters on it so that it can be moved about easily. She believes it to be a bad chair, causing him to work in cramped positions. Working away, he slumped over and fell onto the floor. Fortunately, Mrs. Douglas happened to come in. She found him lying there, mumbling, but could not make out what he was saying. She called Tom and the first-aid man at the Supreme Court building. They lifted him onto his couch and sent for Dr. Kelser, who arrived in about ten minutes. He gave F.F. some glycerine tablets and other emergency treatment, then went with him in the ambulance to the hospital. A second doctor, Bloedorn, went to the house to inform Marion. She says he did it badly and gave her a shock. She reports that he clasped his hands together tightly and said, "The Justice can't do *this* any more." She has been to the hospital three times. F.F. calls her every evening at seven.

The book. We talk about *Felix Frankfurter Reminisces.* Marion tells us that F.F. insisted on the royalties going to the editor. She says, "You know, Felix has always had this strange antipathy toward money. He's always trying to think of some reason not to take a fee, or an honorarium, or a payment. He feels victorious when he avoids money. I suppose he has a feeling that there's something wrong about making money."

The hospital again, after two weeks. There has been a depressing deterioration. It may be that we were expecting too much, but last time we found him sitting up in a chair, chipper and jovial.

This time he is flat on his back. He looks pale and fatigued. He lacks energy. His rate of speech has slowed, and the volume of his voice has dropped several decibels.

There is a photograph of Marion on a table a few feet below the foot of the bed, placed there so that he can see it easily. "One of the nurses," he says softly, "spoke of Marion's beauty." Several other people have done so, and Justice Harlan, who has been visiting Marion regularly, reported to F.F. that she looks more beautiful than ever before. F.F. tells this to Marion on the telephone.

Marion: "Well, people come here and then they leave and say foolish things."

F.F.: "Why do you call that foolish? I think you're *very* beautiful."

Marion: Well, you're getting quite foolish too."

F.F.: "Marion, you must learn to face the truth even when it's pleasant."

He talks about the orderlies here. Again his concern with the individual human being. He describes the ones who come in each morning for the routine of bathing, changing, moving him from the bed, getting him up, and so on. He refers to them with enormous appreciation and affection. "These two young Negroes who begin each of my days now—" F.F. says. "Let me give you a measure of these men. They came in this morning and one of them said, 'It's only sixty-three degrees outside, Justice, so it'll be a nice day for your wife.'"

There is talk of Holmes today and of Mrs. Holmes. F.F. mentions the great admiration which William James had for her. This reminds me, and I say teasingly, "Those James letters you recommended. Thanks. We've been searching for them everywhere and it turns out they've been out of print since 1920." He bristles slightly and says, "No, no." I give him my information:

"A two-volume edition published in 1920, edited by Percy Lub-bock—out of print. There's been a more recent one, a single volume of selected letters, and we've ordered it. Anyway, why do you want us to read them?"

He thinks for a moment before replying. "After you have, you'll know why. They're very fine and they have importance." He pauses. "There is one he wrote to his sister. She was ill. It was serious. Heart, I suppose. Cancer, perhaps—and she was suffering. And he wrote, telling her that if at any time she felt that she wanted to put an end to it all, she would be justified in doing so and why. It's a marvelous letter." He pauses, and says suddenly, "They were not edited by Percy Lubbock, but by his son, Harry. When you go to the house, go into the sitting room, and on the bookshelves on the left-hand side over by the window you'll find a lot of biographical material, and among the William James books you'll find these two volumes of letters. I'll let you cart them off if you like—if you promise to return them. Thin blue books," he adds. I protest that it would be too great a responsibility to have them and to worry about returning them. "No, no," he says, "take them."

Later in the day, at the house, I go downstairs and make my way to that familiar room, now bereft, sad, deserted, and there on the neglected bookshelves, exactly where he said they would be, are the two books. We take them back to the hotel and read them, each of us one of the volumes. Very late that night we see what he meant.

R. asks him about his earliest American theatre memories. He thinks hard before he says, "I suppose it must have been the Irving Place Theatre, run by that fellow Conreid."

I say, "Yes, Heinrich Conreid, who later directed the Metro-politan Opera Company."

He regards me. "How would you know *that?*"

He is fascinated to learn that one of my classmates at the American Academy of Dramatic Arts was the granddaughter of Heinrich Conreid.

He looks at the ceiling, contentedly, floating in recollection: the Irving Place Theatre . . . plays by Lessing . . . *Nathan the Wise* . . . Nazimova . . . Minnie Maddern Fiske as Becky Sharp and in *The New York Idea*, by Langdon Mitchell. Remembering makes him happy. He reaches out and clutches the air before him as though picking an image from the stream of memory. "I shall never forget," he says, his fist still clenched, "Eleonora Duse taking her curtain call. I don't remember the play—isn't that odd?—nor anything about it, but I do remember the moment when she came before the curtain to bow. She did it with—with—" He wants a certain word. It does not come at once. He struggles for it. Clearly, no other word will do except that one which he has momentarily mislaid. He fights for it. At last it comes. He says it, a syllable at a time. "In-eff-able. She took her bows with *ineffable* charm . . . Another? Forbes-Robertson in *Hamlet*. My!" He smacks his lips. "Unforgettable. His presence, his voice—and when he recited 'To be or not to be'—the accent, the feeling— I shall never forget it."

He says that Archie MacLeish came in to see him a few days ago. Answering F.F.'s question as to his present activity, he said, "I am writing another play. I've been at it for a long time."

"What sort of a play?" asks F.F.

"Well, I suppose it might be described as a patriotic play."

"Good," says F.F. "You couldn't make it too patriotic for me."

R. later observes that what makes this illness so poignant, even tragic, is the fact that of all the people we know, he possesses the greatest zest for living. He appreciates the goods of life, and relishes every moment of being.

He used an odd expression when I asked him if he had seen Alice Longworth recently. "No," he replied, "not since I was stricken."

Solicitor General. F.F. tells of Herbert Swope going down to see F.D.R. in 1932 to urge upon him the appointment of F.F. as Attorney General. F.D.R. took it under consideration, but decided against it. Instead, he offered F.F. an appointment as Solicitor General of the United States, which he deemed more important, even though it does not carry Cabinet rank. "Still," says F.F., "Solicitor General may be the most interesting legal job in the country." F.F. declined, but came to Washington to discuss it with the President. The President urged him to accept, saying, "I want you on the Supreme Court, Felix, but I can't appoint you out of the Harvard Law School. What will people say? 'He's a Red. He's a professor. He's had no judicial experience.' I won't be able to do it. I'd never get it by. But I *could* appoint you to the Court from the Solicitor General's office. So take this job and do it as well as I know you can, and then I'll appoint you to the Court." F.F. remembers that he declined again, saying, "Franklin, I believe it to be a faulty rule of human conduct to take one job in the hope or expectation that it is going to lead to another job."

Further, F.F. points out that he thought there were others who could handle the job of Solicitor General and that he felt it was more important for him to stay up at the Harvard Law School and continue to train young lawyers. (Irony. F.D.R. later did appoint him to the Supreme Court from the Harvard Law School, and although people said precisely what F.D.R. expected them to say, nothing prevented F.F. from being confirmed and from having a long and honorable career on the Court.)

He muses quietly for a few minutes and says, "I've turned down many jobs in my life."

R. asks, "Do you regret any of them?"

His answer is immediate and firm. "No, not at all. Not a one." He looks at her. "There's one job I wish I could have had and — But that one was never offered to me."

"What was that?" asks R.

"Well," he explains, "it would have had to do with meeting *you* when I was a much younger man. When I was still at Harvard."

R. smiles and says, "You wouldn't have considered that a *job*, would you?"

F.F. presses her hand and says, "I'd have *turned* it *into* a job!"

He laughs as he tells us that the physiotherapist who works with him daily constantly says, "Stand tall! Stand tall!" This strikes little F.F. as being immensely comic.

R. asks, "Are you a good patient?" He gives himself an excellent review and says that the doctors assure him that he is the most cooperative, uncomplaining, serious, and respectful patient they have ever known. He says that he does precisely what he is told, without reservation, or qualification, or compromise.

For the third time this summer we go down to Washington to see F.F. An extremely hot day. We find him out in the garden of his house. Ralph, the new orderly (a young Negro with a mustache, bright eyes, and a determined manner), is looking after him.

We start on a high note. F.F. looks well, better than last time, and we tell him so at once. His color is ruddy. We cannot see his eyes because he is wearing sunglasses, but he seems lively. His left arm is in a bandage-like sling, with an odd foam-rubber handle close to the elbow. I ask at once, "What's all that?" The

51

question, I fear, angers him. He replies snappishly, "It's a sling! Haven't you ever seen a sling? What's so remarkable about it? You had slings when you were a boy, didn't you? Well, this is a sling." I notice that the arm is, at present, useless, without mobility. From time to time he moves his left arm with his right.

His flare-up passes and he begins to talk about Ralph, his newest interest and enthusiasm. "I picked him out pretty fast over there at the hospital," says F.F. "An exceptional young man; discreet and courteous and so kind. He carries me into Marion's room every evening. When I expressed some concern as to the difficulty of this, Ralph said, 'No, no. It's no trouble at all. It's a great pleasure to be able to put a man and his wife together.' . . . I said to my nurse the other day, the beautiful one, I said to her, 'Miss So-and-so, I know that a stunning girl such as you are has many beaux and I am equally sure that since you are what you are, they are fellows who come from fine homes and who were educated at Yale and Harvard and Princeton and Johns Hopkins. But I am certain that not one of them has the grace, or the elegance, or the manners that Ralph has.' "

He talks about his new training, about learning again to walk. He points off and says, "You see that railing there? Well, that's where I walk. All this is interesting and important to me. We have to know what we are capable of. It's a matter of learning limits and coming to understand weakness and strength and balancing one against the other. I've never known a more fascinating time. You see, the last time I was learning to walk, I had no awareness of what a remarkable act it is."

On Ralph again. He reports that Ralph said to him, "Now, Justice, would you do something for me?" F.F.: "Of course." Ralph: "Well, when you've got your visitors and it's time for them to go, don't add another paragraph." He laughs and remembers that Marion used to call him "a door-hanger."

"Of course you are," says R. "It seems to me I've spent more time on your doorstep while leaving than I have inside the house."

The President. He has an interesting announcement. This Thursday at five President Kennedy is going to call on him. I gather that he is pleased, but he shifts the focus on to Ralph's reaction. "Ralph," he reports, "has been excited about all this and keeps working on plans for the occasion. Where to sit and how. What to serve and when. He said to me, 'Now we've got to talk about this, Justice. I want to make sure you don't get too excited.' And I said, 'Look here, Ralph, when you've known me longer, you'll know that I'm not the kind of fellow who's going to pee in his pants when the President comes! . . . After all, I've known this young man since he was a kid and I had a good deal to do with his education.' "

Dream. He tells us about a dream he had the other night.
"I found myself in the Middlesex Hospital in London. I sent for David Bruce, our Ambassador there, and for his wife, Evangeline. When they turned up, I said, 'I am in a most embarrassing position. I haven't a shilling, or a dollar either, for that matter. Could you let me have some money?' David says, 'Of course,' and I say, 'Would you please call Marion and tell her of my predicament? The number is Federal 3-4171.' Then I say, 'There are some people I want to see. Would you arrange it?' Evangeline says that she will, and I go on, 'I want to see Pat Devlin—he was on that murder case just recently—the Adams? And I want to see Arthur Goodhart.' "

F.F., digressing, says, "Do you know who Arthur Goodhart is?"

"No," I say.

He begins to talk about Arthur Goodhart, and it is half an hour before he returns to tell the weird end of the dream.

I chide him about his rambling. He laughs and quotes Marion. " 'Felix has only two faults. One, he *always* gets off the subject; two, he *always* gets back on to it again!' "

R.: "Do you sleep well?"

Felix: "Oh, yes, perfectly. I have a bad night now and then—two since I came home—but Ralph says, 'Justice, I'm a young man and I have good health and I have more bad nights than you do.'"

All through this garden visit a neighbor has a hi-fi on about as loud as it will play. A single side is repeated again and again: the overture to *West Side Story*. It booms, it rattles the windows, it irritates me. F.F., when I complain of it, looks at me with some surprise. It does not occur to him to question his neighbor's right.

Ralph is in and out all through the hour. There appears to be anxiety about visitors. We start to leave, but Ellen comes out. There is talk of food, of the difficulty of putting together satisfactory menus. F.F. has lost interest in food. (He, who used to sit with us and devour eight courses with joy, and raise hell when anything was less than perfect.) Now and again, Ellen reports, he gets to hankering after some small thing. The other day she went all over Washington looking for what Felix described as "kosher sturgeon."

Ralph again. Plans are made for the evening. We are to return at eight to visit with F.F. and Marion. A long goodbye. I kiss the top of his head and we are off. For the first time since I have known him, he has let us go without delay. I have the feeling that he is glad to see us go. We are tiring him.

We go to Magruder's to buy champagne, and to the Statler to get a bottle of Chanel Eau de Cologne for Marion. After dinner we return to Georgetown, stopping on the way at Duke Zeibert's restaurant to pick up an enormous strawberry cheesecake. Bearing our gifts, we arrive at the house a few minutes before eight. R. goes up the front steps. I follow a minute later with the cheesecake. At the front door I find her standing in the entry, talking to Ralph. I hear him say, "Yes, I tried to phone you at your hotel." A sudden clench. Something has happened. What? It jig-saws itself together. F.F. had been worn out by the visit in the afternoon, and Ralph explains, "I had to put him out." Marion is asleep. I sense that a façade is being presented, that something else has happened. Whatever it is, there is to be no visit tonight. We leave the gifts. In any case, bringing them is something we do for ourselves more than for them. Ralph continues and reveals a bit more. I began to see what F.F. sees in him. A strong, determined, efficient man. He says, "I see him getting tired out because when he gets tired out, he gets to perspiring—you know, sweating?—up here around on his forehead. I noticed that happening this afternoon. He gets pale sometimes, too. He always wants to do too much. He's one of those. I keep telling him, 'Now you just take it easy, man, because you know this world wasn't made in a day,' and I say to him, 'Now you've been sick, but now you're not sick any more. I know all about that because I've been sick too. And I know what it is to have to convalesce and get better after. You've *been* sick but you've got to put it out of your mind now. You've got to stop thinking about it and put your head on what you have to learn. You've got to just learn to walk again just like a little baby. You're just going to have to learn it. It's only natural that you can't walk after being in bed as long as you've been. It's just something to learn.'" (Ralph talks the right sort of nonsense.)

He continues. "Now I know you're his friends—good friends —so I want to tell you something, promise you something. I'm going to have him walking right back into that court!" He speaks passionately. I wonder if he believes what he is saying.

We have been to Washington again to see F.F. This time our opinions of his condition differ. R. feels that he is greatly improved. My impression is that this is an illusion, caused by his perfected techniques in dealing with his situation.

We spend some time separately; R. with Felix, I with Marion.

Referring to some of F.F.'s current activities, Marion says, "His loyalty is sometimes a curse."

F.F. tells of Dr. Herrman Blumgart questioning Dr. Kelser (in his presence) about the case.

Kelser: "Well, sir, as you see, he has only limited use of his left leg and of his left arm."

Blumgart: "No matter. The world has never counted much on this one's abilities as an athlete."

The remark delights F.F. He taps his forehead and says, "Nothing wrong here, you see, nothing at all." He goes on to say that he now wakes early, thinks his thoughts, and by the time Mrs. Douglas arrives is ready to spill out a flow of dictation.

Marion is concerned about F.F.'s newest preoccupation—making arrangements for his funeral. "It worries me," she says. "I must ask the doctor if this is a common occurrence in these circumstances. In all our years I have never known him to give so much as a fleeting thought to the subject, and now he simply won't get off it. Where. And how. And who. I suppose it's because he has seen so many services botched. It troubles him to think that his may be. But, of course, it's most unpleasant. One of the things that seem to worry him is the religious aspect. He is afraid that somehow there will be prayers or words spoken by a rabbi. He says he wants no such meaningless hypocrisy; that right or wrong, for better or worse, he left the synagogue when he was fifteen and has never returned. He recalls that he sat there one morning, looked about him, and realized that the ritual and the prayers meant a great deal to the others and nothing to him. And he felt that he was desecrating the temple by his presence. So he left and has not returned. He wants the service held here in the apartment, and he wants the list of people invited to be limited, and he knows exactly the sort of ceremony he wants, and above all, no prayers."

When it is time to leave today, F.F. points at me and says, "I want to see you privately for two minutes before you go. In the study." The two minutes turn into twenty. The subject—his funeral. He says, "When the time comes that we must, as Holmes used to say, 'bow to the inevitable,' I want to be certain that what happens is right." He goes on at length, outlining the arrangements. Who is to speak, who is to attend. "And I want *you*," he says, "to see to it that none of my instructions are violated." He gives me a commission to execute in New York with regard to the musical part of the services. I promise a report. Finally he names the last of the speakers.

"Do you know why I want *him?*" he asks.

"No."

"Because he is my only close personal friend who is also a practicing, orthodox Jew. He knows Hebrew perfectly and will know exactly what to say."

Remembering Marion's earlier account, I am astounded. Have I misunderstood? I ask, "Do you mean a prayer of some sort?"

"Well, of course, you nut, what else would he say in Hebrew?"

"Then you do mean the Kaddish?"

He waves me off impatiently. "Oh, I don't know, and neither do you, but *he'll* know and he'll do it beautifully. Let me explain. I came into the world a Jew and although I did not live my life entirely as a Jew, I think it is fitting that I should leave as a Jew. I don't want to be one of these pretenders and turn my back on a great and noble heritage. I don't want to—how do they say it?—*pass!* Like that thoroughly reprehensible—well, never mind. That's why. So there's going to be the Hebrew."

I have been trying to handle all this casually, but all at once my resources fail and I become lightheaded. F.F. looks at me. "What's the matter with you?"

"Nothing. Warm in here."

He grasps my elbow and shakes me. "Look here," he says, "I don't expect any of this to be necessary for a long time. A *long* time," he says. "I simply want it *understood* now. But listen to me. Before I'm in the grave—I'm going to be back on the Court. Did you hear me?"

"You bet," I whisper.

His strong right hand clutches my elbow with uncommon strength. It is painful, but I cannot move away. His eyes are brighter than I have seen them in years, and he is smiling as he says, "I am going to be back on the Court before I am in the grave!"

Let us pray.

To Gather Meaning, Not from Reading the Constitution, but from Reading Life[1]

Francis Biddle, *former Attorney General of the United States*

When I began to think about Felix Frankfurter, I realized how much, over the fifty years during which we had been friends, he had done for me. I am therefore glad to have this opportunity to record my gratitude.

We came to know each other in Washington in the winter of 1911–1912, when he was Law Officer of the Bureau of Insular Affairs, under Henry L. Stimson, who was Secretary of War. Fresh out of the Harvard Law School, I was secretary to Mr. Justice Holmes for one wonderful year. When Professor John Chipman Gray wrote me to offer the position in March 1911, he said to me about his old friend, "Judge Holmes is the most stimulating man to talk law with I have ever known" ("or anything else," he might have added). "I have no doubt that when you left Washington you would be a better-equipped lawyer than when you go there." For many years I did not realize how right he was, or what a great influence Justice Holmes had on my outlook and character. He had even more influence on the life and career of Felix Frankfurter.

The Washington of fifty years ago was still a southern town —feminine, casual, friendly. The First World War, psychologically speaking, was incredible. The town—it did not then seem like a city—has always been clothed in my memory of the spring of 1912 with magnolias everywhere, and after an April shower the wet brick sidewalks catching a shimmer of green. I saw a good deal of Felix, on occasional walks together, and once lunching on Sunday with Robert G. Valentine, the Commissioner of Indian Affairs, at his house, where the quality, as Frankfurter remembers it in his memoirs, *Felix Frankfurter Reminisces*, was without "repressions, or inhibitions, or fears, or timidities, or prudences . . . [in] an atmosphere of intellectual liveliness, governed by curiosity and free and high-spirited talk and lovely ladies." The description stirs memories of Felix over the years—Felix, searching, brilliant; full of his subject; with the exhilarating pull and tug of swift exchange; Felix, restless and ubiquitous, stimulating the rest of us to follow the reach and rush of his mind.

Before I went to Washington, I had never heard such talk, and I was spellbound in this handful of young progressives, not much older than I, who gave me a new outlook and a dawning awareness of the conflicts of American life. At Harvard no one of my crowd was interested in politics, or public service, and we thought President Theodore Roosevelt a bore, and caricatured and laughed at him in the *Lampoon*. But here the mood was humane and searching, and the subjects concrete, clustering around the rift between Roosevelt and President Taft which was swiftly developing in the winter of 1911 and spring of 1912. The ferment of the progressive movement had got into men's minds and would culminate in the split at the Republican Convention a few months later, and the formation of the Progressive Party, which nominated Roosevelt to run against Taft and divide the Republicans in half. Gradually the mild conservatism of my overrespectable past dissolved under the impact of a new and more sympathetic outlook to the political currents of the day.

Frankfurter felt those currents, and described them in his reminiscences when he looked back fifty years later. "This was a very fermenting period in American history . . . a minor renaissance in feeling, if not in thinking, of people who either by age, or by native woodenness of mind, weren't absolutely settled and impervious to the new currents that were floating about, the new needs that were asserting themselves."

Frankfurter was on the threshold of a career that would be devoted continuously to public service, for his twenty-five years of teaching at the Harvard Law School were pointed essentially to that end. He interested young men in the deeper satisfactions of such a life, and trained them to use the tools of scholarship and knowledge that might bring them to live humanely and generously in their own communities. For he taught law as a means to noble ends as well as the satisfactions of private practice. As I have said in my book *A Casual Past*, Frankfurter touched my imagination at precisely the time that I most needed the stimulus of his outlook—prodding, searching, lively—and uninhibited by the types of class prejudices that I had not altogether lost. That his influence was casual and indirect made it more telling, and the moral energy behind it carried conviction.

After Washington we saw each other for a good many years only occasionally, and we were never as intimate again. I remember breakfasting with him at the Ritz in Boston when my wife and I were there for a brief visit—I think it was in 1932—

and his excitement about the extraordinary manner in which young David Riesman had dealt with his first-year law examinations, citing from memory to sustain his answers an armful of cases, many of them reaching back for centuries. There had been nothing like it since Brandeis, with undreamed-of honors, had graduated in 1877. Did we know his father in Philadelphia? Felix asked, and I said yes, he was our doctor, a very great doctor, a great diagnostician.

A few years later I appealed to Felix for help in an effort to prevent the Philadelphia Bar Association from adopting the views of a committee which it had appointed to study the proposed Norris-La Guardia Act. It was correctly believed that the committee would vigorously oppose this effort to limit the federal courts' power to punish indirect contempts without trial by jury. Frankfurter sent me immediately a copy of *The Labor Injunction*, a book recently published, which he had written with Nathan Greene. Armed with such convincing ammunition, I helped to persuade the Bar Association to turn down its committee's report and endorse the bill. In 1931, Gifford Pinchot, who was then Governor of Pennsylvania, managed to get the legislature to adopt a law providing for jury trials in such proceedings, modeled on the federal statute. A court injunction was an effective and time-honored way of breaking a strike by summoning picketers into court and sentencing them for contempt without benefit of jury. A trial court disregarded the statute on the grounds that it was unconstitutional, and sent the miners to jail without trials. Representing the labor union, I obtained a reversal in the State Superior Court, and the Pennsylvania Supreme Court granted certiorari. At that point George Wharton Pepper was taken in to argue the case for the owner of the mine.

The historical research on which Frankfurter's book was based showed that at common law indirect contempts—that is disobedience of the court's order outside of the courtroom—were tried by juries, and only direct contempts, those in the actual view of the court, were immediately dealt with by the judge, to keep order and sustain the dignity of the court. Later, however, star chamber asserted authority over individuals by summary proceedings. But there was nothing sacrosanct about the use of such summary punishment, which, if based on common law, would have been protected by the Constitution. Nor did the Pennsylvania statute weaken the whole judicial foundation of society, as Mr. Pepper loftily argued, sneering at my "dusty fumbling with the year books." The Supreme Court sustained the Superior Court's judgment. I doubt whether I could have won the case without the use of Frankfurter's practical scholarship.

President Roosevelt called me on the telephone early in 1939, just after I had completed my work as general counsel for the Joint Congressional Committee investigating the Tennessee Valley Authority, to say that he wanted me to serve on the Court of Appeals for the Third Circuit until he had an opportunity to appoint Robert H. Jackson Attorney General and me Solicitor General, to take Jackson's place. He added that Jackson and Frankfurter were sitting next to him and were "witnesses to the plot." Senator Vic Donahey, the Chairman of the Congressional Committee, had recommended my appointment; but without Felix's endorsement I doubt whether anything would have come of it. It was typical of him that he has never referred to his help on my behalf.

Nor did he ever comment to me on my arguments before the Court when I was appointed. I suspect that he preferred a more objective approach than mine, laying both sides before the Court and asking them to choose, without too much partisanship—but that was not my way. When, as was the custom, I called on members of the Court immediately after I was sworn in, Felix's advice was simple—know your records inside out, and keep out of politics. As to my assistants—tell A not to drop his voice at the end of a sentence, B to be less discursive, and C —well, C was hopelessly dull, keep him out of the Court. Never pad your argument with make-weights, which tend to dilute the power behind it, stake everything on a single issue. Never underrate your opponent's case. . . . When I began to argue cases, my friend followed up his advice by picking out obscure morsels somewhere hidden in the record, perhaps not referred to in the briefs, and discussing them at some length. "Do you see what I mean, Mr. Solicitor?" he would ask, with an indication that the answer need not be simple or the morsel obviously relevant.

When I was appointed Attorney General, on the eve of our entrance into the war, Justice Frankfurter wrote me that Katherine and I should pause long enough "to hear the kind voice of friends," as Holmes had put it. "In succession," he went on, "you have been called to the two offices of State that excite me most and in which my interest and understanding are longest rooted in experience. . . . Dire days are ahead of you, unless I am a very bad prophet—not only those that are ahead for all of us, but those special demands on one's convictions and affections when one has to be indifferent to misunderstanding of friends and to be uncompromising with one's own insights and convictions and to disregard the wishes and views of those with less insight and less disinterestedness. I content myself with saying . . . that I too should like to express the highest praise that Holmes could give to a friend in your situation—'I bet on you.'"

A characteristic of his warmly enthusiastic nature was his encouragement of friends to embark on new intellectual adventures. When in 1950 I was planning, rather vaguely, an analysis of what seemed to me the obsession of fear and anxiety which had spread its ominous fog throughout America, with results perhaps best described by the single word "McCarthyism," I went to see the Justice for his advice and help. He listened attentively to my outline and then asked me a single question: Had I thought about the similar situation that had begun in England in 1792, under the impact of the French Revolution, and particularly the Terror? I had not. He got up, walked over to a bookcase, and pulled out a slim and little-known volume, *The French Revolution in English History*, by Philip Anthony Brown. "Take it along," he said, "but don't forget how precious it is. You can do something important."

It was exactly what I needed. The Alien and Sedition Acts in the United States had been adopted on the basis of a similar law in Great Britain, but fortunately were not re-enacted when they expired in 1799, and the terror of revolution petered out with the election of President Jefferson in 1800. Brown described the same fear in England, which lasted from the Terror in 1792 to the Reform Bill in 1832, long after the French Revolution had spent its force. Such influences in both countries had striking similarities at different times: laws against seditious talk, sedition trials with inflaming charges by the judges, and outrageously long sentences; obsession with the French and, in America after the First World War, with the Russian Revolution; dismissal of professors who were not critical enough of revolution; fear of the free expression of opinion; the use of loyalty oaths; fear of joining suspected organizations—all of these were curiously similar in each country. I drew freely on Brown in discussing in my book *The Fear of Freedom* the impact of the French Revolution in Great Britain and comparing it with a similar nightmare about the Russian Revolution in the United States.

It was natural that Justice Holmes and Harold Laski should have frequently referred to their close friend, Felix Frankfurter, in that long, exuberant correspondence, and that their reaction should express their individual temperaments. During the early First World War years, when Frankfurter was in Washington as assistant to Secretary of War Newton D. Baker and counsel to the President's Mediation Commission, and Laski was teaching at Harvard, the younger man missed his friend's controversial vitality. "With Felix centred at Washington, Cambridge has departed this life. He attracts everyone there and none will come, far less stay, in this grave of youthful hopes," he writes Justice Holmes in June 1917; and three months later: "Mr. Wilson has charge of foreign policy and Felix seems to sponsor the rest of the government. To my certain knowledge he directs the War Department; Mr. Baker is the pale wraith that Felix casts before him in his progress. . . . He has almost annexed the Shipping Board; there are similar rumours about the Department of Justice."[3] Two years later Laski, still in Cambridge, writes his friend that he is amazed at the barriers Felix has overleaped. "People meet him, and the adjective 'dangerous' melts as the snow before the sun. He is very happy—the students, *bien entendu*, are wild about him."[4]

Laski, knowing how genuinely Holmes admired Frankfurter, and how much pleasure the Justice took in hearing about him from the few who counted and knew what they were talking about, took occasion to quote what Joseph Redlich, who was then lecturing at Harvard, said about Frankfurter in 1921, that "three continuous years in Europe would make him the first administrative mind in America." Redlich "thought that Felix was too big for his environment, with the result that he lacked that precision in the details of thinking which would come from being driven every inch of the way by minds as good as his own."[5] Justice Brandeis said about Frankfurter seven years later that in his judgment he was "the most useful lawyer in the United States."[6]

Holmes shared his correspondent's enthusiasm about Frankfurter, who, he believed, brought fire to his students and invited new adventures. When, following the Russian Revolution in October 1917, a wave of panic began to sweep the country and washed at the foundations of the universities, Holmes heard that there was a move to push Roscoe Pound and Frankfurter out of the Harvard Law School. He wrote Laski, who was teaching at Harvard at the time: "If the school should lose Pound and Frankfurter it would lose its soul, it seems to me";[7] and shortly afterward wrote to President Lowell that they imparted "the ferment which is more valuable than an endowment, and makes of a Law School a focus of life."[8] That was precisely what Frankfurter was doing at Harvard.

But the Justice was not sympathetic to the younger man's "excursions and alarums" (such as the Sacco and Vanzetti case) because he was "so good in his chosen business that I think he helps the world more in that way than he does by becoming a knight-errant or a martyr."[9] That was twelve years before Frankfurter took his place on the Supreme Court, where he abandoned the knighthood and martyrdom for the no less important adventures of a judge. Frankfurter when he wrote a charming little foreword to the two volumes of correspondence may have remembered this reference to himself, for he says of Laski: "The world suffers less from knight-errantry induced by a passion for liberty than from prudence dictated by self-regard."[10] They had both broken lances in the same tournament.

Holmes believed in brevity, particularly in judges' opinions, and often said so in strong language; and knowing his friend's feeling for such an admirable habit, Laski indulged in rather cautious criticism of two of Frankfurter's books. Of *The Business of the Supreme Court*, which Frankfurter had written with James M. Landis, Laski thought that Frankfurter "had broken a butterfly on a wheel in devoting 400 pages to an analysis of what really was worth an article."[11] About *The Labor Injunction*, Laski wrote it was most illuminating, "though rather long and a little over-equipped with the scaffolding of research."[12]

Justice Frankfurter, as has often been said, carried on the tradition and approach of Justice Holmes on the Court. What united the thought of the two men was not their social or political outlook, but the view that each had of the judge's function. Both believed that the duty of the Justices on the great Court was not to act on their personal views and predilections, which they were too apt to clothe with the stately if meaningless language of moral principles. One should have, as Frankfurter has remarked in *Government Under Law* (1956), a "sturdy doubt that one has found those standards." Both were highly skeptical of the use of pat phrases, and distrusted ethical and personal reactions. They accepted "compromises with eternity as the essence of the law" so that they could be left free "to learn the lessons that come with self-inflicted wounds."[13]

Holmes was a Massachusetts Republican, an aristocrat, and a conservative. He shared the ideas that were current at the time he was growing up, some hundred years ago, the ideas of Malthus, of Darwin, of Herbert Spencer. He distrusted modern efforts to improve the world, for he did not believe in the Christian precept to love thy neighbor as thyself, which he thought was the test of the meddling missionary. Yet as a judge he would not interfere with efforts to enact the kind of remedial legislation for which he had little taste, for he was a liberal in the nineteenth-century sense of *laissez faire*, not only in the market place but in the realm of ideas.

In contrast to these views was Frankfurter's progressive outlook, which found so wide a scope during the twenty-five years before he went on the bench. He was a reformer, a crusader for causes (by no means all of them lost), bent on trying to make our American society more sanely planned, more responsive to our needs, more fluid and open. But both men when they sat on the Court shared the same conception of their duties as Justices.

The popular view that the nine Justices are divided between conservatives and liberals is misleading. The difference relates to the conception that a judge has of his own job. Professor Mendelson has admirably described the two current beliefs as to the nature of that role in his discussion of Justices Black and Frankfurter. The one seldom "resists the temptation continually to remedy injustice"; the other practices judicial self-restraint, "and seeks less to obtain final solutions than to establish a tolerable balance of interests."[14]

That Frankfurter, like Holmes, recognized reality and faced it made him see the decisions of the Supreme Court as they really were. The Court was not an abstraction, the Justices made history and affected the nation as much as the other two branches of the government. Their opinions were in substance legislation, where construction of the Constitution or of statutes was concerned. In this connection Frankfurter recites a favorite quotation of John Chipman Gray from a sermon of Bishop Hoadley's: "Whoever hath an absolute authority to interpret any written or spoken law, it is he who is truly the lawgiver to all intents and purposes, and not the person who first wrote or spoke them."[15] Frankfurter is fully aware how deeply "the law of the Supreme Court is enmeshed in the country's history."[16]

He did not believe in the "inevitability in history except as men make it";[17] and never forgot that there was no resort to Congress from decisions of the Justices. It was their moral obligation to approach their work with caution, tolerance, and humility.

Frankfurter taught young men in the law school that government—their government—was but an agent of society. Government would be good or bad according to the esteem in which it was held. He attacked the illusion of simplicity, particularly in dealing with the complex problems with which public servants have to deal in our modern industrial world. After Holmes, Justice Brandeis was the chief influence on his career, especially in those early fermenting years at Harvard when the older man was practicing law in Boston. Specifically, Brandeis interested the young professor in labor problems and labor legislation, then almost nonexistent, so that when Frankfurter joined the government in the First World War he was prepared for his work on the President's Mediation Commission, as assistant to the Secretary of Labor, and as Chairman of the War Labor Policies Board. But these were side shows—during the war the law school had been emptied. He felt himself a teacher, in the large sense of the word, and declined Governor Ely's nomination to the Massachusetts Supreme Court in 1932; and even President Roosevelt's offer to appoint him Solicitor General the same year. Professionally it was the most interesting job a lawyer could have, but he did not want to give himself up completely to being a technical lawyer, and believed he could be of more use to the President by staying in Cambridge.[18] He was happy at Harvard, where he combined academic work with public service to a remarkable degree. He was sending the top honor students to fill posts in the government, particularly during the New Deal, in countless numbers. He was "probably endowed with a gift of spotting talent," as he says of himself, and had at Harvard become "the recruiting officer."[19] He was getting law clerks for Holmes after Gray died, for Brandeis, for Learned Hand, and for Judge Julian Mack, also on the Second Circuit. And he could keep his hand on scholarly work to feed into the consuming furnace of his vitality. *And Gladly Teach*, the title that Bliss Perry gave to his autobiography, would have fitted Felix's had he ever wished to write it.

When finally he went on the bench, he must have missed his

life at the university, sending the young men to Washington, with their ardor for difficulties, leaving "absolutely no stone unturned to make the thing they are at a success,"[20] young men who perhaps did not have the sense of shrewdness and feeling for negotiation that age brings, but with their heads up, and in their hands the sharp tools that the law school had given them, each year graduating a group of the ablest lawyers in the country.

Frankfurter was not always restrained on the bench. Occasionally he would lash out in public at one of the brethren in passionate indignation; and I have no doubt that in conference he would sometimes descend to the vernacular, as Holmes once said of his associates. On the Court he would "gather meaning not from reading the Constitution, but from reading life."

How Justice Frankfurter Got His Spasm

James Reston, *New York Times*

Dr. George A. Kelser, Jr., of Washington said yesterday that Justice Felix Frankfurter had suffered "an acute cerebrovascular insufficiency," and was "resting" in the hospital, but this could not possibly be true.

Judge Frankfurter has never had an "insufficiency" of anything in his life. His problem is not "insufficiency" but over-sufficiency. He has more surpluses than the Department of Agriculture. His difficulty is not a shortage of anything, except maybe size, but too much blood and energy, too many ideas, interests, and opinions racing too fast through too small an area.

What clearly destroys the doctor's medical bulletin is his reference to the Justice "fainting" and then "resting." He has made strong men faint all his life, but he has never done the thing himself, and as for "resting," this is obviously ridiculous. He has never rested, night or day, and he's not likely to start at seventy-nine.

The explanation of what happened to the judge is really very simple: he blew a gasket. He has been doing it all his life, and the reason is clear enough. Every man has some weakness, and Mr. Frankfurter has a weakness for olives and newspapers. He is incontinent about both.

He is not a secret drinker but a secret reader. He has a little second-floor study in his Victorian house in Georgetown, and when his lovely wife, Marion, and his faithful friend Matilda are not looking, he sneaks in there and reads newspapers from all over the world.

What is worse, he thinks newspapers should be logical or at least sensible—an obviously preposterous idea—and over the years this has had certain medical effects on him, which Dr. Kelser did not mention. The judge has taken an overdose of printer's ink into his blood stream. His memory is overdeveloped, and when he reads some particularly outrageous bit of nonsense the ink momentarily clots the blood.

Thus, as Dr. Kelser explained, there can be a "temporary narrowing of blood vessels in the brain, rupture of a brain artery, or blockage of a brain artery by a clot. The Justice is believed to have suffered a spasm, a sudden narrowing of a brain artery, which relaxed before any real harm was done."

Precisely. But it was not an "insufficiency" of blood that did it, but an oversufficiency of ink and nonsense. This city is an intellectual midden of illogical rubbish, and anybody who has ever watched the judge read a newspaper about events in Washington knows that he gets an average of at least one spasm on every page.

Dr. Kelser was no doubt right about one thing. He said that Judge Frankfurter's condition cleared up "spontaneously." This is precisely the word that describes most things about the judge. He is a "spontaneous" character given to "spontaneous combustion." This explains why he has an oversufficiency of both friends and enemies.

The other night Robert Frost was here for a big, splashy eighty-eighth birthday party, and the judge was there till one in the morning, singing the old poet's praises and listening to Frost's remarks.

"All there is to life," said Frost, "is getting a meaning into a lot of material. . . . You've got to be sweeping and you've got to be pointed. You've got to come out somewhere, just as plain as a wisecrack or a joke."

Frankfurter was so enthusiastic in his applause that he probably overdid himself right there, and no wonder, for this is precisely what F.F. has been doing all his life—getting a meaning into a lot of material, reducing diversity to identity, coming out somewhere, plain as a wisecrack, to the delight of many and the despair of many more.

Maybe the doctors are right that age has something to do with the judge's physical problem, though not because it has narrowed the arteries but because it has widened the mind and deepened the memory. The judge, bless him, can't help thinking that the Constitution is important and that people are important. His enthusiasms are boundless. If he is a little tired, it is because he has paid attention to so many things and inspired so many youngsters here and in Cambridge over so long a time.

There is now some talk here of replacing him on the Supreme Court of the United States, but this is as silly as the doctor's bulletin. They may eventually put somebody in his place, but they won't replace him.

A Fifty Year Friendship

Edmund Morris Morgan,
School of Law, Vanderbilt University

For me to write an article worthy of inclusion in a *Festschrift* to Mr. Justice Frankfurter would be impossible. All that I can do is to tell briefly some impressions left by a friendship of more than half a century, which began when we were both students at the Harvard Law School. During one whole academic year I was in position to limit the volume of what he published. I did not realize what a unique distinction I was achieving in compressing each of his contributions to the Note Department of the Harvard Law Review into five hundred words, or what it must have cost him to suppress his characteristic enthusiasm about anything or anybody that challenges his intellectual or emotional interest. And at that time we had on the faculty some men of such outstanding quality that only a dullard could have failed to be aware that they were of great intellectual stature and high character. They had in addition both the capacity and the desire to discover in the student body men of unusual intellectual ability and attractive personality. That Felix obviously

75

fitted these specifications was shown by two incidents. (1) When Ames[1] learned that Felix was to remain in Cambridge during the Christmas recess of his first year, he invited him to dinner on Christmas Day. Felix declined because his acceptance would have left alone for the day his roommate, a Jewish boy of unusual ability but of rather unattractive personal appearance. Ames made this reason inapplicable by inviting the roommate, who was in fact a person of lovable disposition and keen discernment. (2) In the summer recess following the first year, Gray[2] asked Felix to assist him in the preparation of a new edition of his casebook on property. At the end of the summer Gray sent him a check for $125, which was at that time fair compensation for the time spent. Felix returned the check with a note saying that his profit and pleasure in doing this work more than repaid him. Gray sent back the check with this message: "Dear Frankfurter, Don't be a damn'd fool!"

Typical of both!

I left the law school in June 1905. Because I had been a member of the *Law Review* Board of Editors, I was offered a job in the office of what I then knew as the Hornblower firm, but I declined. I had spent a summer in New York City following my graduation from Harvard College and determined that I would not live there regardless of any financial rewards it might offer. But Felix wanted to practice in New York, and though he had led his class during all three years, he had to make the rounds of the offices in which he thought he might like to begin. He was quickly made to understand that his extraordinarily high law school record was not a ticket to a reserved seat in an established law office and that his being a Jew was a handicap not overcome by his demonstrated ability to understand legal propositions. But he finally was interviewed by a member of the Hornblower firm who had some appreciation of the value of a Harvard Law School education and of an extraordinarily strong recommendation by Dean Ames. Frankfurter began in the Hornblower office—Hornblower, Byrne, Miller & Potter—at a salary of a thousand dollars a year. He had been there only a few months when he received a communication from Henry L. Stimson, then recently appointed United States Attorney for the Southern District of New York, as a result of which Mr. Stimson asked him if he would "come over" as an assistant at a salary of $750 a year. He was anxious to do so, but felt some sort of obligation to the Hornblower office, although he was not under any legal duty to remain there. One of the two senior partners was violently opposed to his leaving, counting it no justification for such an unwise and immoral performance that he was leaving to take a position in a public office at a reduced salary. After thorough consideration he went with Mr. Stimson. His experiences as Assistant United States Attorney under Mr. Stimson and his personal contacts with him made this one of the most fruitful periods of his life, and has had a profound influence upon his conduct to this day. In the crash of the banks during the panic of 1906–1907, the investigation which Stimson made was thorough and painstaking and time-consuming. President Roosevelt wanted action and wanted it fast. But Stimson, to Frankfurter's delight, refused to be hurried, and told Loeb to tell the President that if he didn't like it he could get another District Attorney.

I lost track of Frankfurter's later activities until I found him in the office of the Secretary of War during the First World War, when I went to Washington as an officer in the Judge Advocate General's Department. I know nothing of his secret missions abroad, but I well remember the misinformation I had of his role in the Mooney case. I believed that the President had sent him to California for the express purpose of looking into that case and making his personal recommendation concerning the President's contemplated intervention therein. The facts are that strikes in Arizona and California were interfering with the supply of materials badly needed in preparation for expected participation in the First World War. The President appointed a Mediation Commission, with Labor Secretary Wilson as chairman and Frankfurter as the lawyer member. In stating the duties of the Commission the President, after referring to the current labor disputes, added, "There is one more matter I want this Commission to look into, and as a lawyer of the Commission, Mr. Frankfurter, this will be particularly your concern. That is the Mooney case, which is greatly disturbing to our allies, Russia and Italy. When you get to California, I hope you will look into that and report to me about it."

Felix has said that the reference to Russia and Italy caused him to infer that the man in question was an Italian or a Russian. But he soon learned what the case was about and wired a classmate in San Francisco to get together for him the documents, the record, and a statement as to the then existing situation. His receipt of several replies pleading lack of time and the pressure of other business warned him that the subject called for no run-of-the-mine or perfunctory investigation.

On July 22, 1916, a so-called Preparedness Day Parade was marching up Market Street in San Francisco. It had started at the Embarcadero Plaza at 1:30 P.M. Units of marchers stationed at the intersecting streets were to join the line of march. At 2:06 P.M. the Spanish-American War veterans were coming into Market from Stewart Street when a bomb exploded, killing nine persons and injuring many others. Mooney, a labor leader, was arrested, indicted, and convicted of murder. There was and is no question that the proceedings against him were blatantly irregular, and that his conviction was accomplished by the use of perjured testimony. By the time the Mediation Commission reached San Francisco, he was in prison and the status of his case was the cause of much debate. Frankfurter was extended every courtesy by the judges of the Supreme Court of California, but the result was an affirmance of the conviction. The recommendation of the Commission written by him was "in case the Supreme Court should find it necessary (confined as it is by jurisdictional limitations) to sustain the conviction of Mooney on the trial, that the President use his good offices to invoke action by the Governor of California and the cooperation of its prosecuting officers to the end that a new trial may be had for Mooney whereby guilt or innocence may be put to the test of unquestionable justice. This result can easily be accomplished by postponing the execution of the sentence of Mooney to await the outcome of a new trial, based upon prosecution under one of the untried indictments against him." The President sent such a message to Governor Stephens, who commuted Mooney's sentence to life imprisonment. This action was contrary to the Commission's recommendation, and as long as Mooney was in prison he was the source of propaganda here and abroad against the government and its Department of Justice. To some who should have known better, it furnished an opportunity to attack Frankfurter. The Solicitor General, James M. Beck, made the attack formidable by publishing in the *New Republic* a letter asserting that in his investigation Frankfurter had seen only Mooney and his adherents. This justified, if it did not require, a public answer stating the facts. As usually happens in such circumstances, the answer published in the *New Republic* convinced those who wanted to know what actually happened and those who had already made up their minds in Frankfurter's favor, but left his opponents with still another grievance against him.

After the war Felix returned to the Harvard Law School and I to Yale. During the next few years I had several opportunities to join the Harvard Law School faculty; as to none of them did Felix communicate with me. I was happy at Yale, Swan was a wonderfully fine Dean and Corbin a colleague who not only inspired me to put forth my best efforts professionally, but also won my affection and admiration. Walter Wheeler Cook later came back from Columbia, and his intolerance toward all who failed or refused to accept his theories made me receptive to the invitation brought to me at the 1924 annual meeting of the Association of American Law Schools by Ed Warren. After I had written my acceptance, conditioned upon the unanimous approval of the invitation by the Harvard Law School faculty, and had received assurance from the Dean that the condition was satisfied, I resigned from Yale. When I had made final arrangements for moving from New Haven to Harvard, I received from Felix a note saying that no one would welcome me more warmly than he, but he wanted me to know that he had voted against me (because he was opposed to further expansion of the law school). He was as good as his word, and our relations as colleagues were in no manner less pleasant than if he had been the initiator of the invitation.

To write of his participation in the Sacco-Vanzetti case might well expose me to comment upon the danger of speaking out of the abundance of my ignorance. I knew that he was writing his article (afterward published in book form) because he consulted me about a specific ruling by Judge Thayer upon a matter of evidence. I knew it was not subject to review because it was within the discretion of the trial judge, and could not under Massachusetts contemporary practice be termed an abuse. I also knew that to urge him to refrain from publication until the Supreme Court had said its final word would be like blowing against the wind; it would be asking him to order his conduct by considerations of mere etiquette or of the hostile personal criticisms that would almost certainly follow. What I have written about it was written without any previous consultation with him although he was a colleague of mine during much of the time.

What I have said before, and said publicly and in law school classes in universities in the East, in the Middle West, on the Pacific coast, in Texas, in North Carolina and Georgia, and am now repeating in Tennessee is that I have been a close friend of Felix Frankfurter's for more than a half a century, and I have never heard him utter an unkind word about any man merely because that man's views on a problem of legal or economic or philosophic or social policy were contrary to his own. The only requirement he has imposed is that the views be honestly held and honestly expressed. Recently he has been classified as a conservative. While he was being branded a Red, I was preaching that he was and always had been a conservative, who regards and has always regarded the Supreme Court as an institution composed of all members, past and present, where a member's personal predilections are to be submerged in the collective judgment of the Court. His retirement has deprived the Court of an influence for stability which it has acutely needed and will continue to need.

F.F.C.C.N.Y.

Nathaniel Phillips, *Counselor at Law*

The title of this slight tribute to Felix Frankfurter is no letters game. It means much in the life of Frankfurter. It brings to mind his devotion to his alma mater and the pride of the college in the achievements of her illustrious son.

I remember Frankfurter at the college. He was a year ahead of me. He had come from his native Vienna at the age of twelve. There never seemed a trace of an accent, and his speech had a limpid quality and an engaging timbre that charmed his listeners.

We were members of the Clionia Society, one of the college's two leading literary societies. The annual debate between Clionia and Phrenocosmia aroused a keenness of rivalry that quite dwarfed the emotions roused by our present-day World Series. The rule was universal that only seniors were to be debaters. But even then universality of regulation did not apply to Frankfurter. Though he was only a member of the junior class, we chose him to represent Clionia. How handsomely he justified our breach of tradition! Of course Clionia won, and we all felt that he brought us the triumph. I wrote him about that many years later. I'll tell about that in a moment.

I shall never forget his stunning performance. He looked so boyish, his neatness was striking. He spoke such sense. It was as though no opposition could have any significance. He was extremely courteous in manner, but he pierced the arguments of his opponents with a deftness and finality that was devastating.

He was never fulsome in his greetings. But he impressed you with his sincerity, and his gaiety was a delight. There was a rare sparkle about him. He inspired warm affection.

C.C.N.Y.—locally known as City College—is now an awe-inspiring (I just refuse to use the word "complex") group of buildings on St. Nicholas Heights, in the upper reaches of New York City. Its roster numbers 34,080. In Frankfurter's student days the entire college was housed in a tiny Gothic structure at Twenty-third Street and Lexington Avenue. The number of students was 774. His classmates included descendants of early settlers, as well as representatives of the other races that make up our mixed society—Irish, Germans, Russians, Poles, Italians, Hungarians, Austrians, Rumanians; Catholics, Protestants, Jews, and doubtless nonbelievers. The examination for admittance to the college was most severe. The curriculum was a demanding one, the discipline harsh. The saying was that anybody who was graduated from City College was entitled to his diploma. The college was free. And there is little doubt that most of the students would have had no college education had there been any charge for tuition or for textbooks. Bernard M. Baruch of the class of 1889 has said, "If there were no C.C.N.Y., I never would have an education beyond the public schools."

The financial status of Frankfurter's classmates was something like this: the parents of about ten percent were well-to-do, twenty percent did fairly well. The rest were poor—actually poor—the family income barely sufficient to make ends meet, all the boys in the family working after college hours and on Saturday and Sunday to help meet the family needs. Luncheon at the college food counter consisted generally of an apple, a pretzel, and a cup of coffee. Few could afford much more.

The affluent undergraduates rode to and from the college. Most walked to save the five-cent carfare except in extremely stormy weather. Many will remember on such days, as they rode uptown, passing one of Frankfurter's classmates walking under the elevated road for a bit of shelter. He afterward became a noted writer and an English professor in an important college.

Frankfurter's was a good class. It numbered an able judge of New York's highest criminal court, two archaeologists who made important studies of the Indians of the western reservations (one of them became a highly respected paleontologist), an outstanding Associate Superintendent of the city schools, a leading landscape artist, a painter whose work is in the Corcoran Art Gallery and other famous galleries, two members of the House of Representatives, and there were others who made substantial contributions to the life of the community. But Frankfurter's name "led all the rest."

In Frankfurter's time C.C.N.Y. was a small college, and in his love for the college, Mr. Justice Frankfurter must often have been minded of Webster's pleading for his alma mater in the Dartmouth College case, calling upon the great Chief Justice to save Dartmouth: "She is a small college, but there are those who love her."

Frankfurter's devotion to his small college continued through the years, and in our exchange of letters there was always a reference to the college. An opinion he had written for the Court moved me to write him a word of admiration while expressing doubt as to whether that was quite the right thing to do. His reply was characteristic.

NATHANIEL PHILLIPS

Supreme Court of the United States
Washington, D.C.

CHAMBERS OF
JUSTICE FELIX FRANKFURTER   February 4, 1952

My dear Phillips:
   You rightly infer that a judge is not to be praised for any
opinion he may render, because he is not a judge if he renders
them for any consideration other than the compulsion of mind
and conscience.
   But in any event I was glad to get a note from you and to
recall days of old which, in their way, were not less filled with
anxiety and hope than the present.

                                   Sincerely yours,
Nathaniel Phillips, Esq.   FELIX FRANKFURTER

   After a visit to Gray's Inn in London some years ago, I was
delighted to write him:

                         New York, October 15, 1956
My dear Judge,
   I am happy to have the opportunity to write you this little
note. I do so to tell you how thrilled I was recently when I
visited Gray's Inn, to behold in the robing room, on individual
coat rings, the names "Mr. Churchill," many of the leading
British jurists, and "Mr. Frankfurter."
   My mind went back to a time, oh so many years ago, when a
young lad debated for Clionia and gave to us then the promise
of his later distinguished career.
   With warm regard, I am,

                              Most sincerely,
                              NATHANIEL PHILLIPS

Here's his gracious response:

FELIX FRANKFURTER—*A Tribute*

Supreme Court of the United States
Washington 25, D.C.

CHAMBERS OF
JUSTICE FELIX FRANKFURTER   October 27, 1956

My dear Nathaniel Phillips:
    Your generous thoughts leaped across half a century, and more, and across the ocean to make a single story and stir happy memories.
    With much appreciation and all good wishes.

Very sincerely yours,
FELIX FRANKFURTER

I have heard it said that when Justice Frankfurter would come into the courtroom, it would be with a certain "bounciness." That being so, it will not be sacrilegious to say he walked just that way in his college days. He seemed to be going forward with a slight leap, as though he were too impatient to get there to trust himself to mere walking. Well, he did get there. And the affection and pride of his fellow alumni of C.C.N.Y. have been with him throughout the years. They have been awed, but not surprised, at his elevation to the exalted post of Justice of the Supreme Court of the United States.

A Mirror of Friendship

Alexander Meiklejohn,
former President of Amherst College

As a layman in the law I have no valid claim for "freedom of speech" in the company of those who critically assess Felix Frankfurter's judicial achievements. But I can and must express my lifelong regard and affection for him. (The time reference here relates to the length of his life, which is not so long as mine.)

Many years ago—I think vaguely that it was at the Inauguration of Ernest Hopkins as President of Dartmouth—he and I met as fellow members of a seminar on the question, "How can the social sciences be so studied that they will unite in genuine significance for one another?" (We probably used the new word, "integration.")

The young fellow from the Harvard Law School fascinated me then, and ever since, we have been friends. We have differed much in opinion, and at times seriously. But those differences, focusing on shared issues, have given us the solid basis for the friendship which springs up in men as they meditate on the same problems, search for the same truth. Very happily—if I may borrow a word from one of his letters—we have "teased" each other. For example, he has suggested to me that our common interest might be better served by me if I would spend three years in a "good" law school. And to that I have replied that, ideally, I would be glad to do so if I knew that he was spending the same three years in a school of philosophy.

What I am trying to say or suggest was summed up by him in the final paragraph of a letter which he sent me on March 22, 1961, when we were reflecting together about our mutual friend, Zach Chafee. The sentence which I venture to quote reads as follows:

"What a joy you have been to me all these many years and how often I regret that we don't live round the corner from one another."

As I have known and enjoyed F.F., however right or wrong he may have been in his theories of constitutional freedom, he has been clearly and persistently right about the way in which free men may hold different views as to what freedom really is.

Felix

Herbert B. Ehrmann, *Attorney*

I first heard of Felix Frankfurter in 1911, when I was an under-graduate at Harvard. At the time, I was president of the Harvard Menorah Society, a student organization which crowned its season's program with an annual dinner addressed by a "name" speaker. Judge Julian W. Mack was to be the orator in that year. The day before the banquet, however, we received a telegram from Judge Mack regretting that he could not come because of the illness of his wife. We were in a panic. Many tickets had been sold on Judge Mack's reputation to awesome law school students. Reservations had been made at the hotel for a guaranteed number of dinners. A major tragedy of youth impended.

In this quandary I consulted my friend, Max Lowenthal, then one of the demigods attending the Harvard Law School. Max did not hesitate.

"Get Felix Frankfurter!" he said immediately.

Hearing this odd and unfamiliar name, I asked Max who and what was Felix Frankfurter. Max opened his eyes wide and looked at me in marked astonishment. Nature had already endowed Max's face with a fixed expression of wide-eyed astonishment, but this time it went further and managed to convey a sense of shock that anyone existed who had never heard of Felix Frankfurter.

"Felix Frankfurter," he declared, "is the greatest man in the world."

At the moment, I thought this a slight exaggeration. Today I am not so sure that his appraisal went beyond the fact. Max went on to say that Felix was then Law Officer of the Bureau of Insular Affairs in Washington and a powerful influence in the set governing the capital. Chiefly I recall that he pictured Felix as hobnobbing with titled Englishmen, even rooming with some of them, and as riding horses in Rock Creek Park with noble young women. Years later I came to know that kind hearts meant more to Felix than coronets, and also that those in high-sounding positions not only left him unimpressed, but that he was more severely critical of their behavior than of those in humbler ranks.

We did not have Felix as our speaker at the dinner because I wanted to make a try first at securing Louis D. Brandeis, then "the Tribune of the People" practicing law in Boston. I did not then know Brandeis, but I had hopes because we both came from Louisville, Kentucky, and I had been a close friend of his uncle, Louis Dembitz, some sixty years my senior.

I do not know whether Felix would have come on one day's notice because Brandeis surprised all of us by accepting the invitation. His talk was inspiring, but the evening acquired memorable importance for another reason. Harry Wolfson (later Professor Wolfson) recited an original Hebrew poem, and I read an English version, which I had laboriously translated. Years later Brandeis stated that Wolfson's fervor and eloquence were the start of a series of experiences which kindled within him an interest in Jewish affairs leading eventually to his historic espousal of Zionism, in which Felix joined with him. That, however, is another story.

Felix remained a Lowenthal myth for me until 1914, the year I was graduated from the law school. In September of that year I had suddenly decided not to practice law in Louisville, and returned to Boston to find a start in my profession. Like most recent graduates from the law school in a similar situation, I immediately sought out Richard Ames, Secretary of the school. Mr. Ames greeted me with the statement that I already had a position. He seemed surprised that I did not know about it—but not as surprised as I was to hear it. Then he explained.

"We have a new professor at the law school. The United States Attorney General asked him to recommend a recent graduate as an assistant. He wanted someone unspoiled by experience. Pound suggested your name to him and the recommendation has gone to Washington. You are as good as appointed." I asked Ames the name of the new professor.

"Frankfurter," he said. "Why don't you introduce yourself to him? He's in his office now."

Thereupon I met Felix. He created instantly an atmosphere of warm friendliness. The charm, electric energy, and quick perception which have marked his life were evident at once. He was so youthful-looking that he appeared more like a student than an august faculty member. In fact, a few months later a Boston matron entertained him under the impression that he actually was a student. This deception was furthered by what Felix did not tell her. Hearing that he was at the law school, his hostess had asked him, "What year?" and he had told her the fact, but not the truth. "This is my first." Subsequently the lady asked me in trepidation whether the young guest she had entertained really was a professor, as she had heard. She was somewhat a collector of celebrities, so that the truth threw her into a double dejection. I suggested revenge to restore her ego to health. She was to invite Felix, as a new student, to another dinner to meet with several second- and third-year men. It would be nice for him to know a few upper classmen. Unfortunately, the lady was not for lying and Felix's deviltry went unpunished. It usually did.

But to return to his office in September 1914. After asking me a few personal questions, he apparently decided that I was inexperienced enough to satisfy the most exacting requirements of the Attorney General. He called in his secretary and dictated a follow-up letter to Washington, filling in the biographical gaps left in his letter of recommendation. A few days later he received a reply. The Attorney General had changed his mind and now wanted an assistant with experience. Perhaps we had overdone it.

After dictating the letter, Felix called up his close friend, Arthur D. Hill, a prominent State Street lawyer, and asked him to see me. Hill consented immediately. He not only saw me in the afternoon, but invited me to dinner that evening at his home. This began one of the most delightful friendships of my life, one of several for which I am indebted to Felix.

Arthur Hill was quite special. Conversation with him was a stimulating experience. His bold generalizations were always brilliant, although occasionally a trifle inaccurate. He had the gift of making his point in epigrams remarkable for wit and wisdom. He was definitely a Boston Brahmin, but had lost a bit of caste by fighting for Teddy Roosevelt in the battle of the Moose against the Elephant. This had hurt him somewhat in his professional and social relations with the upper crust, sometimes defined by those who do not belong as a "bundle of crumbs held together by dough." After being wounded at Armageddon, Arthur became somewhat gun-shy. Thereafter he continued to support some unpopular causes, including Sacco and Vanzetti in the last few hopeless weeks. However, he explained his actions to the George Apleys in terms of their own code. He sought to bury his idealistic motives beneath a heap of talk about professional duty or the nebulous prospects of a large fee. He may have fooled some people, even himself, but not Felix. Nor me, either, as time went on.

Felix and Arthur were brothers under the skin. In both men unusual moral courage came from sympathy with humanity and devotion to the basic principles of justice. Arthur, however, covered up these motivations, somewhat suspect in his set, lest he be classified as a rebel against the "establishment" or, even worse, as a "do-gooder." After Sacco and Vanzetti were executed, he even defended President Lowell of Harvard, whose garbled report to the Governor killed all hope of commutation. Felix was free of any concern about probable disapproval of his conduct in publishing his condemnation of the trial. When the Lowell report justifying the proceedings was released, he was asked whether he would resign from the Harvard faculty. "Why should I resign?" he replied. "Let Lowell resign." Arthur concealed his sense of outrage under a characteristic cynical epigram: "Sacco and Vanzetti received as fair a trial as possible—consistent with the determination to convict them!"

September is not the month for a recent law school graduate to look for a position in a good law office in Boston or with the government. The openings are almost invariably filled before graduation. Nevertheless, there appeared to be a number of possibilities. However, the attractive ones did not materialize, and I did not want to start professional life with the others. I was like the maiden who remains single for years because the men she could love did not propose and those who proposed she couldn't love.

At the time, my friend and fellow law school mate, Reginald Heber Smith, was Chief Counsel of the Boston Legal Aid Society. After several weeks of watching my frustrations, Reginald offered me a position in his organization.

"My budget won't permit me to pay you anything the first year," he said, "but next year I can pay you five dollars a week." I accepted the offer.

For me the decision was fateful. Looking backward, I can now see how those two years shaped my career. A lawyer cannot spend so much time trying to bring legal relief to the victims of poverty, of oppression, of misfortune, or of their own bad habits or mental quirks, without realizing that the law must have purposes beyond solving individual problems and furnishing a livelihood for lawyers. More specifically, some of the experiences which I had during this period were setting an unknown train which eventually led to activities then undreamed of, such as industrial relations for the U. S. Shipping Board, the Cleveland Crime Survey, and even the Sacco-Vanzetti case. Felix had a hand in these developments.

When I telephoned to report to Felix that I had joined the Legal Aid Society, he managed to let me know that I was a member of what has since been called the "Distinguished Club" by Geoffrey May in the April 1963 number of the *Harvard Law School Bulletin.*

"Is this Professor Frankfurter?" I asked. There was a moment's pause, and then came the answer:

"This is Felix," and it has been "Felix" ever since. Thereafter also Felix always called me by the nickname "Brute," which had followed me from Louisville to Boston.

From the lawyer's point of view, work in the Legal Aid Society had volume and variety, but scarcely any depth. There was no time to be thorough. We were continually doing too little on too much. Nevertheless, we learned many things about the practice of law that were not in the books. When people have little or no money, they must often compromise with harsh reality, and one of our principal functions was to work out such

94

practical adjustments. This meant dealing with many different kinds of people, and so we grew, or thought we grew, in our knowledge of human nature.

Some of the cases which I handled took unexpected turns, not entirely without humor. These experiences I would relate occasionally to Felix, who would greet the recital with such boisterous joy that I found a new pleasure in my work. One such matter was the case of Mr. Nolan, the repentant but bibulous street cleaner, whom we charged with nonsupport of his wife. As a gesture of atonement, he bought a turkey for Thanksgiving—on credit, "to save money." However, his wife wanted to keep the turkey for a family weekend and served ham on Thanksgiving. Ham on Thanksgiving! Mr. Nolan stealthily stole the turkey from his own home in the hour before dawn, traded it for a bottle of whiskey, and then in sulky solitude sought to drown the memory of such insolence in many a draught of the forbidden liquor. Whenever Felix had the chance, he would egg me on to tell the Nolan story and other selected bits from my Legal Aid practice. Once at dinner in the Brandeis home at Otis Place, he slyly started me on some of my adventures in Legal Aid and led the responding laughter with his own sudden and infectious bursts.

One afternoon at the Legal Aid office I was visited by a man and a woman who introduced themselves as Arthur N. Holcombe and Mabel Gillespie, two members of the Minimum Wage Commission of Massachusetts. They were setting up a board whose purpose would be to establish a minimum wage in the women's clothing industry. The board was composed of representatives of labor, the manufacturers, and the public. The commissioners asked me to be a public representative and to act as Chairman. I accepted. It never occurred to me to ask how it happened that they should request a young man of twenty-four to take on such a responsibility. Many, many years later I learned the answer to my unasked question. Through other work I had become a good friend of Amy Hewes, Secretary of the Commission. She told me that my two visitors had emerged from my office in a dazed condition. They had stood at the top of the stairway in our old building for over an hour, discussing what they should do. They agreed that Professor Frankfurter must be crazy to recommend such a kid for the chairmanship of a Minimum Wage Board. They finally decided that having asked me, they had to see it through. I became Chairman of the Board, but their fears did not subside. Fortunately I was able, after long negotiation with both sides, to secure the first unanimous finding in the history of the Commission. I believed then, and have always believed, that a divided decision in a labor dispute greatly dilutes its moral strength. The result of my first essay was gratifying, of course. However, the belated news imparted to me by Miss Hewes gave me a powerful ex post facto satisfaction in the knowledge that I had not let Felix down because of his rash recommendation.

Another outside activity that engaged my energies during the Legal Aid years was the organization of an open forum in the South End of Boston, modeled after the Ford Hall Forum. The South End in those days was ridden with squalor. It was almost totally devoid of intellectual or cultural interests to relieve the sordid physical environment. Many of the inhabitants, however, were recent immigrants who hungered for an opportunity to lift themselves above their surroundings—and to express their individuality. Our Sunday evening meetings in the vestry of the old Temple Ohabei Shalom on Union Park were crowded with eager residents of the neighborhood. Many of the youth of the South End helped to run the meetings. Some of America's ablest speakers came willingly, without honorarium, to thrill and stimulate the auidences and to stand cross-examination by questioners who frequently were passionate speechmakers.

Felix addressed the forum twice. On each occasion he was

badgered a bit by the perennial socialists who dominated the question period. As chairman, I thoroughly enjoyed putting their questions to him. His answers were always thought-pro-voking. He never spoke down to his audience, but always up. His vocabulary remained unique Frankfurtiana. He never yielded to the temptation to give smarty answers. This was not because Felix was naturally a mild man. It was merely because he understood the background and the experiences which prompted the questioners. He could be caustic enough and even arrogant when he felt that those who had every advantage of position and education pontificated without knowledge or covered the principles which they professed with complacent acceptance of their violation. On such occasions the contempt in his voice and words was unrestrained. In the South End forum, however, he remained the patient teacher.

I remember well one answer. After he had discussed the public interest in many current industrial matters, he was asked the inevitable question:

"Professor Frankfurter, since you believe these things, why aren't you a socialist?"

Felix replied instantaneously:

"Because I cannot compress life into a formula." He then spent some time discussing the complexity of modern life, point-ing out that difficulties in different industries required distinct remedies—some public ownership, some governmental control, some free competition, some various incentives, and so on. For me, at least, Felix in eight words had banished isms forever. He had also compressed his own philosophy into a phrase.

The idea that Felix could be tagged a "liberal" or a "radical" never had validity. He was as progressive as science, as reaction-ary as the multiplication table, and as conservative as the Deca-logue. He had only one ready-made approach—get the facts. In 1920 he was the principal speaker at a rally to protest the raids and suppressions of the anti-Red hysteria of the Mitchell Palmer era. The air was charged with emotion. Instead of voicing the excitement and indignation of the assembled crowd, however, Felix used up his time urging the group to withhold action until they had verified the rumors of illegal official conduct on which they proposed to rely. He then concluded:

"And now, having said this, I will unscathingly sit down." And that sat us all down.

Felix also showed surprising patience with some of his favorite disciples. I remember an incident that occurred in his seminar on administrative law in 1939. I was welcomed as an old alumnus who wanted to learn something. One of the youngest members of the group was the ebullient Edward F. Prichard, a third-year man whose mind and wit endeared him to everyone—especially to his "Perfessor." It was the session immediately following President Roosevelt's nomination of Felix to be a Justice of the Supreme Court. Felix had just suggested an original approach to a problem in administrative law and asked "Prich" what he thought of it.

"That," ejaculated Prich, "is the most tenuous legal proposition I have ever heard!" We waited for the cutting rejoinder None came. Instead, Felix merely admonished mildly:

"I hope, Mr. Prichard, that your capacity for surprise has not been exhausted."

"No, it has not," snapped Prich, "and I'll tell you why. You can never tell what one of these new judges may decide!"

The class roared with glee, Felix leading all the rest. Prich later became Felix's first law clerk in Washington.

As a teacher, Felix was accused of favoring the brilliant scholars and forgetting that the average student needed more help. This was true only south by southwest. It was natural that he would respond to the intellectual talents of others. He was attracted by minds that could cope with his own. Since he was a teacher of young men, he encountered many such minds. But he also found such congeniality among those who were not his students. In fact, his friendships include the intellectual elite of the world.

Appreciation of Professor Roscoe Pound's legal stature led to a warm friendship between them which lasted until Felix's famous review of the Sacco-Vanzetti case was published in the *Atlantic Monthly*. One evening in 1916, I was having dinner with Felix at the Harvard Club of Boston. He was being constantly paged with telephone calls. After he had left our table several times, I asked him what it was all about. He answered, "I am trying to get Pound appointed Dean of the law school." The try was successful.

However, although Felix was personally attracted to the top students, it is not true that they monopolized his concern as a teacher of the law. He knew that the future of the profession would be largely in the hands of the average students. The quality of the bar as a profession, quite apart from legal acumen, was always a matter of grave concern with him. Many years later, in a letter dated February 18, 1929, to William Marshall Bullitt, a former Solicitor General, discussing the Sacco-Vanzetti case, Felix was to write:

"I am a devotee of the law and my life is given to the endeavor of quickening in young men a realization of the forces of truth and justice which law seeks to express."

This was his basic credo as a teacher.

Admirable qualities of the mind and spirit could stir up in Felix his warm appreciation, but not circumscribe it. His enthusiasms included many things in addition to human virtues or abstract principles. Sometimes they took a surprising turn. It was a unique experience to walk with him in the retail section of the city. No matter how late we were to keep an appointment —promptness to Felix was a waste of time—he would sometimes stand enraptured before the display of women's dresses in the show windows of Stearn's or Hollander's. After a moment of silent contemplation—while I fidgeted—he would then point out the most beautiful garment in the window with something approaching ecstatic pleasure.

As we entered the penumbra of World War I, I saw less and less of Felix. He began to commute to Washington, doing his extra work in his berth on the Federal Express. Later came his trip to the West on behalf of Secretary of Labor Wilson, studying the effect on labor morale of the Bisbee deportations and the Mooney-Billings case. When the War Labor Policies Board was established, Felix was named its Chairman.

Meanwhile I was serving in the United States Fuel Administration, under Massachusetts' first citizen, James J. Storrow. In June 1918, I received a telegram from the United States Shipping Board, requesting me to assist Robert P. Bass, formerly Governor of New Hampshire, then Chairman of the Board's Marine and Dock Industrial Relations Division. The call was undoubtedly the result of my Minimum Wage experience. My proposed title was "Expert," but since this carried a salary too low to support a family of three, a higher rating was created—"Special Expert." This changed nothing except my salary, but the nebulous concept of an expert who was also special entertained by friends, particularly Max Lowenthal.

I then began to see Felix again and to seek his advice on occasion. He had me to dinner at the famous "House of Truth." The talk was fast and sprightly, although a number of Harvard College professors seemed more interested in scuttle butt about their colleagues back home than in the "Truth."

Governor Bass became ill, and resigned. The Shipping Board then named me in his place. Thereby I found myself, at the age of twenty-seven, entrusted with wartime responsibility for industrial relations with the longshoremen's and the various seamen's unions. As acting director of a division, I automatically became a member of the War Labor Policies Board, where I had the opportunity to follow the discussions among the heads of other divisions and departments, including generals, admirals, Cabinet members, and their deputies. There I discovered for the first time that rank and talent do not necessarily go together like a horse and carriage. I reported to my wife that on the whole Board I could discern only two first-rate minds. One was the Chairman's and the other belonged to a handsome young Assistant Secretary of the Navy, named Roosevelt. I really deserve a foreseer's medal for this prejudgment of a future President. Felix refers to this incident in his book *Felix Frankfurter Reminisces*.

My own part in the Board's deliberations was quite negligible. I respected my years by remaining silent. After one session Felix asked me why I did not contribute something. I responded by handing him a quarter "to buy Louis Howe a haircut." This brought a chuckle, but Howe remained unshorn.

The war over, I returned to Boston to practice law. My friend Reginald Heber Smith was then managing partner of the long-established firm of Hale and Dorr. For a second time he asked me to join his organization, and again I accepted. For a while I was besieged with offers to represent industry or the public in industrial relations. My standing as a "Special Expert" in such matters had been publicized by my appointment as Director of the Division of Industrial Relations. In each case the salary was several times that of a young lawyer. Since I needed the money, I was torn between the law and lucre. In my dilemma I sought the advice of Felix. He asked me what I wanted to be. "A lawyer," I answered.

"Then," said Felix, "you have no problem. Be a lawyer."

As I turned to go, Felix, with his quick perception, saw that I was suffering.

"Brute," he admonished, "always remember that when you have a decision to make, do it easily. Don't torture yourself." I have always remembered this sage advice, but never followed it.

The years immediately after the close of World War I were marked by the rise of violent crimes in the United States. Part of this was due to the general reaction after a period of idealism and self-denial, and part to the huge profits in bootlegging available to criminal gangs because of prohibition. The situation was particularly aggravated in the city of Cleveland because of the laxity in law enforcement during the preceding era of Mayor Tom Johnson. The wholesome humanitarian thrust of Johnson's leadership had become diverted by sheer sentimentality.

In retrospect it almost seemed as if criminals had been viewed as noblemen who had gone wrong, like the Pirates of Penzance. The postwar disillusionment therefore was more intense. The discovery that the preceding public apathy had nurtured the alliance between crime and politics raised the indignation of the citizenry to the boiling point. The explosion came when the Chief Judge of Cleveland's Municipal Court shot and killed his favorite bootlegger in the center of the city on the crossing of Ninth and Euclid avenues. An additional sensation was added when it was found that the principal witness was the mistress of the judge, who had trailed him to the spot out of mistaken jealousy concerning the purpose of his trip into the city. That did it. The Cleveland Foundation organized a committee to survey the administration of criminal justice and undertook to finance it. Amos Burt Thompson of the firm of Thompson, Hine and Flory, was Chairman, and Raymond Moley was Secretary.

Dean Pound of the Harvard Law School and Felix were named to head the study. The field was subdivided into the police, the prosecution, courts, correctional and penal treatment, medical science, legal education, and the newspapers. Reginald

Heber Smith, whose pioneer book *Justice and the Poor* had been received with just acclaim as a basic treatise, was asked to take over the assignment on the courts. Smith declined, and Pound and Felix recommended me in his stead. Felix knew that I had written a number of reviews of the most recent books on criminology for the *Harvard Law Review*. I have always suspected him of suggesting my name to the *Review* editors. The Foundation accepted the change, provided Smith's name remained in the survey. The arrangement worked satisfactorily. I spent four months in Cleveland, gathering material, interviewing judges, lawyers, prosecutors, clerks, police, probation officers, and a host of others, and making daily memoranda to myself for use later in writing my final report.

Smith wrote a summary chapter. The entire series of studies was later published in a single volume under the title *Criminal Justice in Cleveland*. It was the first of a number of scientific surveys of the actual working of the criminal law in a great metropolitan community.

Felix's natural enthusiasm for the work of others was a great encouragement to me as the survey progressed. When I showed him the first written product of my study, he approved it warmly, and immediately took the manuscript to Pound. The Dean leafed through the pages rapidly and handed back the manuscript, exclaiming, "Very good, very good indeed!" As we returned to Felix's office, I remarked that Pound hadn't really read a word of the manuscript. Felix observed that I was quite mistaken, that Pound had the gift of photographing an entire page as he read and of understanding its contents. I had known that Lord Macaulay was supposed to have had this unusual ability, but I was always skeptical. Pound was proof that such a talent actually existed. In his case, no doubt, this accounted for his almost unbelievably vast scholarship.

Pound spent several days in Cleveland, shut up in an hotel

room, writing his views on "Criminal Justice and the American City." He drew on his colossal stock of juristic lore and hardly needed to leave Cambridge to put his thoughts on paper. Felix came to Cleveland on several occasions and maintained close contact with the Survey Committee. He wrote the Preface and a chapter on "Newspapers and Criminal Justice." On his first visit he was able to clear away certain doubts about my methods of working. Unknown to me, the Chairman was disturbed because I frequently came to the office after nine o'clock in the morning. Felix explained that survey work differed from routine law practice and that most of my time had to be spent away from the office. Actually, I was working about twelve hours a day. The Secretary also was disappointed that I was not seeking to expose individual crooks and scoundrels. This gave Felix, the teacher, an opportunity to develop an understanding of our purposes in combing through voluminous court and police records and in interviewing scores of knowledgeable persons. We were seeking for causes of the failure of law enforcement, not acting on individual results like a local grand jury. He put his point across so successfully that Mr. Moley later became a writer and lecturer of note on the Cleveland study and the subsequent crime surveys which it evoked. In the end the Committee was well satisfied with the total result. Unlike the case in many surveys, some of our recommendations were adopted, apparently with beneficial results. If nothing else, the survey alerted the civic leadership of Cleveland to the truth that law enforcement, no less than liberty, requires eternal vigilance.

While we were engaged on the Cleveland project, two anarchists were being tried for murder in Dedham, Massachusetts. I knew nothing about the case other than some vague awareness of the names, "Sacco" and "Vanzetti." Felix never mentioned the proceedings, and apparently took little or no notice of them at the time of the trial or for several years thereafter. Meanwhile the historic case was moving on its way toward the tragic climax.

On April 15, 1920, Frederick Parmenter, paymaster of two shoe companies in South Braintree, Massachusetts, and Alessandro Berardelli, his guard, had been shot down on the street in front of the factories and robbed of the payrolls in excess of $15,000. On the previous December 24, 1919, there had been an unsuccessful attempt to hold up the pay truck of another shoe company, in Bridgewater, Massachusetts. On the night of May 5, 1920, Sacco, an industrious shoemaker, and Vanzetti, a preaching fish peddler, were arrested on an interurban streetcar. Neither man had any criminal record.

In June 1920, Vanzetti was convicted in Plymouth for the Bridgewater attempt. Although at least four bandits were involved, Vanzetti alone was tried. A year later Sacco and Vanzetti were put on trial in Dedham for the South Braintree murders. There had been at least five robbers involved, but Sacco and Vanzetti alone were tried.

In 1923, Felix first became aware that something might be wrong with the Sacco-Vanzetti case. He read in the daily papers a summary of a motion for a new trial containing a charge that the District Attorney had framed misleading testimony with one of the most important witnesses. The state's chief ballistics expert, Captain Proctor, had given his opinion at the trial that one of the bullets (No. 3) allegedly extracted from the body of Berardelli, was "consistent" with having passed through Sacco's pistol. The jury and the judge could have understood this to mean that Proctor believed that the bullet had been fired through Sacco's pistol. Trial Judge Webster Thayer charged the jury to this effect. Actually, Proctor had told the prosecution there was no evidence to justify such a conclusion. In conference with the District Attorney, the precise wording of

Proctor's opinion had been deliberately prepared for the trial so that Proctor could side-step his real opinion. What shocked Felix was that *the District Attorney answered the accusation by admitting the truth of Captain Proctor's revelation.* Once interested in the case, Felix began to investigate the trial record and found much besides the Proctor affair that outraged his sense of justice. The results of his study are embodied in his *Atlantic Monthly* article, published by Little, Brown in 1927 in booklet form and titled *The Case of Sacco and Vanzetti.* The case then leaped the boundaries of Massachusetts and captured the attention of the civilized world.

It was early May in 1926 when I received a telephone call from Felix which was to alter drastically the direction of my life and thought. He stated that William G. Thompson, counsel for Sacco and Vanzetti, had just received word that the Massachusetts Supreme Judicial Court had overruled the defendants' bill of exceptions, that Thompson had carried on alone for several years, and now needed help to continue with the defense. He asked me if I would assist. I said that I would if Thompson asked me. Within an hour Thompson made the request and I was in his office for a first conference.

My initial assignment was to investigate the story of Madeiros, then a prisoner in the Dedham jail, that he and a group of professionals from Providence, easily identified as the "Morelli gang," had committed the payroll robbery and murders in South Braintree of which Sacco and Vanzetti had been found guilty. Madeiros stood convicted of the murder of a cashier in an attempted bank robbery at Wrentham, Massachusetts. He was then awaiting the outcome of his own exceptions in that case. They were sustained; he was granted a second trial and convicted again. Although under pressure to retract, Madeiros stoutly maintained the truth of his story to the end of his life in the electric chair.

Felix probably suggested my name to Thompson because he knew of my work in the Cleveland Survey. Indeed, that experience proved to be very helpful. In Cleveland, I had acquired some familiarity with the way of professional criminals with the law—and the techniques of their trade. I was able, therefore, to follow the six-year-old trail of the Providence criminals with some capacity to make a realistic evaluation of the evidence which was uncovered. The Cleveland experience was also useful to Mrs. Ehrmann, who assisted me by studying the records of the case of United States v. Joseph Morelli *et al.* in the United States District Court for the District of Rhode Island, a prosecution based on freight car thefts of shoes and textiles.

I began the investigation with skepticism, but soon became convinced that the South Braintree crimes were the work of the Morelli mob indicated by Madeiros. So massive was the confirmation obtained, despite the hostility of the Massachusetts authorities, and after passage of six years from the affair, that coincidence was utterly impossible. The search for this evidence is told in my book *The Untried Case*, published in 1933 and again in 1960.

Felix shared with me my rising excitement as the investigation turned up fact after fact—never disproved to this date—that Madeiros had "pointed the finger" at the real criminals. I believe he also shared our conviction that the evidence would compel a new trial for Sacco and Vanzetti. However, at no stage did Felix attempt to advise Thompson or me concerning what we should do as lawyers. When Dean John Wigmore of Northwestern University Law School publicly attacked him for the *Atlantic Monthly* article, Felix asked me to check the accuracy of Wigmore's piece and his own reply. This I did, and found to my astonishment that the great master of the law of evidence had injected his opinions into the case without looking at the record, had misstated the facts, and even cited nonexistent "question and answer" testimony.

Lawrence Lowell, then President of Harvard University, was quoted by Norman Hapgood as saying, "Wigmore was a fool. He must have known that Frankfurter would be shrewd enough to be accurate."

Some weeks thereafter Lawrence Lowell was appointed by Governor Fuller to be Chairman of an "Advisory Committee" to review the case. Had we known then what we later learned about Lowell, we would have recognized the ominous import of his remark. The accuracy of Felix's article in depicting the proceedings did not register in Lowell's mind as proof of unfairness and injustice, but as evidence that Felix was "shrewd."

This evaluation foreshadowed the Committee's view of trial judge Thayer's talk off the bench. On unimpeachable testimony, he was quoted as referring to the defendants as "anarchistic bastards," as calling attention to what he had done to them and what he would do to them. At the time of these remarks Judge Thayer was passing on various motions as to which his decisions were both discretionary and final. According to the Committee report—written by Lowell—this talk by the trial judge merely indicated "a grave breach of official decorum."

In Lawrence Lowell's mind it was a matter of manners, but not of morals. Basic concepts of justice and decency apparently had nothing to do with it.

Early in the hearings before the Advisory Committee (from some of which we were excluded) we received word from persons on the State House staff that they had overheard conversation among the members of the Advisory Committee indicating that they had already decided against Sacco and Vanzetti. We believed the report to be quite accurate. Thompson and I then decided to withdraw so as not to lend an air of fairness to a farce. When Felix heard of this, he went into action immediately. He and Judge Julian W. Mack invited us to a dinner. They pleaded with us not to give up even the remote chance of changing Lowell's mind. The argument that convinced us to go on, however, was the consideration that our withdrawal might be regarded as indicating lack of faith in our cause. Felix followed up the dinner by writing to me a long letter of encouragement, probing more deeply into Lowell's character and suggesting ways of breaking through the shell of incomprehension which seemed to deflect whatever we said. The task was beyond our powers.

It was the Committee report which rendered the deaths of Sacco and Vanzetti acceptable to scores of troubled consciences. Lowell was the head of a great university, and it was known that he had sturdily defended the tradition of academic freedom at Harvard. What was not so well known, however, was that he had excluded Negroes from the (then) new freshman dormitories and had tried to impose a quota on the number of Jews to be admitted to Harvard. He was a prisoner of class prejudice. Felix later quoted the comment of one of Lowell's closest friends, John F. Moors, also a Boston Brahmin, a member of the Harvard Corporation, and a man of great breadth:

"Lawrence Lowell was incapable of seeing that two wops could be right and the Yankee judiciary could be wrong." No doubt the same incapability silenced others whose voices could have saved the reputation of the Commonwealth. Fiery protest against injustice which had so often stirred Massachusetts into action was left largely to a band of fearless women. Among the highborn ladies who kept alive the glorious tradition of the Commonwealth were Elizabeth Glendower Evans, Cerise Carman Jack, Katie Codman, Gertrude Winslow, Zara Dupont, Lois Rantoul, and Jessica Henderson. However, without the voice of the men in their group they were unable to affect the course of the impending tragedy. The Lowell report stopped the late but growing protest in responsible quarters.

There were blocks other than class prejudice in the way of

our breaking through to Lowell. To explain this fully, however, would require a different article, and this is a story about Felix Frankfurter.

The analysis of the case in the *Atlantic Monthly* had made Felix the center of admiration and suspicion. He continued patiently to write long letters explaining misconceptions of the evidence and mistaken assumptions. This continued long after the executions.

Through his friends Bernard Flexner and Emory Buckner a most distinguished committee was organized to publish the transcript of the record of the Sacco-Vanzetti case. Felix raised part of the money himself. In 1928 the record was published by Henry Holt and Company in five volumes and a supplement. This publication is now the prime source for all writing about the case. This massive contribution to history is almost entirely due to the foresight and initiative of Felix.

The deaths of Sacco and Vanzetti did not still the abuse heaped on Felix because of his exposure of the failure of our judicial processes. In fact, it snowballed for many years. Before and after the executions Communist agitation exploited the Sacco-Vanzetti case with characteristic hypocrisy. According to what Vanzetti told me, the Bolsheviks had shot about one hundred and sixty anarchists, without trial, for no reason other than that the executed men were anarchists. This alone would have been a crushing answer to Communist propaganda. Instead, Sacco and Vanzetti were pushed relentlessly into the chair despite the agonized protest of much of the civilized world. The manifest unfairness of the entire proceeding against the men was then depicted as an illusion created by Communist lies. The necessary result of this was to pillory Felix as a diabolical fellow traveler. This abuse continued for years and spread throughout the country. Campaign literature in three elections made Felix Frankfurter, rather then Franklin Roosevelt, the target of low political attack. The slanders grew more vicious as the Goebbels-Coughlin anti-Semitic line was added to violent anti-Communism.

Early in this campaign of vilification Thompson and I decided to do something about it. Joseph B. Ely had been elected Governor of Massachusetts. He was a top-notch trial lawyer, had been a District Attorney, and was convinced that Sacco and Vanzetti were innocent. He was also an admirer of Felix's from a distance. We decided that an effective answer to the slanders was for Ely to put Felix in the Supreme Judicial Court of Massachusetts. We brought them together at our home for a number of dinners and very enjoyable evenings. Nothing was said on these occasions about Felix going on the bench, but the Governor and Felix soon established a warm personal relationship. Thompson and I did our soliciting on nonsocial occasions. I think Felix knew what we were up to, but he made no effort to stop us. Either he thought nothing would come of it or that if it did an offer to make him a high justice was important whether he accepted it or not.

Suddenly, without warning or even word to Felix, the Governor named him to the Supreme Judicial Court. Ely said later that he did not want to give Felix a chance to refuse. The nomination was a sensation. Those who resented his part in exposing the Sacco-Vanzetti story were in a frenzy. Those who believed that Massachusetts was shamed in the eyes of civilization felt as if Ely had purified the air of the Commonwealth. On hearing the news, I rushed to Cambridge and walked with Felix from the faculty club to the law school. He seemed happy about the nomination, but hardly spoke during our stroll.

Later I telephoned his home in Cambridge. His wife, Marion, answered. She said that Felix would be away for a day or two. "Has he gone to Chatham?" I asked. Marion hesitated, and then replied that he had. Chatham was the summer home of Justice

Brandeis. When Felix returned, he had decided not to accept. I do not know his reason, but he reported to me that Brandeis urged him to continue teaching for another ten years and then to consider the bench. This is just about what happened, except that when the call came it was to the Supreme Court of the United States.

A booklet lies on my desk before me. It is *The Case of Sacco and Vanzetti*, by Felix Frankfurter, a reprint of the *Atlantic Monthly* article. It is inscribed, "For Brute, in happy memory of an unhappy past, affectionately, Felix."

As I glance at its pages, I can see that it tells an unfinished story. The full impact of unfairness, of prejudice, and perhaps of mere stupidity was not known when Felix wrote the booklet. For instance, Felix was stirred to action when he read that Captain Proctor gave a prepared answer to a question so that the judge and jury could believe his expert opinion to be that bullet No. 3 passed through Sacco's pistol. Felix then knew that Captain Proctor had found no evidence that it had been so fired. What Felix did not know was that Captain Proctor had a *positive opinion that the bullet had not gone through Sacco's pistol*, that during the trial he had exclaimed to his associates in the Court House corridor, "These are not the right men. Oh, no, you haven't got the right men," and that two years after the trial he disclaimed any further participation in the case, exclaiming, "*I'm getting too old to want to see a couple of fellows go to the chair for something I don't think they did.*"

These things were not then known to Felix, although he knew in a general way that Proctor believed the crime was the work of professionals. Nor was he aware of the fact that Captain Proctor, the senior police officer of the Commonwealth, was removed from direction of the preparation of the case for trial. His experience with crime and criminals was vast. He had been in charge of the investigation of the South Braintree murders and knew what evidence, if any, there was against Sacco and Vanzetti. Yet the preparation of the prosecution's case was taken from him and placed under the direction of Michael E. Stewart, Chief of Police of the small town of Bridgewater, a man with scarcely any knowledge of professional criminals or their ways, but with fresh experience in rounding up radicals for deportation. To Stewart criminals and radicals were synonymous. He believed firmly in the guilt of Sacco and Vanzetti. Had Proctor remained in charge, it seems certain that the presentation of the Commonwealth's case would not have taken the course it did. Also, Proctor's death just as he was beginning to talk about the case was another calamity. Had he lived, he might well have saved their lives.

Another example of a most important understatement in the booklet concerns a cap found at the scene of the crime, allegedly immediately after the shooting and claimed by the Commonwealth to belong to Sacco. Except as to general color resemblance, practically the only evidence purporting to identify the cap as Sacco's was a tear in the lining which the prosecution contended was caused by Sacco's habit of hanging the cap on a nail. So crucial was the cap evidence regarded that Judge Thayer cited it in three separate opinions denying motions for a new trial, in two of which he specifically pointed to the tear in the lining.

Felix mentions the cap, but was not then aware of the following facts: In 1927, before the Lowell Committee, Jeremiah F. Gallivan, Chief of the Braintree Police in 1920, testified that the cap had been found about thirty hours after the shooting (the area had been crowded with hundreds of people), that he had kept it under the seat of his car for more than ten days, and that *he himself had ripped the lining looking for identification marks*. Ordinarily Gallivan should have been called as a prosecution witness if only to trace the custody of a vital exhibit. He was not called. *His testimony would probably have eliminated the cap entirely as evidence against Sacco.* Failure to call him might well be responsible for the deaths of Sacco and Vanzetti.

In many other respects knowledge of the unfairness of the prosecution has grown with the years. Felix kept in touch with most developments, and has learned much that he did not know when he wrote the original article. An updated edition of his book today would make the original seem like a tepid understatement. History has fully justified his 1927 judgment. Among most responsible writers unfairness of the proceedings against Sacco and Vanzetti is no longer questioned. It is not surprising that some authors turn instead to the question of guilt. Even for this question, however, the original case has now been largely abandoned as the rot within it becomes exposed. Reliance is now placed on a synthetic case, built on contentions and witnesses rejected by the prosecution, on post-trial ex parte voluntary experiments, on armchair speculation and on hearsay tittle-tattle, none of which was ever subjected to defendants' investigation, cross-examination, rebuttal, or the evidential safeguards of trial. The need to use these leavings of the original case to support the theory of guilt is strongly suggestive of innocence. Although Felix, as a Supreme Court Justice, no longer expressed himself in public about the case, there can be no doubt concerning his low evaluation of any conclusions based on this kind of material.

Ten years after the deaths of Sacco and Vanzetti, I recorded my impression of Felix and the case in *Unity* magazine, issue of August 16, 1937. Today I would reaffirm this appraisal except that I would note that Felix voluntarily curbed his own freedom of speech when he changed from teacher to judge. The article said in part:

> The Sacco-Vanzetti case brought no crises to the life of Felix Frankfurter. . . . He was never counsel for the men, nor did he

ever undertake to advise their lawyers. So far as I know, he never talked with either Sacco or Vanzetti. His interest was wholly that of a student of the administration of justice, sharpened by indignation and a natural quick sympathy for the unfortunate. His contribution to the actual conduct of the case was limited to a sustaining faith in Thompson and to a buoyancy of spirits which relieved many a dark hour for counsel of the defense.

Accustomed as Frankfurter was to adulation and curses from the mighty, he was impervious to both. For years he had been the close friend of the intellectual leaders of two continents. He was no stranger to miscarriages of justice or to the fate of those who speak out when the mob is raging. At President Wilson's request he had investigated the Mooney case and reported in terms which now seem conservative in the light of the subsequently admitted perjuries. He had survived that earlier outburst from those who want order at the price of law and justice. When he decided to write about the Sacco-Vanzetti case he knew what was coming and did not care. To him the all-important thing was a proper administration of justice. He spoke, and the civilized world listened.

The only thing which could disturb Frankfurter was the claim that he had been unfair or inaccurate. So great was his passion for exactness that not one of his critics has been able to show that he omitted a single important detail or made any misstatement whatsoever in his presentation of the evidence in the case. . . .

After the close of the Sacco-Vanzetti case my contact with Felix was largely social, but not entirely so. For instance, in September 1929 there occurred a bit of history that never happened. I had just returned from a six-week absence in Scotland and England, and found a message on my desk that Professor Frankfurter wanted to see me immediately. We arranged to meet the same day for lunch at the Harvard Club.

Felix opened our talk with a question: "Brute, can you go to the Middle East for a few months?" When I protested that

I had just landed, he added, "I mean, on business," to which I replied, "That's different."

Indeed it was. The British Government had just appointed a High Commission to investigate the massacres of Jews by the Arabs in Palestine and to report its findings. Under the Balfour Declaration in 1918, Britain had bound itself to favor a national home for the Jewish people in Palestine. The spirit of the Declaration had been incorporated in the Treaty of San Remo, under which Britain held the mandate to govern that region. It was important to Jews that the Parliamentary Commission should not recommend any impairment of the treaty obligation. Looking backward today through the Nazi miasma, we now know that this was not merely important, it was crucial. To assure an impartial investigation, Felix stated first it was advisable that the different interests should be represented by counsel. He and Brandeis felt that the Jewish side could be more effectively presented by counsel not identified with the Zionist cause, one of whom should be an English conservative and the other an American lawyer. They wanted to recommend my brother-in-law, Sir Reginald Mitchell Banks, as senior counsel and me as his junior. Was Sir Reginald available?

A cable to London brought an affirmative response, and Felix promptly sent our names to Lord Melchett. Word came back immediately that he had just engaged the services of a K.C. high in British conservative politics as senior and the young son of a prominent English lawyer as junior.

The Passfield White Paper that resulted from the report of the Parliamentary Commission began the eclipse of Jewish immigration into Palestine. This was later followed by a second White Paper, which produced a complete blackout of such immigration just at the time when Palestine would have offered to the Jews of Europe the only escape from being murdered.

I do not know whether Reginald and I could have secured

any better results. It is not easy to influence decisions affected by power politics. However, Reginald possessed certain special qualifications not possessed, I believe, by the counsel chosen for the task. He spoke and understood Arabic; therefore needed no interpreter to translate the Arab presentation into English. During World War I he had commanded a Ghurka regiment in Mesopotamia. He knew the customs, manner of thought, and modes of expression of the other side. It is just possible that he might have been able to induce a more penetrating perspective in the minds of the commissioners. At the time, however, we did not foresee the outcome. My chief emotion was simply one of great disappointment at losing out on high adventure which also offered the opportunity of great service. So I remained in my Boston office and Sir Reginald in the Temple.

During most of the 1930's, however, my ultra-office activities were not associated with Felix. They were, however, gratifying. Some were in philanthropic and social service organizations. Others included membership on the Massachusetts Judicial Council, on the Massachusetts Civil Service Commission, and Chairman of the Parole Board for Shirley Industrial School.

In the fall of 1938 the news of Munich burst on an anxious world. Mrs. Ehrmann and I, together with millions of people outside of the Chamberlain government, knew what that surrender presaged. In our mood of hopeless frustration we did an irrational thing indicative of nothing except our feeling of affectionate affinity with Felix. We bought a bottle of the oldest port wine available and made a pilgrimage to the Frankfurter home on Brattle Street. However, even Felix could do nothing now to halt the march to manifest disaster. We held communion as the port vanished, and finally left in a lighter, if still pessimistic mood. Sometime later I received from Sir Reginald an explanation of Britain's incomprehensible surrender. He,

Churchill, and the Duchess of Atholl had constituted a trium-
virate trumpeting warnings about Hitler to the Baldwin-Cham-
berlain governments. Their call to arm went unheeded. Reginald's message was laconic and British: "We had no defence
against an air attack and so we funked it!"

In January 1939, Felix went to Washington and our close
personal contact lapsed. This was not only because of distance
but because he insulated himself against outside activities. My
own interests, however, continued to supplement my law practice.

In the early forties my voluntary activities were in aid of
the war effort. At the same time, the Hitler holocaust and the
first appearance in our own country of virulent anti-Semitism
led me to the conviction that human relations was the most
important problem in the postwar world. I joined the American
Jewish Committee, the oldest organization in America fighting
prejudice and discrimination. We soon concluded that no permanent solution could be found that was limited to the rights
of any particular group. Lasting safety lay only in a society in
which all were safe. This concept opened up boundless opportunities for cooperation with others and research in depth.
Today the Committee has grown into one of the foremost
human relations agencies in the entire world.

Although we saw little of Felix after he went on the bench,
his correspondence with us was considerable. Because of the
Sacco-Vanzetti case Mrs. Ehrmann had studied the question
of capital punishment. Like practically all serious students, she
came to the conclusion that it accomplished little good, if any,
but created much evil. She ultimately became the national leader
in the fight to abolish the death penalty. Felix was of great help
in this movement, both judicially and as a most impressive witness before various investigating commissions. He maintained
for Mrs. Ehrmann a stream of significant news items from here

and abroad, touching on the subject. This one-man clipping service was of inestimable value to her work.

On two occasions I argued cases before the Supreme Court challenging the constitutionality of state statutes under the First and Fourteenth amendments. In each case the state statute was upheld. In all probability, both decisions were influenced by Felix's philosophy that a state statute should never be upset if the Justices can possibly find some rational basis for its existence. Never? Well, hardly ever. Some members of the bar consoled me by explaining the adverse decisions on the ground that my clients were unfortunately white.

After both decisions Felix wrote most gracious letters to me, containing warm praise for my presentation. In effect they said, "The fault, dear Brutus, lay not in yourself, but in the stars." His sympathetic perception saw that I needed a lift and he gave it to me. This reversed my low spirits, but not the judgments.

In one of the cases, Crown Kosher Supermarket v. Gallagher, I lost by a margin of two Justices, but with an assist from Felix, I managed to win what is probably the biggest laugh in Supreme Court history. The case involved the constitutionality of the Massachusetts Sunday Closing Law. I represented not only the kosher market, but also Orthodox Jewish organizations. It was the first Sunday law case to receive a plenary hearing by the Supreme Court on First and Fourteenth Amendment grounds. The courtroom was crowded with lawyers from all over the country. I had tried the case in the United States District Court, and the three-judge court had found the Massachusetts Sunday Law unconstitutional. Chief Judge Calvert Magruder, in the majority opinion, had found that the statute had a primary purpose to establish Sunday as a Christian sabbath and also that its categories of exceptions were so arbitrary as to be a denial of equal protection of the laws. Among the latter, he cited that the act prohibited dredging for oysters, but not digging for clams. Joseph Elcock, Esq., for the appealing Commonwealth, in arguing constitutionality, answered by explaining that digging clams was a pleasure, but dredging for oysters was an industry. In reply, I commented that in Massachusetts clams constituted one of the biggest food industries in the Commonwealth, whereupon Felix interjected one of his mischievous questions. "Is there, Mr. Ehrmann," he asked in feigned seriousness, "any *religious* difference between a clam and an oyster?"

When the laugh subsided, I answered with the same ostensible gravity, "Not for Orthodox Jews, Mr. Justice Frankfurter."

The entire courtroom, including the nine Justices, exploded with such a roar that neither Chief Justice Warren nor any court officer called for order. The next morning the New York *Times* featured the episode and solemnly explained to its readers that the eating of *all* shell fish was forbidden to Jews who observed the dietary laws of kashruth.

When Felix posed the case of Clams v. Oysters, he was not being entirely frivolous. He was apparently probing the contention that the Massachusetts Sunday Closing Law had a primary religious purpose. This Socratic process of testing legal assumptions had characterized his teaching in the law school and followed him to the bench. As a teacher-justice, Felix was pre-eminent. It is remarkable, however, that his popularity survived this roughing up of the talk and thought of lawyers during their great moment before the United States Supreme Court. Equally surprising is the durability of his popularity as a person among his many friends who accepted the false notion that the judicial restraint he imposed upon his decisions indicated that he had become a "conservative." In an earlier period, when the Congress and the states were passing radical social legislation, this reluctance to interfere would have stamped him as a "liberal." Felix was able to separate his personal views of life from his own concept of judicial responsibility. This is a process hard to understand or to apply—even by judges.

More amazing still is the fact that Felix survived his repeated denunciations of injustice at the gates of power. During the Sacco-Vanzetti case Justice Brandeis observed to me that physical courage is the commonest human virtue and moral courage the rarest. By its very exercise, moral courage defies or challenges the popular prevailing opinion. This quality rarely wins laurels for the living, however many monuments its memory may evoke for the dead. Nevertheless, it did not blast Felix's career as it has that of others who attacked the established order. On the contrary, it may have enhanced it. Only recently Felix was included in a Presidential list of those deserving the Presidential Medal of Freedom. Was it accorded to him as a teacher, judge, or prophet? No doubt the author of *Profiles in Courage* could have given us the answer.

Yet none of the roles played by Felix explains the universal affection for him felt by his host of friends. Perhaps, like Abou ben Adhem, he heads the list because of his love of his fellow man. Whatever the explanation, he stands high on my own list because he is uniquely "Felix."

Felix Long Ago

Max Lowenthal, *Attorney*

In 1912, when F.F. was thirty and a name familiar to aspiring
Harvard Law students, I was one of the many introduced to
him at the twenty-fifth anniversary dinner of the *Harvard Law
Review*. That autumn I saw him the second time, in Washington. By then, his second Washington year, he was a favorite
in influential circles in the executive branch. He had been
brought thither by President Taft's Secretary of War, Henry
L. Stimson. Before that, in the years 1906–1910, Stimson had
been U. S. District Attorney in Manhattan, and selecting his
staff on a merit basis (as Wickersham did in the Justice Department thereafter), he recruited Felix from a leading Wall Street
law office whose clerkships were prizes of *Harvard Law Review*
editors of that period—the office to which Felix went from
the law school, and where he spent the few months constituting
his sole participation in private practice.

I learned more about Felix's career when I began to know
him and some of his friends during his earlier Washington
years. I mention a few fragments, chiefly in the political setting
of the two decades from 1894, when he was brought to the
U.S.A.—decades which are the frame for some of his wartime
and postwar attitudes and actions to which this paper is devoted.

In 1896, two years after America acquired him, Felix at fourteen was campaigning for William Jennings Bryan. Besides his cross-of-gold views, Bryan's platform favored such innovations as a graduated income tax, for which the Populists had stormily propagandized. That fear-engendering statute had been successfully described to the United States Supreme Court in 1894, the year of Felix's arrival, as Communistic.

Many incidents were occurring that stirred the alarm of the well-to-do and the powerful. The Homestead riots and pitched battles in the steel industry had marked the year 1892, the Pullman and nationwide rail strike the year 1894.

In the 1894 election Populist candidates won a great many seats in the national and state legislatures. A number of the Populist policies were taken over by Bryan's Democratic Party —policies which the Populists themselves had taken over from the earlier agrarian revolt.

The perturbation of better-to-do citizens was lessened if not stilled during McKinley's four years (Felix was then in high school and entering City College). But fright returned when a deranged young man shot the President. Conservative newspapers such as the New York *Sun* blamed the Hearst press for inflaming the irresponsible by its violent campaign against McKinley. Hearst shifted the blame and stressed the fact that the assassin had previously sought solace from his failures in life in lurid preachings of doctrines labeled "socialism," and later in advocacy of anarchism. Hunt down the anarchists, demanded the Hearst press; send the United States Army to discover and destroy every one of these "hellholes" where evil doctrines were preached, one statesman adjured the United States Senate; other legislators advanced similar views.

The more immediate cause of fright for entrenched conservatism of the time was not, however, the beliefs which Hearst attributed to the assassin. Supreme power over the executive branch now fell into the hands of Vice-President

Theodore Roosevelt, admired by Felix but feared by powerful politicians and financiers. Trust busting and indictment of wealthy violators of law followed T.R.'s rise, and continued into the regime of William Howard Taft and his United States Attorney in New York, Henry L. Stimson, Felix's first government employer.

It was during the pre-Taft years that Felix completed his term at City College and entered Harvard Law School. It was a time when the perceptive could hardly have failed to notice and devalue the bitterness of heated political invective. How much this may have influenced Felix in the broadening of his outlook I can not say. Certainly in his later years, when he himself was the occasional target of such bitterness, he was able to disregard it.

An occasion for distress of a much milder sort arose when Felix arrived in Cambridge and talked with the roommate he was to have. This was the lovable Sam J. Rosensohn, whose brilliance was already recognized in the previous, his first, year of attendance there. The conversation between the two opened innocently enough. What clothes had Felix brought with him? Felix did not know; he said his mother had packed his bag. But then came the disclosure that Felix was not going to follow the customary practice of slaving at law studies, to the exclusion of all else. He wanted to savor the courses in literature and other disciplines at Harvard College. Sam was shocked. The shock was not dissipated until Felix's first-year examination blue books put him in the front rank of his class. I remember that at least as late as five years thereafter, in 1909, first-year students were being given by Professor Jeremiah Smith, elderly ex-judge of the New Hampshire Supreme Court, a reading of a brilliant passage on a law problem, which our then oldest professor followed with these words: "I have been reading to you, gentlemen, from the first-year blue book of Felix Frankfurter, of the class of 1906."

Under U. S. Attorney Stimson, Felix enjoyed the opportunity to develop his unusual capacity for administration. I cite an instance in which sound judgment prevailed over the seduction of problems of lawyers' law. Stimson was prosecuting one of the big-time financier-industrialists of that unregenerate period. The juniors were Felix for the government, his onetime roommate, Sam Rosensohn, for the defense. Sam conceived and elaborated, in requests to the judge to charge the jury, minute gradations of law points wherein quietly reposed bases for appeal from a possible conviction—Talmudic splitting of hair after hair even more refined than Sammy Williston's classroom spinning of Socratic hypotheses. Stimson turned over to Felix the book-size series of requests—which should the government accept, which oppose? Felix saw that the very multiplicity of the proposed charges to the jury would have a benumbing effect, undoing the extremes to which the defense was trying to carry legal doctrines for the protection of accused persons. Agree to all the requests, said Felix to Stimson; the defense got its every theory, the prosecution got its conviction.

Good sense and talent in public affairs were to become more crucially needed than men foresaw during Felix's first Washington service—two years under Stimson, and two more in which the Woodrow Wilson Administration continued him as Counsel to the Bureau of Insular Affairs, until he was called to the Harvard Law faculty. His nominal job in the Bureau was complex enough, dealing with the issues of colonialism bequeathed to the United States Government by our last century's Cuban adventure. But Stimson used Felix for much beyond the limits of his nominal post—beyond the extraterritorial issues in our new island possessions. Stimson's insight, plus Felix's genius for sensing character and capacity and cementing relationships wherever such talents were to be found, led him into friendship with some of the finest personalities in our military establishment—men like Enoch H. Crowder. This proved useful in America's wartime when Felix was recalled to Washington in 1917. Garrison, and afterward Newton D. Baker and civilians assisting Baker, found Felix invaluable in pointing to the men within the Department and outside it who should be charged with tasks novel in nature or scope.

Between his two periods of service in the War Department, Felix had become professor of law at Harvard and had seemingly turned pure law lawyer. Yet he was innovating. There was need that practitioners and scholars should recognize the differences and distinctions in the semiadministrative, semijudicial functioning of such bodies as the Interstate Commerce Commission—a prevision helpful to the present generation of law offices and business concerns a large portion of whose time is absorbed by dealings with government administrators. When Felix went back to the law school in 1914, he set about the preparation of a casebook in this field.

Felix had been the beneficiary of the creation of the Commerce Court. That had been the occasion for President Taft's appointment of Julian W. Mack, an Illinois judge, and for Mack's frequent sitting in Washington during Felix's first term there. Though Mack was forty-five years old to Felix's twenty-nine, they took to each other at once, and formed the closest and warmest of friendships—an abiding love. Both men possessed deep sympathy for character, the older was a law judge par excellence as well as a forerunner in important social fields, and his appeals to Felix's interests thus touched Felix from all sides; and the younger man's charm and attractiveness and quickness in thought and expression swept the older man off his feet. And both, with so many similarities of interest and a gregariousness that was a passion in each of them, were contemporary newcomers to the Washington scene.

It was a good time for social life in the grand style of a Europe known to both Felix and Mack. Washington was then a comparatively small city; the house that Felix and several kindred young spirits were to take on S Street, not far from White House and executive departments, was accessible by the common transportation of the time, though then considered far out. It was the day of carriages and horses; the square adjoining what one now thinks of as the old Justice Department building was surrounded by these vehicles and steeds.

In this Washington, Felix and his young associates from various posts in the government set up what in time became a salon in the Continental spirit, which became known as the "House of Truth." Into their dinner parties, where wit and intelligence reigned, Judge Mack was drawn—and with the kindness of Felix and Mack toward youth, I, then the judge's law clerk, was given some opportunity to come along.

However errant such remembrances are likely to be after fifty years, some at least have been recounted by me so often that they seem to me deep-seated truth. Of one I have not had occasion to speak often. That was when Felix, for his casebook on administrative law, bestowed on me, a clientless lawyer on the fringes of Wall Street, the benison of invoking my assistance. It was one of the earliest of his uses of younger men in his successive scholarship enterprises. Possibly my present memory is ex post facto, but I think I remember that Felix was generous to me, encouraging and stimulating me to do the best I was then capable of. And—*mirabile dictu*—ever patient.

Something must have clicked. When Felix was back in Washington in 1917, and was assigned to several departments and was commandeered to expedite various government enterprises of a somewhat novel nature, he sent for me. So it was that I saw him close up in a number of wartime and postwar undertakings in which he was chief actor—about which I have some sketchy memories that are the *raison d'écrire* of this paper.

In the autumn of 1917, President Woodrow Wilson drafted Felix to become Secretary of the President's Mediation Commission, a temporary undertaking to settle major strikes in major wartime industries of the Far and Middle West. Felix called me. I warned him that I knew no economics, had had only a boring half year in that field at college, and had no knowledge of labor relations. The reply: "Neither does anybody else. Come along." Thus began eighteen months of almost continuous observation of the Felix of World War I and of post-Armistice months of preparation of material for the American staff at Versailles.

The Mediation Commission was headed by William B. Wilson, the kindly first Secretary of Labor, who had been a Pennsylvania coal miner, and been elected to Congress. Born in Scotland, brought to America at age eight, in his mid-fifties he still retained some of his Scotch burr. More Scotch in his accent was the chief labor member of the five-man Commission, John H. Walker, Illinois coal miner. The chief capitalist member was Verner Z. Reed of Colorado, whose fortune, measured by stock market quotations, shrank a mere few millions in the first few days of our train journey to the struck copper mines of Arizona.

Those isolated, desert-encircled mining hamlets were the Commission's first destination. The reopening of the mines, essential for prosecution of the war, depended on much more than mediation for adjustment of wages and conditions of work. This industry, like many others of those years, suffered from a deeply imbedded hate of labor unions and fear of anything that might be considered recognition of a union by an employer; recognition was considered to be involved merely in a meeting of strike leaders and employers' representatives in the same room —even in their physical presence in the same room on request of government mediators.

Felix addressed himself to this problem before leaving Washington. Making use of his wealth of acquaintanceship in many and varied circles, he persuaded two copper managements to direct local cooperation with the Mediation Commission. With their presence assured and the solid industry-wide wall thus breached, the job became that of relieving the warring sides of their animosities, by giving them every opportunity for airing their views, and reducing heat and venom whenever the excitement of the hearings rose too high. At that stage the most effective were Commission Chairman Wilson and Commissioner Spangler—Colonel, as he was then called—an elderly retired coal mine operator. Both had infinite capacity for quiescence, even for seeming to become drowsy during protracted hearings; their bearing, their slowness of utterance, their arts in appealing for considerateness and forbearance, constituted the process of conciliation at its highest.

Felix's contribution at this later stage was his resourcefulness in devising expedients to undo the knots tied by the power of hated words and by the irrationalities of strife.

As the Commission continued on its work of mediation, more and more duties devolved on Felix. Chairman Wilson's health was not of the best, and the working conditions were not calculated to enable men in their fifties and sixties to perform this task week after week—long hours of hearing every day, sleep and meals in a railway car on sidings in remote mining hamlets, all the labors before and after each day's public hearing to smooth out difficulties. At the same time, the chairman had to keep in touch with his Department in Washington.

Of the entire party, with the exception of the Chairman, the only one equipped to do an all-around job, even in the best of conditions, was Felix, early promoted from Secretary to Counsel. By the time the Commission tackled the west coast telephone strike, the proceedings unavoidably revolved around

Felix, and if he happened to be off on any of the side jobs (to which I shall refer below), all waited for his return. An instance was the evening when the union leaders from Washington State had finally been persuaded to come to San Francisco; an informal meeting with them was essential at the earliest possible moment; Felix was notified, and hurried back, and talks began at once.

Two main factors affected the settlement of that strike. Foremost was the conduct of Commissioner Verner Z. Reed. His career had accustomed him to making decisions rather than listening to recital of grievances and arguments. Of that he had had more in Arizona than he cared to take. Receiving the Chairman's permission to absent himself from those proceedings, and to take preliminary steps in behalf of the Commission in California, he undertook to demonstrate in San Francisco the procedure, antithetical to the Commission's, which he considered appropriate. When the Commission reached the west coast and read the newspapers, it discovered what he had done. He had summoned telephone management and unions to his hotel suite, allowed them a brief time to say their say, and dismissed them with orders to return in two hours, "when I will give you my decision." At the time appointed he read, from a sheet of hotel stationery, terms of settlement he said he prescribed, and without giving the parties time to point out that some of his prescription was impracticable, said, "You can either obey these terms or, in the name of the Government of the United States, I will commandeer the plants, the managements, and the men. Good day, gentlemen."

To be sure, not even the full Commission had such power, or any power other than that of persuading management and labor to reach an agreement. But no one could be sure of the direction which Congress might take, how fast it might move, and whether the entire Bell Telephone System might not pass under government control for the duration. Management was so eager to settle that if it could find anyone who spoke its language it would go far in yielding.

This led to the second chief factor, that the company lawyers knew of Felix and his practicality. They met him as the train drew into San Francisco and said, "We will agree to anything workable."

The problem then became principally that of the attitude of the telephone unions in the states north of San Francisco, where feeling had a barrier-like bitterness. Felix advised, and Chairman Wilson agreed, that the Commission must insist on conferences outside that bitter atmosphere. When the northern union leaders finally arrived at the Commission's hotel room, they said as they crossed the threshold, "We're ready to go to Alcatraz." Instead, Felix invited them to have a drink with him.

After copper, after telephones, after oil, the Commission's task became tougher. The logging camps of Oregon and Washington states were the scenes of homeless men in isolated small groups, and of unyielding employers. There the Commission could do no more than to hold public hearings in which camp working conditions were described by Pacific coast college teachers who had conducted surveys on the spot.

This gave the Commission a foretaste of the toughness of the meat packers' strike in Chicago. The managements would have nothing to do with the unions or their leaders, would not be seen anywhere near them, considered even a chance encounter a mortal danger to what the managements called "high principle." The most that Felix could effect in Chicago was an attempt to soften the management lawyers. Finally, as the war continued, the managements agreed to send their top men to Washington, to the office of the Secretary of Labor, and without conversing with the union leaders, to suffer their presence in that office. Before an hour had passed, both sides were indulging in polite handshakes—not the least of them being the chief company lawyer, on whom Professor Frankfurter, teacher of some

FELIX FRANKFURTER—*A Tribute*

of the brightest of that lawyer's juniors, had exerted his persuasion.

Returned to Washington, and appointed Chairman of a new agency, the War Labor Policies Board, Felix tackled the biggest and least touchable of the important managements of the day, the United States Steel Corporation. Considerable maneuvering with the help of men influential in steel and in finance generally finally persuaded Judge Gary, head of that corporation, to come to Washington to talk with Felix. But the talk was private, without presence of labor or public. A big issue was the eight-hour day, favored by Felix's board and recommended in the reports written by him for the Mediation Commission. The steel companies said this was an impossibility in their industry, which must continue the prevailing ten- and eleven-hour day. As for dealing with the steel union—it was dominated by syndicalists, by the IWW, by the wild-eyed leaders, the steelmakers said, and the American Federation of Labor was not much better. Felix's offer to Judge Gary of a bridge to a peaceful future was rejected, and disturbance and strife in steel continued years more, until the prematureness of Felix's offers of 1918 had become the actuality he forecast.

For one interested in the trappings and *mise en scène*, the Gary-Frankfurter conference offered striking contrasts and some similarities. The two lawyers, one seventy-two and the other thirty-six, were both small-bodied, but in most respects dissimilar in career and manner. The one was born on a midwestern pioneer farm during Abraham Lincoln's Springfield lawyership, in the year of Lincoln's election as a Whig to the Thirtieth Congress, the other in one of the most cultured European capitals when the Austrian Empire was in power and glory. Gary had served as peacetime small-town mayor and rural county judge before moving to the big city, Chicago, and ultimately directing a midwestern steel company and at last the biggest merger in the

132

land; Felix went directly from law school to a law citadel of American finance and then into the Government of the United States when the pioneering century was already giving way to the "big stick" and to assaults in the courts upon massive combinations of capital. Behind Gary was the most powerful banking house in the world; behind F.F. was win-the-war sentiment which Gary could also claim.

Judge Gary came to the conference obviously on guard, prepared to say as little as possible, his small eyes carefully watching his interlocutor, coolly aware of his superior position as one who needed nothing more than to bring the conference to an end and to nothing. F.F. was warm, eager, charming—all unavailing against a negotiator schooled in the arts of indifference.

They met in the small room off Felix's office. Judge Gary could barely see the White House across Lafayette Park. But he was accustomed to disagreements and even conflicts with the relatively short-term occupants of the Presidency and to almost invariable success for his methods and for reliance on the United States of aforetime. Time, not Felix, was to prove the victor over the seemingly ageless ex-lawyer, ex-judge, young as long ago as the time of the American Civil War, a power in steel as far back as the nineteenth century.

Felix's official position and his wealth of relations with men in power enabled him to take some effective part toward combating "patriotic" lawlessness. Thus he was in a position to persuade the Mediation commissioners that, in addition to restoring the production of copper, they ought to report publicly on the corraling and deportation into the desert of hundreds of striking copper miners, and to condemn illegalities committed in the name of patriotism or the necessity of winning the war. He wrote a revealing report, and it was issued by the Commission, despite initial inclinations of some of the commissioners to restrict their actions to settling strikes.

A more delicate task was the persuasion of those commissioners who were members of the American Federation of Labor to speak for correction of wrongs where the IWW was the chief labor organization in an industrial battle. This younger organization, a native American labor body, had rushed in to fill the vacuum in industries which had defeated, crushed, and stilled AFL efforts for correction of intolerable working conditions. The militant IWW became a thorn in the side of the older labor body, and also the target for attacks by employers and legislators. After the United States entered the war, the IWW was called treasonable, and before long was slowed up and enfeebled by indictment and conviction of its leadership under wartime sedition law.

In the Mediation Commission's report on the strife between loggers and lumbermen, Felix pointed out that if the IWW was rising in power in 1917 and prior thereto by radical methods, managements had only themselves to blame for driving out the AFL, and for continuing conditions that should long before have been remedied.

A different tactic was necessary in the Mediation Commission's action relating to the Mooney case, which the Commission had been instructed by President Wilson to investigate. Our government, in need of alliances against the Central European empires, was being seriously embarrassed abroad by widespread agitation to free Mooney, a California AFL official who had been convicted for bomb throwing in the San Francisco Preparedness Parade of 1916. The AFL in America, and working groups abroad, claimed that he was a victim of hysteria, that the crime had been fastened on him because of his labor union work.

Felix carried the load of personally investigating the case in the few days the Commission spent in California, and wrote the report. He advised against the Commission's endeavoring to arrive at a verdict of guilt or innocence, and in favor of recommending a new trial, on the basis of the evidence of subornation of perjury against Mooney. As a result, Felix became the target of bitter criticism in an atmosphere already heated by wartime excitement—an incident which was a forerunner of the opprobrium visited upon him when, a few years later, he wrote his report on the conduct of authorities in the Sacco-Vanzetti case.

Private and unpublicized actions by Felix during and after the war have too long remained generally unknown. I have in mind two examples. One consisted of his efforts to secure reversal of the summary wartime dismissal of a university professor as an alleged pro-German traitor. At a star chamber proceeding the governing board of the University of Minnesota, under the pressure of its most forceful member, discharged the long-time head of its Political Science Department, who was of German descent and had publicly opposed America's entering the war. Felix privately sought to obtain, for the broken professor, due process by the university's board. This failing, Felix tried to get other universities to employ him—an almost impossible undertaking amid the frenzy of the times. The case did not die; it became a byword, and a warning to other universities, even as late as World War II, to avoid similar dismissals.

In the second incident I have in mind, Felix again took a role currently unpopular in powerful places. He tried to persuade Coolidge's Attorney General, Harlan F. Stone, to drop a political prosecution instituted by Stone's discredited predecessor, Daugherty, against United States Senator Burton K. Wheeler. The prosecution was a weapon to force Wheeler to give up his investigation of Daugherty and Daugherty's so-called "Ohio gang." The only charge which the Justice Department detectives dared to trump up was a claim, with the help of dubious informants, that Wheeler, while Senator, had represented private clients before government departments. Felix's attempt to have the prosecution dropped was embarrassing to the party in power, and proved unsuccessful. But the trial jury corrected this wrong, throwing the case out in record time.

Prior to Daugherty's Attorney Generalship, Felix had been one of twelve eminent lawyers to issue a report on the illegal conduct of the Department of Justice under A. Mitchell Palmer and his political police against alleged "Reds." This report was followed by investigation of that Department at public hearings under direction of the senior Senator from Montana, Tom Walsh. When Felix thus evidenced his concern, in the early 1920s, over maladministration by the Justice Department, he was not holding public office. He was back at the law school—as a teacher.

It may not be amiss to recall some of the specifications of the indictment of the Attorney General and police agents contained in the lawyers' report; similar specifications appear later in decisions written or approved by Mr. Justice Frankfurter. "Wholesale arrests . . . without any process of law"; holding men and women "incommunicado without access of friends or counsel"; federal police entrance into private homes and seizure of property without search warrants; shameful abuse and maltreatment of persons "suspected of radical views"; Justice Department introduction of its agents "into radical organizations for . . . informing upon their members or inciting them to activities"; publicity "in support of these illegal acts," thus converting the Justice Department's officialdom into "a propaganda bureau designed to excite public opinion against radicals."

The lawyers' report reminded the Department of Justice of basic beliefs in the United States: "Free men respect justice and follow truth, but arbitrary power they will oppose until the end of time. There is no danger of revolution so great as that created by suppression, by ruthlessness, and by deliberate violation of the simple rules of American law and American decency."

Felix Frankfurter at Harvard

Roscoe Pound,
former Dean of the Harvard Law School

It was my good fortune to be a colleague of Mr. Justice Frankfurter's in the twenty-five years of his experience as a law teacher
before he began his exceptional career upon the bench. I am of
a somewhat older generation of law teachers, graduated from
college in 1888, student at Harvard Law School, 1889–1890, admitted to the bar in 1890, Professor of Law at Harvard Law
School in 1910, and Dean in 1916. He graduated from college
in 1902; studied at Harvard Law School, 1903–1906; LL.B. *cum
laude*, 1906; was admitted to the bar in 1906; Professor of Law
at Harvard Law School in 1914; Byrne Professor of Administrative Law in 1924, and resigned to take his seat upon the bench
in 1939. In the practice in New York he had been associated with
Hornblower, Byrne, Miller and Taylor, and later with Winthrop
and Stimson, and in law school he had been a classmate of
Grenville Clark and Elihu Root, Jr.'s, and a close friend of each.
Moreover, James Byrne and Henry L. Stimson, who were among
the leaders of the bar, and Grenville Clark, who had become the

head of one of the leading firms in New York, had urged his appointment to a professorship, and when James Byrne endowed the Byrne Professorship of Administrative Law, Professor Frankfurter, for whom the chair was intended by its founder, was at once appointed. He came to law teaching auspiciously, and his career as teacher and as judge has but confirmed the expectations of those who promoted it.

In his first year as a law teacher he taught the first-year course in criminal law. The time was one of exceptional interest in that subject. The juvenile court, probation and parole, modernized prison administration, and reformed procedure in the criminal courts were in the air. As a result, there came to be surveys of the administration of criminal justice, of which the Cleveland Survey, conducted by the Cleveland Foundation, a summary report of which was published in 1922, was outstanding. I was asked to be director of this survey. But as serving as director would take up my whole time for a year, to the detriment of my teaching work, I accepted the appointment only on condition that Professor Frankfurter be appointed co-director. This was agreed to. Accordingly, I went to Cleveland from Monday to Wednesday of each week, and he from Thursday to Saturday of each week until the survey was complete. We felt that this work was a needed step toward effective teaching of a very important branch of the law.

But after two years of teaching criminal law he felt that his time could be more effectively employed in teaching advanced rather than elementary legal courses, and after 1916 he ceased to teach criminal law and more and more taught only advanced subjects. In the meantime the graduate curriculum leading to the degrees of LL.M. and J.S.D. had been established, and provided an opportunity for full development of his powers.

From 1895 to 1909–10, Professor Gray taught a course called "Comparative Jurisprudence," the scope and purpose of which is indicated by his book, *The Nature and Sources of the Law, 1909; 2nd ed., 1927*. The course was taught in 1909–1910 by Professor Beale, under the title "Jurisprudence: The Nature of the Written and Unwritten Law." A course in Roman law was offered also in 1898–1899, and in some years thereafter, but got no permanent place in the undergraduate curriculum. International law was taught in 1898–1899 by Professor Strobel, but got no permanent place in the law school curriculum till later. In 1909–1910, International Law as Administered by the Courts was taught in the third year by Professor Wambaugh.

Out of these beginnings with the advent of Dean Thayer, and my appointment as Story Professor of Law, came a full course of what became graduate instruction leading to a degree of Doctor of Laws. Candidates for this degree were required to have completed the course for the degree of Bachelor of Laws with high rank. It was open to graduates of the Harvard Law School and of other law schools qualified to be members of the Association of American Law Schools upon one year after receiving the Bachelor's degree. The courses to be offered for this degree were stated as: "Roman Law, and the Principles of Civil Law and Modern Codes as Developments Thereof—An Introduction to Comparative Law; Administrative Law; History of the Common Law; International Law as Administered by the Courts; Interpretation of Statutes; Introduction to the Year Books; Jurisprudence—The Province of the Written and Unwritten Law; and Theory of Law and Legislation—including the relation of legislation to other agencies of lawmaking according to the different theories of jurisprudence, the limitations of effective legislation in matters of private law; Codification; Problems of Law Reform in America."

This preliminary plan for graduate instruction, the work of Professor Beale and Professor Wambaugh, was not carried out as at first announced in 1910. But in the catalogue of 1911–1912 it was stated thus: "Roman Law and the Principles of the Civil Law and Modern Codes as Developments Thereof—An Introduction to Comparative Law; Administrative Law; History of the Common Law; International Law as Administered by the Courts; Introduction to the Year Books; Jurisprudence: The Province of the Written and Unwritten Law; Theory of Law and Legislation—including the relation of legislation to other agencies of lawmaking according to the different theories of jurisprudence; Problems of Law Reform in America."

By 1914–1915, when Professor Frankfurter came to the school as Professor of Law, the graduate curriculum had been reorganized to six subjects: Jurisprudence, International Law, Roman Law, and the Civil Law and Modern Codes, Penal Legislation and Administration, History of the Common Law, and Administrative Law. He taught Criminal Law three hours a week in the first half of the first year; Public Service Companies two hours a week in the second year; and Penal Legislation and Administration, a two-hour graduate course. In 1915–1916 his teaching schedule was the same. But the resignation of Professor Wyman in 1914 had left open the course in public utilities, which had been developed as one on public service companies by Professor Beale and later by Professor Wyman; and Professor Frankfurter, finding the course open, had taken it over and renamed it "Public Utilities." It became his favorite course for the remainder of his teaching career. For the rest, he taught in the third year, Partnership, two hours a week in the second year, Jurisdiction and Procedure of the Federal Courts in the third year, and Administrative Law two hours a week in the second half of the graduate year. He had the same teaching program in 1917–1918, except that in place of Partnership he gave Municipal Corporations, from Beale's *Cases on Municipal Corporations*, two hours a week in the first half year. In 1918–1919 he was on leave of absence for the school year, for the period of the war, but was back at his teaching post in the year 1919–1920, teaching Public Utilities in the second year, Contracts and Combinations in Restraint of Trade, a full course, and Municipal Corporations (a half course) in the third year, and as a graduate course Administrative Law. In 1920–1921 he gave in the second year Public Utilities, using his own book, *Cases Under the Interstate Commerce Act*, in the third year Contracts and Combinations in Restraint of Trade, and a half course on municipal corporations. He taught Administrative Law as a graduate course. In 1921–1922 and 1922–1923 his teaching program was the same. But in 1923–1924 the course on public utilities was put over into the third year, so that he finally gave advanced courses, his program being, for that third year, Public Utilities, Contracts and Combinations in Restraint of Trade, Municipal Corporations, and Administrative Law. His teaching program for 1924–1925 was the same.

But a significant change was made in the provisions as to graduate study and graduate degrees. When I came to the Harvard Law School as a teacher in 1910–1911, the only graduate degree was Doctor of Laws, conferred upon graduates of the Harvard Law School upon one year's residence after receiving the Bachelor's degree, and upon graduates of the schools qualified to be members of the Association of American Law Schools after one year's residence after obtaining the Bachelor's degree. In that year the catalogue records two resident graduates: one from Harvard, 1910; the other from Yale, 1909. In 1911–1912 three are recorded: one from Harvard, one from Cincinnati, and one from St. Louis University. In 1913–1914 there were six: two from Harvard, one each from California, Chicago, Iowa, and Michigan. In 1914–1915, five, all but one from Harvard; in 1915–1916, eight: two from Harvard, and one each from Michigan, Chicago, Idaho, Kansas, and Stanford; in 1916–1917, ten: five from Harvard, and one each from Columbia, George Washington, Indiana, and Texas. From then the number and distribution remained about the same—twelve in 1922–1923: three from Harvard, two from the University of California, and one each from Chicago, Cincinnati, Iowa, Minnesota, North Carolina, Southern California, and Virginia. In 1924–1925 the number of graduate students was seventeen from Harvard Law School, eleven from the University of California, two from the University of Iowa, the University of Missouri, Syracuse University, the University of West Virginia, and from Yale one.

By this time the catalogue began to present adequate recognition of what had become prescribed graduate work. In the catalogue for 1925–1926, two graduate degrees are described; Master of Laws (LL.M.) and Doctor of Juridical Science (S.J.D.), and the work to be done for each is laid out in detail. In that year the number of graduate students rose to twenty-nine, of whom eleven held the degree of LL.B. from Harvard, ten were graduates of other American law schools, the remainder from Canadian, European, or Anglo-Indian institutions. When Professor Frankfurter resigned to go upon the bench of the Supreme Court of the United States in 1939, the number of graduate students had risen to forty-one, graduates of thirty-four American, two Canadian, and five European law schools.

Thus the graduate courses had come to be in some sort a law school in itself, in which the teachers met the students individually more than in large groups and could develop special subjects and individual talents.

Professor Frankfurter's appointment to the newly instituted Byrne Professorship of Administrative Law, which first appears in the catalogue for 1922–1923, is marked also by the transfer of the course on public utilities from the second to the third year. From this period on his teaching work was confined to third-year and graduate couses; for six years Public Utilities and for five years Jurisdiction and Procedure of Federal Courts as third-year courses, and for five years Administrative Law as a graduate course. But he taught Public Utilities from the beginning of his teaching career.

In the last five years of his teaching he developed fully his power of teaching the individual student rather than the class, especially adapted to graduate as compared with undergraduate instruction. His class took on something of the character of Socrates' "thinking shop." Teacher and student were cooperating in juristic development of the details of a branch of the law in the light of an assured grasp of the whole. Applied to Public Utilities, Contracts and Combinations in Restraint of Trade, Federal Jurisdiction and Procedure and Administration, this method of instruction developed a remarkable body of writing by students, both in their third year and in their graduate years, which many continued both as practitioners and as teachers. A catalogue of such dissertations left in the law school library after his resignation shows 161 items.

Some of these student papers were published while the writers were students. For example: "Judicial Review of Administrative Action," by E. F. Albertsworth, 35 *Harvard Law Review*, 125 (1931); Laurence Curtis, Jr., "Judicial Review of Administrative Regulation," 34 *Harvard Law Review*, 862 (1930); Frank A. Ross, "The Application of Common-law Rules of Evidence in Proceedings Before Workmen's Compensation Commissions," 36 *Harvard Law Review*, 263 (1923); Arthur E. Sutherland, "Federal Police Courts," 11 *Massachusetts Law Quarterly*, No. 5, 43 (1926); Maurice Finkelstein, "Judicial Self-Limitation," 37 *Harvard Law Review*, 338 (1923); Thomas G. Corcoran, "Petty Federal Offenses and the Constitutional Guaranty of Trial by Jury," 39 *Harvard Law Review*, 917 (1926); James M. Landis, "Power of Congress Over Procedure in Criminal Contempts in 'Inferior' Federal Courts—A Study in Separation of Powers," 37 *Harvard Law Review*, 1010 (1924); "The Historic Basis of

Diversity Jurisdiction," Henry J. Friendly, 41 *Harvard Law Review*, 458 (1928); W. Barton Leach, "State Laws of Evidence in the Federal Courts," 43 *Harvard Law Review*, 554 (1930); Judson A. Crane, "Jurisdiction of the United States Court of Claims," 34 *Harvard Law Review*, 161 (1920); Armistead M. Dobie, "Jurisdictional Amount in the United States District Court," 38 *Harvard Law Review*, 733 (1925); W. E. McCurdy, "The Power of a Public Utility to Fix Its Rates and Charges in the Absence of Regulatory Legislation," 38 *Harvard Law Review*, 202 (1924); Lester P. Schoene and Frank Watson, "Workmen's Compensation on Interstate Railways," 47 *Harvard Law Review*, 389 (1934).

In the past many a great teacher of law in the Harvard Law School, after a generation of teaching some particular subject which he had made particularly his own, published a textbook upon that subject which has taken its place among the classics of our American law. Beginning with the books by Judge Story, there are Greenleaf on evidence, Parsons on contracts, Washburn on real property, Beale on conflict of laws, Williston on contracts, and Scott on trusts. Professor Frankfurter did not continue to teach any one subject of the law for a generation before leaving law teaching to become a great judge upon our highest court. But he had while teaching proved a prolific and fruitful writer in the *Harvard Law Review*. Some of the items are: "Hours of Labor and Realism in Constitutional Law," 29 *Harvard Law Review*, 353 (1916); "The Constitutional Opinions of Justice Holmes," 29 *Harvard Law Review*, 683 (1916); "Twenty Years of Mr. Justice Holmes's Constitutional Opinions," 36 *Harvard Law Review*, 909 (1923); "A Note to Advisory Opinions of National and International Courts," 37 *Harvard Law Review* 1002 (1924); "Mr. Justice Brandeis and the Constitution," 45 *Harvard Law Review* 33 (1931); "Taney and the Commerce Clause," 49 *Harvard Law Review*, 1286

(1936). Also in collaboration with students and colleagues: "Felix Frankfurter and Nathan Greene, Labor Injunctions and Federal Legislation," 42 *Harvard Law Review*, 766 (1929); Felix Frankfurter and Henry M. Hart, Jr., "The Business of the Supreme Court at the October Term, 1932, 1933, 1934," 47, 48, 49 *Harvard Law Review* (1933-1935); Felix Frankfurter and James M. Landis, "Power of Congress Over Procedure in Criminal Contempts in 'Inferior' Federal Courts, A Study in Separation of Powers," 37 *Harvard Law Review*, 1010 (1924); "The Business of the Supreme Court of the United States—A Study in the Federal Judicial Sytem: I. The Period Prior to the Civil War; II. From the Civil War to the Circuit Courts of Appeals Acts; III. From the Circuit Courts of Appeals Act to the Judicial Code; IV. Federal Courts of Specialized Jurisdiction; V. From the Judicial Code to the Post-War Judiciary Acts; VI. The Judicial Conference; VII. The Judiciary Act of 1925; VIII. The Future of Supreme Court Litigation," 38, 39, 40 *Harvard Law Review* (1925-1927). Also "The Supreme Court Under the Judiciary Act of 1925," 42 *Harvard Law Review*, 1 (1928); "The Business of the Supreme Court at the October Term, 1928," 43 *Harvard Law Review*, 33 (1929); "The Business of the Supreme Court at the October Term, 1929," 44 *Harvard Law Review*, 1 (1930); "The Business of the Supreme Court at the October 1930 Term," 45 *Harvard Law Review*, 271 (1931); "The Business of the Supreme Court at the October Term 1932," 46 *Harvard Law Review*, 226 (1932).

This writing of itself, done while in full tide of active teaching, is remarkable evidence of fruitful activity.

Finally, in the last year of his teaching, he was one of a group of teachers in other departments of the university who arranged a program of joint seminars, to be limited to not more than twelve students in each, admitted with the consent of their teachers.

Thus Professor Frankfurter had already done what would amount to a reasonable life's work as a jurist and teacher of law when he resigned to take on a new role as a Justice of the Supreme Court of the United States. In that role he has also, so far as that has been possible, distinguished himself even more.

May we not believe that as a worthy successor of Story and of Holmes as contributors to the building of American law, with them he will be reckoned as one who has built toward a law of the world that is to come.

Mr. Justice Frankfurter

Paul A. Freund, *Harvard Law School*

Felix Frankfurter is by temperament and conviction preeminently a teacher. He himself enjoys telling of an incident not long after he went on the Court when in the course of an animated discussion at conference one of the brethren referred, not in entire forgetfulness, to the views just expressed by "Professor Frankfurter," to which the Justice interposed that he could not imagine a more honorable or flattering title.

Thirty years ago Oxford University recognized his position in the great community of legal scholarship by conferring on Professor Frankfurter its degree of Doctor of Laws. Indeed, the university orator in composing the citation was able, with donnish wit, to suggest that the event had been foreshadowed by Vergil: *"Felix qui potuit reorum cognoscere causas."* However that may be, whether the ascription of happiness to one who understands lawsuits is a Roman or only an Oxonian philosophy, surely no Supreme Court Justice has been more solicitous of the place of our law in the whole current of Anglo-American legal history or more anxious that the Court guide with the lamp of learning.

What picture of Felix Frankfurter as a teacher can be conveyed to those who did not have the fortune to know him in the classroom? To describe the special qualities of a great teacher almost eludes the power of words; in this, testimonial evidence is much less effective than real evidence. Perhaps the most touching description of a great teacher that I have seen is the picture given of Willard Gibbs, the Yale mathematician, by his biographer, Muriel Rukeyser. She tells of Gibbs standing in front of a class, beside a blackboard on which an abstruse equation had been worked out, tears streaming down his face and the students gazing at the board with the look of those who had just seen angels. The sight of angels is an image that is denied to most students of the law, even at Harvard. But what we did see was the illumination created by an incandescent mind, sometimes by the darting gleam of fireworks.

Professor Frankfurter taught a course in public utilities known affectionately as the "Case of the Month Club." For him a case was not the illustration of some principle or point of law; to approach it thus would for him have been a sacrilege. A case was explored as a process, through the record, the briefs, the counsel, the judges, the statute, its legislative background, indeed the geography of the area involved, preferably to be reported on by a student who came from that locality. The law of public utilities was learned almost by osmosis as you breathed it in while absorbing the insights of lawyership.

Then there were the seminars in administrative law and federal jurisdiction, where the intensity of a smaller group narrowed the gap over which the sparks traveled, and where the most recondite research became as exciting as the most recent Supreme Court advance sheets because it was felt that the voices of the past, if only they were unlocked, would have something vital to say to us about our urgent problems. Paging the reports, paging the statute books, even paging the statute books of the American colonies, was for many a student an enthralling adventure.

History was always a primary interest of Professor Frankfurter's, but not history as inert knowledge. He viewed the study of history much as Holmes did, as a way of emancipating ourselves from fetters forged of our own misunderstanding.[1] Two of his most notable law review articles were of this character. One, the study of jury trial for petty federal crimes, showed that the Constitution viewed historically allowed a classification of crimes that would tolerate trials without jury in a substantial group of cases.[2] This at a time when the enforcement of the Volstead Act posed serious problems of judicial administration for the federal courts on their criminal side. The other paper, curiously cognate to this, was a historical study of criminal contempt to determine whether jury trial might constitutionally be provided, and this at a time when the validity of the jury provision of the Clayton Act was actively in litigation.[3] It is interesting that in each instance the study demonstrated that constitutional history left scope to Congress to settle the issue without coercion by the supposed compulsion of the Constitution. In the article on petty offenses Professor Frankfurter concluded with words which, though written in 1926, could be matched in his opinions today. He said this:

> One can say with assurance, then, that so far as history is a guide, those multitudinous infractions of the detailed rules of modern society which we significantly group as police regulations need not be enforced with all the paraphernalia of jury trials. The profound reasons for a popular share in the administration of criminal justice did not cover this extensive range of petty offenses. Such is the verdict of the history that went into the Constitution. But it does not consider the influences which modify the sway of the common law in the application even of constitutional clauses rooted in its history. Still less are we here concerned with the wisdom of doing what the Constitution allows. American social policy suffers all too much from the dictation of abstract questions of constitutional powers. The historic availability of summary judgment is by no means proof

of its desirability in the enforcement of a particular law. That
is a problem for statecraft, whatever may be the opportunities
which the Constitution affords. But Congress should know the
alternatives which constitutionally are open to it. . . . If [this
paper] be lacking in the definiteness of a yardstick, we can
only conclude by saying that history presents a body of experience expressive of the judgment of its time, but does not save
Congress nor the Supreme Court from the necessity for judgment in giving past history present application.[4]

As one reviews Professor Frankfurter's scholarly works one is
impressed with their dominant concern for procedure in the
large sense: that pioneering volume, *The Business of the Supreme
Court*, the casebooks on federal jurisdiction and administrative
law, the fruitful study of the labor injunction, and the courageous book which reflected the most painful experience of his life,
The Sacco-Vanzetti Case. These were all studies of procedure in
the context of very concrete issues which transcended procedure
but which are made more tractable through the lawyer's contribution of a right structure for their solution.

Significant as his scholarly writings have been, it would be
hard to place them higher in importance than his evocative
powers with his students. What he said of Judge Cardozo, as
Chief Judge of New York, will best convey what I mean. "One
is told," he said, "that the same men were somehow or other
better when he was chief judge than they were the next day,
after he had ceased to be chief judge. That's a common experience in life. One man is able to bring things out of you that are
there if they're evoked, if they're sufficiently stimulated, sufficiently directed."[5] It is fair to ask whether Frankfurter was not
thinking of the formative influences on himself when he spoke of
a common experience in life. Of these influences, beyond the
intimacies of family life, one would have to include the teachers
in the public schools of New York (his feeling for the public

schools can be seen in the flag-salute cases and in the released time for religious education cases) and the Harvard Law School faculty, in particular Dean Ames, who conveyed a deep sense of legal history and ethics under the rubric of torts or trusts, and the shade of James Bradley Thayer, the teacher of Brandeis and the colleague of Holmes, whose spacious view of constitutional powers and whose correspondingly guarded conception of judicial review has been high in the consciousness of Judge Learned Hand and of Mr. Justice Frankfurter. Then there was Henry L. Stimson, Frankfurter's chief as United States Attorney in New York and as Secretary of War in Washington, whose standards of austerity and integrity in the enforcement of the law are strongly reflected in the Justice's own outlook. And above all, there was the long and intimate friendship with Holmes and Brandeis, of which the Justice's own unstinting tributes make it superfluous to speak.

And yet a man is more than the sum of influences playing upon him. These do not so much instill as they evoke. The relation is not merely influence, but affinity. And so in the end we are brought back to the mysterious alchemy of the self. None of us can know another in the way we know ourselves. We cannot transcend the limitations of our own consciousness and project ourselves into the consciousness of another any more than we can jump out of our own skins, though to try to know another who is an altogether richer being than oneself is a healthy exercise in stretching one's mental and spiritual integument.

This digression on the nature of the self is perhaps as good an introduction as any to the judicial philosophy of Mr. Justice Frankfurter. The cardinal themes in that philosophy can be viewed under the aspect of those objects to which Justice ought to owe the profoundest respect. Of these there are three, I would suggest, that are basic in the thought of Mr. Justice Frankfurter: first, respect for the integrity of the individual; second, respect for the structure of government with its distribution of what the military call roles and missions; and third, self-respect. Let me touch on each of these in turn.

First, the integrity of the individual. The philosophers put it that a man is a subject, not an object. The British speak of the liberty of the subject. Bills of rights, with their due process clauses, are yet another mode of formulation. Mr. Justice Frankfurter has never been fearful that adherence to those guarantees would weaken society's defenses. Twenty-five years ago while he was at Harvard, in his introduction to the Gluecks' early study of juvenile delinquency he wrote this:

> In the main our whole process of criminal justice is crude and amateurish, economically costly and morally cheap. But the center of gravity of our problems of crime lies outside the courtroom. The crucial difficulties are unrelated to defects in trial procedure, and we are doomed to deep disappointment if we look for substantial diminution of crime to departure from those essential safeguards of liberty that have been enshrined in our Bill of Rights.[6]

The integrity of the person is the principle which underlies his McNabb[7] opinion on the fruits of questioning an accused during a period of unlawful detention. The same principle can be discerned in the very different context of Sibbach v. Wilson,[8] where in a dissenting opinion he questioned the federal rule of civil procedure authorizing a compulsory physical examination for a party in a personal injury case. Such a requirement, he believed, touched so sensitively the interests of personality that it ought to await a clear authorization by the legislature and not be imposed by mere rule of court. He has found himself dissenting also from judgments upholding federal searches and seizures without a warrant: violation of the integrity of one's papers and effects, an extension of one's personality, is justified only under the strict safeguards of a specific warrant. In the Harris case, in a dissenting opinion, he said:

> If I begin with some general observations, it is not because I am unmindful of Mr. Justice Holmes' caution that "General propositions do not decide concrete cases. . . ." Whether they do or not often depends on the strength of the conviction with which such "general propositions" are held. A principle may be accepted "in principle," but the impact of an immediate situation may lead to deviation from the principle. Or, while accepted "in principle," a competing principle may seem more important. Both these considerations have doubtless influenced the application of the search and seizure provisions of the Bill of Rights. Thus, one's views regarding circumstances like those here presented ultimately depend upon one's understanding of the history and the function of the Fourth Amendment. A decision may turn on whether one gives that amendment a place second to none in the Bill of Rights, or considers it on the whole a kind of a nuisance, a serious impediment in the war against crime.[9]

And from the same case:

> For me the background is respect for that provision of the Bill of Rights which is central to enjoyment of the other guarantees of the Bill of Rights. How can there be freedom of thought or freedom of speech or freedom of religion if the police can, without warrant, search your house and mine from garret to cellar merely because they are executing a warrant of arrest? How can men feel free if all their papers can be searched, as an incident to the arrest of someone in the house, on the chance that something may turn up, or rather, be turned up? Yesterday the justifying document was an illicit ration book, tomorrow it may be some suspect piece of literature.[10]

Even when the issue involved the procedure of a state rather than that of the federal court, with the corresponding latitude that he insisted a state enjoys to admit or exclude illegally obtained evidence, to employ or not to employ its rules of evidence to keep out relevant and trustworthy evidence because of its origin, even here he balked when the illegal source was grossly offensive to standards of decent official behavior. In the stomach pump case he said:

Due process of law, "itself a historical product," . . . is not to be turned into a destructive dogma against the States in the administration of their systems of criminal justice. However, this Court too has its responsibilities. Regard for the requirements of the Due Process Clause "inescapably imposes upon this Court an exercise of judgment upon the whole course of the proceedings in order to ascertain whether they offend those canons of decency and fairness which express the notions of justice of English-speaking peoples even toward those charged with the most heinous offenses. . . ." These standards of justice are not authoritatively formulated anywhere as though they were specifics. Due process of law is a summarized constitutional guarantee of respect for those personal immunities which, as Mr. Justice Cardozo twice wrote for the Court, are "so rooted in the traditions and conscience of our people as to be ranked as fundamental," . . . or are "implicit in the concept of ordered liberty." . . . The Court's function in the observance of this settled conception of the Due Process Clause does not leave us without adequate guides in subjecting State criminal procedures to constitutional judgment. In dealing not with the machinery of government but with human rights, the absence of formal exactitude, or want of fixity of meaning, is not an unusual or even regrettable attribute of constitutional provisions. Words being symbols do not speak without a gloss. On the one hand the gloss may be the deposit of history, whereby a term gains technical content. . . . When the gloss has thus not been fixed but is a function of the process of judgment, the judgment is bound to fall differently at different times and differently at the same time through different judges. Even more specific provisions, such as the guarantee of freedom of speech and the detailed protection against unreasonable searches and seizures, have inevitably evoked as sharp divisions in this Court as the least specific and most comprehensive protection of liberties, the Due Process Clause.[11]

This stomach pump case, you will recall, produced a great debate within the Court. Two concurring Justices took the position that the evidence dredged up by the stomach pump must be excluded under the specific guarantee of the privilege against self-incrimination. They bridled at what they regarded as the natural-law and subjective analysis of due process by Mr. Justice Frankfurter. But once the privilege against self-incrimination is applied beyond the sphere of oral testimony, there is no literal guide to its stopping place. The concurring Justices acknowledged that to compel an accused to stand up in court, to turn this way and that, or to put on an article of clothing before the jury would not violate the privilege against self-incrimination. But they would rule out the results of a scientific blood test if carried out without the consent of the defendant. What, then, of the cutting of a strand of hair? They would draw the line somewhere on the basis of physical integrity, and though they might draw it more restrictively, it is hard to see how the invocation of the privilege against self-incrimination furnishes that objective and unmistakable criterion that is lacking in the due process clause.

The same fundamental respect for human integrity comes through the Justice's opinions on the question of the right to a hearing, as when a claim of insanity is made on behalf of a prisoner condemned to death.[12] Here again he found himself in a minority. Of a piece with this concern is the Justice's position on capital punishment. Again he sees the issue in terms of procedure. He said in testimony before the British Royal Commission on Capital Punishment a few years ago:

I am strongly against capital punishment for reasons that are not related to concern for the murderer or the risk of convicting the innocent, and for reasons and considerations that might not be applicable to your country at all. When life is at hazard in a trial, it sensationalizes the whole thing almost unwittingly; the effect on juries, the Bar, the public, the judiciary, I regard as very bad. I think scientifically the claim of deterrence is not worth much. Whatever proof there may be in my judgment does not outweigh the social loss due to the inherent sensationalism of a trial for life.[13]

This is a rather different view of the issue of capital punishment than you will find expressed in the conventional discussions.

The same emphasis on fair procedure as the Court's fundamental concern is to be found in his opinions on administrative law. An alien against whom a deportation order has been issued ought, he felt, to be able to invoke the declaratory judgment procedure and not be confined to habeas corpus; the alien ought, that is, to be able to challenge the order even though not in custody, provided that the governing statutes are susceptible of a reading either way.[14] Once more he was in dissent.

The whole subject of standing to challenge administrative action received full-scale treatment in one of his most massive and deeply felt opinions, that in the Joint Anti-Fascist Committee case:

Man being what he is cannot safely be trusted with complete immunity from outward responsibility in depriving others of their rights. At least such is the conviction underlying our Bill of Rights. That a conclusion satisfies one's private conscience does not attest its reliability. The validity and moral authority of a conclusion largely depend on the mode by which it was reached. Secrecy is not congenial to truth-seeking and self-righteousness gives too slender an assurance of rightness. No better instrument has been devised for arriving at truth than to give a person in jeopardy of serious loss notice of the case against

156

him and opportunity to meet it. Nor has a better way been found for generating the feeling, so important to a popular government, that justice has been done.[15]

A procedural guarantee which is at the core of the rule of law, of Dicey's Rule of Law if you please, is the suability of public officials for illegal actions which they have taken or threatened. How to reconcile this essential of the rule of law with the traditional doctrine of sovereign immunity from suit has been the subject of some of the Justice's most important and revealing opinions. When issues of fundamental human liberty are discussed, the problem of immunity of the sovereign or suability is frequently overlooked, but to me, and I surmise to the Justice, it is at the very core of the guarantee of liberty. It is fitting therefore that one of the two opinions the Justice delivered on his first opinion day twenty years ago was on this theme, and another of his massive dissents, in the Larson case,[16] was in protest against an extension of sovereign immunity.

I have said nothing thus far of the liberty of speech, which many would regard as the cornerstone of respect for integrity of the individual. Surely no one can read Mr. Justice Frankfurter's opinion in the Michigan obscenity case[17] striking down a law which made the test of legality for all distribution the effect of the printed matter on the susceptibilities of youth, or his concurring opinion in the Sweezy case[18] setting up the freedom of the academic lecture room against an attenuated claim of the internal security of the state, no one can read these opinions without recognizing his sensitivity to freedom of expression. But he has not been prepared to regard this freedom in as absolute terms as some of his brethren, as, for example, in the case of contempt of court by newspapers in the Los Angeles *Times*-Harry Bridges affair.[19] This is not the occasion to deal in detail with the issue of freedom of speech and the press. I can do no better for present purposes than to quote from a piece by Philip Toynbee, the English literary critic, which appeared in the London *Observer*. I quote this with the thought that it will be sufficient to illuminate the issue of freedom of expression as seen by an observer with the disinterestedness of distance and with another professional background. What Philip Toynbee wrote with specific reference to obscenity and the law could be taken *mutatis mutandis* as a more general commentary on our problem.

The smut-hounds are guilty of elevating personal prejudice above both art and freedom. The art-heretics are guilty of elevating art above life, the part above the whole, the by-product above the living process of creation. It is the old argument which divided some of us at the time of Monte Cassino, when a few held that the monastery should be spared even at the cost of soldiers' lives while the same majority considered this to be the most odious of blasphemies. Suppose that after an air raid a man had lain buried under St. Paul's in such a way that he could be rescued only by the demolition of the whole cathedral. Who but a monster would have hardened his heart against the victim's cries rather than against the man-made monument above him? And just as there is a lunatic fringe of art lovers, so there is a lunatic fringe of libertarians who hold that the freedom to talk or print is, in all circumstances, sacrosanct. They would protest against any action being taken to prevent the publication of anti-Semitic pamphlets in modern Germany or of incitements to race-violence in Notting Hill. It is another heresy which prefers the part to the whole and attempts to deal with the complexity of life by a single supreme simplicity.[20]

A "single supreme simplicity" is exactly what Mr. Justice Frankfurter is wary of.

This is a convenient point at which to turn to the second kind of respect in the Justice's philosophy: respect for the structure of government and the assignment of roles and missions. If a judge could think only of respect for integrity or personality, all would be peace and quiet in the dovecote. As soon as you introduce such considerations as the federal system, the relation of courts to legislatures, the limits of effective judicial action, and the congeries of cautions known as political questions, you have indeed set the cat among the chickens. The Francis[21] case from Louisiana is an illustration. That was the case of the unfortunate criminal defendant who, upon being placed in the electric chair pursuant to a death sentence, found that the current failed and that the electrocution was therefore frustrated, and who maintained that to be subjected to a second ordeal would violate the guarantee against double jeopardy and cruel and unusual punishment as well as the standard of due process of law. Mr. Justice Frankfurter, with his avowed and deeply felt repugnance toward capital punishment, must surely have felt sympathy for the defendant's claim, and yet he was unable to find in the clauses of the Constitution a ground for preventing a second attempt on the part of the state. He more than implied in his opinion that the case ought to commend itself as one for executive commutation.

The most vexing problem of judicial review in terms of the structure of government is the question of a double standard or a preferred position for certain constitutional guarantees. Mr. Justice Frankfurter has resisted the claim for any such priorities, though he has described approvingly a scale of values which he discerned in the opinions of Mr. Justice Holmes. He said this in writing of Holmes:

> Social development is an effective process of trial and error only if there is the fullest possible opportunity for the free play of the mind. He therefore attributed very different legal significance to those liberties which history has attested as the indis-

pensable conditions of a free society from that which he attached to liberties which derived merely from shirting economic arrangement.[22]

This is not the occasion to examine the myriad judgments arrived at by Mr. Justice Frankfurter in this troubled area. Doubtless no two thinkers would stand in complete agreement, given the complexity of the issues. But it may be important to notice the frank and ever present concern of the Justice that the issues be seen in the full on their several levels, and his cognate concern lest a purely private judgment of preference be taken as a constitutional command. To avoid this he relies heavily, may it not be too heavily, on the teachings of history. Now history can show us a number of things. First, it can show us specific events: what was done, for example, about habeas corpus in the Act of 1679. In the second place, history can give us a narrative; it can tell us what was the practice regarding jury trial for contempt in the centuries preceding our Constitution. But when history is called on to furnish a guide to the priority of values, I wonder whether it is being given a burden heavier than it can bear alone. Here, as it seems to me, history becomes the creative art of the historian. Santayana has spoken of an "estimate of evolution" as "a sort of retrospective politics," engaged in as one "might look over a crowd to find his friends."[23] From Lord Acton has come a similar warning against confounding the historian with the history:

Whatever a man's notions of these later centuries are, such, in the main, the man himself will be. Under the name of History, they cover the articles of his philosophic, his religious and his political creed. They give his measure, they denote his character: and, as praise is the shipwreck of historians, his preferences betray him more than his aversions. Modern history touches us so nearly, it is so deep a question of life and death, that we are bound to find our way through it, and to owe our insight to ourselves.[24]

I wonder whether history does not have to yield here to philosophy. History or historians may suggest, to be sure, some lessons about the effectiveness of institutional arrangements. But would it really matter, for constitutional law, if a historian argued persuasively that English literature had its greatest flowering during a period of the licensing of books and plays?

A philosophy, of course, need not be merely personal. In large terms our professed philosophy is that of representative self-government, a secular state, a division of authority, and the protection of minority rights. While important variances within these very broad conceptions are inevitable, we are not without safeguards against excessively personal judicial judgments. One safeguard is the practice of deciding no more than is necessary to the case—in constitutional law to decide, if possible, on a non-constitutional rather than a constitutional ground. The whole tenor of the Supreme Court's decisions in the last few years in the field of internal sceurity reflects this caution, by giving to the legislature or to the executive an opportunity for sober second thought. And this practice, it must be clear to any reader of the opinions of the Court, is particularly congenial to, and characteristic of, Mr. Justice Frankfurter. Another safeguard is craftsmanship—the careful articulation of the grounds of decision and a re-examination from time to time of the assumptions on which rules and doctrines rest. If the unexamined life is not worth living, the unexamined premise is not worth its implications.

This is the meaning of the third and final form of respect of which I have spoken, namely self-respect, and I shall let Mr. Justice Frankfurter describe it in his own words from the Larson case on sovereign immunity.

Case-by-case adjudication gives to the judicial process the impact of actuality and thereby saves it from the hazards of generalization insufficiently nourished by experience. There is, however, an attendant weakness to a system that purports to pass merely on what are deemed to be the particular circumstances of a case. Consciously or unconsciously the pronouncements in an opinion too often exceed the justification of the circumstances on which they are based, or contrariwise, judicial preoccupation with the claims of the immediate leads to a succession of *ad hoc* determinations making for eventual confusion and conflict. There comes a time when the general considerations underlying each specific situation must be exposed in order to bring the too unruly instances into more fruitful harmony. The case before us presents one of those problems for the rational solution of which it becomes necessary, as a matter of judicial self-respect, to take soundings in order to know where we are and whither we are going.[25]

One is reminded of the moving and profound story told of Gertrude Stein on her deathbed. She was heard to murmur, "What is the answer?", and when there was an awkward and prolonged silence there came from her lips another murmur: "In that case, what is the question?"

Some of Mr. Justice Frankfurter's greatest opinions have inquired into and reformulated "the questions"—his opinions, for example, on standing to challenge administrative action, on review of negative orders in administrative law, on sovereign immunity, on intergovernment relations. The value of these opinions makes one all the more regretful that the volume of the Court's business requires that these explorations be undertaken only now and then, and against undue pressure of time. The full potentialities of the Court for the clarification and advancement of fundamental law may well entail a more selective granting of review and more systematic procedures within the Court for consultation, interchange, and collaborative endeavor leading toward persuasive and scholarly exposition. Mr. Justice Frankfurter, at all events, places his ultimate faith in articulated reason, though he has no illusions about the fragile instrument that reason is. As he has more than once put it, "How slender a reed is reason, how recent its emergence in man." He must have relished the innuendo of President Lowell of Harvard in awarding an honorary degree to William Morton Wheeler, the eminent entomologist, with this citation: "Profound student of the social life of insects, who has shown that they also can maintain complex communities without the use of reason."

For an infusion of a modicum of reason into its relationships the human hive, in its less recalcitrant moments, looks to its teachers and its judges. Mr. Justice Frankfurter has shown, for many more than his twenty-three years of judicial service, how this highest of human enterprises can be carried on at once without illusion and with buoyancy, courage, and faith.

Applied Politics and the Science of Law: Writings of the Harvard Period

Alexander M. Bickel, *Yale Law School*

When Felix Frankfurter was called to the Harvard Law School faculty in 1914 he was already a public figure of significant stature. *The Outlook*, a magazine of which Theodore Roosevelt was a contributing editor, published a full-page picture of Mr. Frankfurter and remarked editorially:

> The Harvard Law School—whose preeminence is unquestionable [and at the time, no doubt, it was]—is a leader in rendering the law modern. One of the signs of its leadership is the recent appointment of Felix Frankfurter as Professor of Law, charged with the duty of dealing with this relationship between law and modern social and industrial conditions.[1]

The decision to return to Harvard was not, as the Justice later told us in his *Felix Frankfurter Reminisces*, altogether easy and automatic.[2] The young government official and man about

ALEXANDER M. BICKEL

Washington was much concerned with the social and economic problems of his day, which he saw as urgent and complex, and which enlisted his abundant resources of intellect, sympathy, and creative energy. He was exquisitely attuned to the need for vast changes in society, and I think one may say that he conceived it to be the *duty* of a lawyer trained and experienced as he was to participate in the crucial process of bringing these changes about, and bringing them about in orderly and wise fashion—that is, by law. As he was to write later: "Lawyers have a special responsibility in breaking these new paths and allowing free travel upon them. In this country, theirs is probably the greatest power for good or evil."[3] If he hesitated about the call to Harvard, one may surmise that he did so in part because of what Holmes had written him in July 1913:

> [A]cademic life is but half life—it is withdrawal from the fight in order to utter smart things that cost you nothing except the thinking them from a cloister. My wife thinks I unconsciously began to grow sober with an inarticulate sense of limitation in the few months of my stay at Cambridge. . . . Business in the world is unhappy, often seems mean, and always challenges your power to idealize the brute fact—but it hardens the fiber and I think is more likely to make more of a man of one who turns it to success.[4]

Mr. Frankfurter's decision to teach law we may attribute to considerations he had expressed in 1912, when addressing the Twenty-fifth Anniversary Dinner of the *Harvard Law Review*. He indicated very briefly the enormous legislative tasks he saw looming ahead. The resulting legislation, he noted, must in our system "pass challenge in the courts, it must have the visé of our judiciary. Having regard to things and not words, the fate of social legislation in this country rests ultimately with our judges." Constitutional law, as it affects social legislation, is "applied politics, using the word in its noble sense." Lawyers must come to know this not merely abstractly, but as "a dynamic part of our professional equipment." It was essential

> that a correct appreciation of the problems raised by social legislation should become a vital part of our professional thinking. . . . In so far as these questions are necessarily questions of fact, dealing with actual conditions of life and current dominant public opinion, it is essential that the stream of the Zeitgeist must be allowed to flood the sympathies and the intelligence of our judges. . . .

The solution, Mr. Frankfurter concluded, lay in professional education.[5]

This early speech marked the opening of a theme to which he often recurred. Legal education plays the chief role in shaping the outlook and the skills of bench and bar, and thus it is legal education that defines the possibilities of law, which is to say, the possibilities of ordered social action. Exactly one year after returning to Harvard, Mr. Frankfurter told the American Bar Association:

> It is not enough that young men should come from our schools equipped to become skillful practitioners, armed with precedent and ready in argument. We fail in our important office if they do not feel that society has breathed into the law the breath of life and made it a living, serving soul . . . a vital agency for human betterment.[6]

In the concluding chapter of *The Business of the Supreme Court*, which is entitled "The Future of Supreme Court Litigation," he wrote:

> An adequately equipped professional bar is the mainstay of the Anglo-American legal order, for it is a necessary adjunct of our courts. If the bar is to fulfill its duties . . . it must realize the

nature of issues raised by constitutional controversies. . . . The intellectual direction of the bar will certainly in the future be decided by the law schools. . . . With legal education rests the responsibility for training men fitted for constitutional adjudications.[7]

As the New Deal was coming to office, he told a bar group:

> To realize that there is a new economic order and to realize it passionately, not platonically, is the central equipment for modern statesmanship.[8]

Achievement of this passionate, not platonic, realization was the important office of legal education. It was the job of the law schools, far from complete or from justifying complacency, as he wrote at about this same time, to produce "lawyers and judges sensitive to the demands of society upon law, and equal to fashioning ideas and instruments with which to make the accommodations necessary for a gracious civilization."[9] When, also in 1932, he declined appointment to the Supreme Judicial Court of Massachusetts, it was on these grounds:

> The future direction of bar and bench will be determined by the quality of our law schools.
> Moreover, the fabric of the law, particularly our public law, we have been told repeatedly by the most farsighted in the profession must be designed chiefly by the law schools.
> This work must go forward. . . .[10]

This, and no less exalted than this, was Mr. Frankfurter's conception of his mission as he went to teach law at Harvard. It may be said of his twenty-five years there that he did not ever, in Holmes's morbid phrase, "grow sober with an inarticulate sense of limitation." After no more than a decade Brandeis, who had an eye to see, was writing to Harold J. Laski: "The year has been for Felix, also, one of happy usefulness, with an ever widening appreciation of his rare qualities. His students are becoming teachers. Given another 20 years of such activity, and he will have profoundly affected American life."[11] So it came to pass through Mr. Frankfurter's teaching, and through his students, who multiplied him. It came to pass also through a body of writings, both scholarly and journalistic, which is . . . well, incredible in volume, range, and consistent quality. Most assuredly the law schools have not produced its like since. The teaching, the scholarship, and the extremely vigorous journalism were an organic unity, operating in the midst of the world's "unhappy" business, never withdrawn from it, and true throughout to the high, vital, and engaged educational purpose that Mr. Frankfurter had set himself upon going to Harvard. And so, as early as 1929, Brandeis was able to convey, again to Laski, this estimate: "He seems to me clearly the most useful lawyer in the United States."[12]

Regarding his career as a whole, at Harvard and on the bench, and not forgetting a Holmes or a Brandeis among his elders, or a Black among his contemporaries, one can say without exaggeration that Felix Frankfurter has been in his time the single most influential figure in American constitutional law. My purpose in this paper is to recall one aspect of the total career on which such a statement as I have just permitted myself is founded. That aspect is the scholarly and journalistic output dating from the twenty-five years at Harvard. I have indicated that the body of this work—none of it from the cloister, not a word of it representing thought divorced from action—is immense. There are the books, leaving out a number of casebooks: the two most massive ones—*The Business of the Supreme Court*, with James M. Landis (1927), and *The Labor Injunction*, with Nathan Greene (1930)—as well as, in chronological order, *The Case of Sacco and Vanzetti* (1927),[13] *The Public and Its Government* (1930), *The Commerce Clause Under Marshall, Taney and Waite* (1937), and *Mr. Justice Holmes and the Supreme Court* (1938).[14] This list also excludes two collections of essays, one on Holmes and the other on Brandeis, that Mr. Frankfurter edited, the study on *Criminal Justice in Cleveland* (1922), which he directed together with Roscoe Pound, and briefs in court cases. Then there are the scholarly articles, also sometimes written with collaborators (not counting those later included as part of one of the books): nineteen of them, running from 1916 to 1939, in the *Harvard Law Review* alone[15]; some five falling in this classification in other journals[16]; and five very substantial and important entries in the Encyclopedia of Social Sciences.[17] Then the numerous speeches, book reviews, and other papers falling for purposes of classification somewhere between formal scholarship and journalism.[18] And finally the journalism, by no means all of it in the *New Republic* alone, and by no means all of it represented in *Law and Politics*, the anthology edited by E. F. Prichard, Jr., and Archibald MacLeish in 1939.[19] Here is a body of work that would unquestionably have endured even had its author not become what he became. Much of it might indeed be more widely read now were it not for the later writings, which to the profession at least are more accessible and, of course, more authoritative. But the later and the earlier writings are a unit, as are the scholarship and the journalism. The themes of this work are there in the opinions of the Justice. This organic coherence is one aspect of the work that I shall try to emphasize. But it is true also that some of the themes of the Justiceship were not yet evolved in the earlier work, because the problems in question were not yet ripe. This also is a matter of some interest and will bear some attention.

From the first, Mr. Frankfurter set out to rethink the Supreme Court and its place in the American government. He opened and pursued, as we shall see, some entirely new lines of inquiry.

The first note that insistently strikes the ear, however, is a powerful, steady realism, which was quite original in the execution and in the insights it produced, but which took its inspiration from Holmes and perhaps from John Chipman Gray, as no doubt did the realism of Mr. Frankfurter's colleague, T. R. Powell. Throughout, with the emphasis of repetition and with inventive variety of formulation, Mr. Frankfurter taught that "the Constitution is not a literary composition but a way of ordering society."[20] Therefore "American constitutional law is not a fixed body of truth, but a mode of social adjustment."[21] In the beginning, he wrote with reference to the commerce clause, "were not the words but the warm and lively issues which engendered them."[22] As for the framers, so for the Justices, warm and lively facts of life are the materials of judgment. The Justices are compelled

> to gather meaning not from reading the constitution but from reading life. It is most revealing that members of the court are frequently admonished by their associates not to read their economic views into the neutral language of the constitution. But the process of constitutional interpretation compels the translation of policy into judgment, and the controlling conceptions of the justices are their "idealized political picture" of the existing social order. Only the conscious recognition of the nature of this exercise of the judicial process will protect policy from being narrowly construed as the reflex of discredited assumptions or the abstract formulation of unconscious bias.[23]

Thus the process is "applied politics," and the Justices are everything. "The Supreme Court is the vehicle of life latent in the letter of the Constitution."[24] "In good truth, the Supreme Court *is* the Constitution."[25]

> Moreover, the work of the Supreme Court is the history of relatively few personalities. However much they may have

represented or resisted their Zeitgeist, symbolized forces outside their own individualities, they were also individuals. The fact that they were *there* and that others were not, surely made decisive differences. To understand what manner of men they were is crucial to an understanding of the Court.[26]

A bold achievement of John Marshall was to establish the dormant commerce clause "as the censor of state regulation." "But clauses are not truly censors; the men who apply them are."[27] Both under the commerce clause and under the due process and equal protection clauses, what happens very often is that:

> The inclination of a single justice, the buoyancy of his hopes or the intensity of his fears, may determine the opportunity of a much needed social experiment to survive, or may frustrate for a long time intelligent attempts to deal with a social evil.[28]
>
> Too often not even the judges who purport to apply principles are aware of what compels choice when competing principles bid for favor, nor are they alert to the concrete determinants for which an indeterminate doctrine is the avowed explanation.[29]

Mr. Frankfurter battled unceasingly against the twin tendencies of "abstract reasoning and canonizing the familiar into the eternal."[30] He was forever warning against that "process of self-delusion" to which judges are so prone "when casting grave issues of public policy into the mold of law."[31]

All this, and more that could well be quoted, is realism as hard-nosed as any that came after, from writers who spent more time and effort priding themselves on the hardness of their noses. But realism is not a philosophy, it is not a program; it is merely a first wisdom, one of the necessary methods for dealing with the materials. Once we have recognized that the Supreme Court deals with "political issues to be discussed like other political issues,"[32] what then? What comes after, as Mr. Frankfurter remarked in 1920, "the door to the Holy of Holies has been opened"?[33] Mr. Frankfurter never suggested that the Supreme Court in fact did—let alone should—behave as if it were part of the political market place. The word politics has many meanings, and he always used it with reference to the Court in a special sense. As early as 1916 he wrote in the *Harvard Law Review:*

> But there are differences between this body of constitutional decisions [having just alluded to their "political" nature] and the judgments of a Kadi or the foreign policies of a Secretary of State. Just these differences entitle the decisions to be called law.[34]

In 1930, writing for a wider audience, he again emphasized that the Court "exercises political and economic control," but pointed out also that the control is exercised "in a different atmosphere and under different circumstances than those which apply to legislature and Congress, to governors and President." And he added, "To the success of our scheme of government an independent and statesmanlike Supreme Court is vital."[35] What was Mr. Frankfurter's conception of the proper functioning of this vital organ of final decision making?

It is well to start by emphasizing that Mr. Frankfurter believed the function of the Court to be vital on principle, not merely unavoidable as an established historical encumbrance. "The Supreme Court," he paused to say in 1933, in the course of a vigorously critical essay, "is indispensable to the effective workings of our federal government. If it did not exist, we should have to create it."[36] This unwavering commitment, on principle, to the Court as both a necessary and a beneficial institution had reference chiefly to the function under the commerce clause, but it was not, as we shall see, entirely so restricted. And with reference to the commerce clause, the commitment leans on, but never altogether adopts, the qualification of Holmes's famous dictum that he did not think the United States would come to an end if the Court lost its power to declare acts of Congress unconstitutional, although he would fear for the Republic if state legislation could not be passed on by the Supreme Court. Mr. Frankfurter's view was less grudging:

> Under the Commerce Clause the Supreme Court maintains the equilibrium between states and nation by determining when a state has sought to project its authority beyond its state lines and when, on the other hand, Congress has interfered with the purely domestic concerns of the individual states. Here is a power that must be left with the Supreme Court although its exercise is not at all a necessary deduction from "principles" hidden in the Constitution, to which only the Supreme Court has the code.[37]

He took no leave of his fierce sense of the realities of the judicial process in this area any more than elsewhere:

> The simple truth of the matter is that decisions of the Court denying or sanctioning the exercise of federal power, as in the first child labor case, largely involve a judgment about practical matters, and not at all any esoteric knowledge of the Constitution. Therefore it is that the decisions of the Court must be subjected to relentless scrutiny to save them from pedantry and sterility, as the unconscious rationalizations of the economic and social biases of individual justices. . . .[38]

Much the same was to be said of the function of the Court in passing on state measures under the commerce clause. Mr. Frankfurter was wont frequently to cite T. R. Powell's analyses showing that these decisions were also "at bottom acts of statesman-ship."[39] In his article on this subject in the Encyclopedia of Social Sciences, written with Paul A. Freund and constituting perhaps his most concerted and deliberate statement about the commerce clause, Mr. Frankfurter wrote:

> Practical necessities and shrewd judgments about practical mat-ters decide the fate of state legislation when challenged by the power or the action of Congress. State necessities, the fitness of state relief as against nation wide action, the limited manifesta-tions of a given evil or the limited benefits of its correction, the actual interest of the whole country in a phenomenon especially virulent in a particular state, the advantages of local regulation balanced against the cost or inconvenience to interests outside the states—these and like questions are involved in the process by which the Supreme Court in concrete cases has held for or against state and national action in the interacting areas of state and national interests.[40]

Thus the virtue of Cooley v. Board of Wardens,[41] a decision to which Mr. Frankfurter assigned the full importance conven-tionally attributed to it, lay not, as was conventionally thought, in its novel and resolving doctrine, but in the fact that Justice Curtis cut through "scholastic reasoning" and offered a candid recognition that what was called for was the judgment of five men on practical matters:

> By making the question of constitutionality turn not upon ab-stract notions regarding the nature of state powers but upon their concrete and multifarious applications the decision in the Cooley case shifted the center of attention to actualities in the disposition of questions under the commerce clause.[42]

Seeing the process in commerce clause cases for exactly what it was, Mr. Frankfurter nevertheless insisted time and again that "the power of the Supreme Court to mediate between the states and the nation in interpreting the Commerce Clause must be left intact."[43] Not only that, but in discussing state taxation, he forecast and explained certain somewhat hard-and-fast attitudes that he would later take on the bench, at not a little cost, in some quarters, by way of loss of "liberal" and "realist" status. No general formula could hope to solve the state taxation cases, but on the other hand, "unbridled empiricism" would not do either:

> The state must have in advance some reasonable assurance of the permissible incidence of the tax. Moreover to invoke standards of reasonableness with reference to an individual taxpayer presents a logical solecism; and practically a large tax on an interstate business may be less burdensome, where a similar tax is borne by businesses generally, than a small tax the impact of which is particularly upon interstate commerce. This will explain why although a carrier engaged in both interstate and intrastate commerce may successfully resist a tax levied in part on gross receipts from interstate commerce, it may be required to pay the same amount of taxes under a statute increasing the general tax rate but confined in application to gross receipts from intrastate commerce. The distinction between the taxation of a subject and the use of that subject as a measure of taxation has a real economic significance, in that the subject will indicate in the light of experience and analysis whether the tax will fall disproportionately upon interstate commerce. A broad subject is a reasonable guaranty that the incidence of the tax will be equitable.[44]

But there was an area of the Court's work in which Mr. Frankfurter, far from thinking the Court's function vital and indispensable, attacked it as such, at wholesale. The attack was sustained and, shall I say, brutal, culminating at one point in the cry that "the due process clauses ought to go,"[45] and in any event, never leaving it in doubt that the Court was unfit to perform the function, that it ought to abandon it, and that its continued performance was a menace to the Republic. The function in question was, of course, that of measuring state and federal social and economic legislation (the word "social" here is to be read as modified by the following term, "economic") against the vague commands of the due process and equal protection clauses. This, in importance if not in volume, was the chief public business of the Court during the years we are discussing, and was the cause of the storms that swirled about the Court, which in turn cannot be viewed as mild even by the generation that lived through the 1950's. In this area Mr. Frankfurter's radical critique proceeded from the foundation work, as he called it, of James Bradley Thayer. "The great master of constitutional law"[46] taught that the widest discretion should be allowed legislatures to effectuate, and respond to, changes in social and economic conditions. What was required of the Court was humility. There is little qualification in Mr. Frankfurter's criticism here; the position is uncompromising, and the admonition is not "restrain," but "abstain." However, this was criticism, time and again, of specific cases, and so a qualification of context must be read in. We may presume that at some point, for Frankfurter as for Holmes and Brandeis themselves, a principle would be found in the Constitution to protect rights of property. Similarly, as we shall soon see, if this critique is read out of context, it might lead to the mistaken assumption that "the due process clauses ought to go" in their application to matters other than socio-economic legislation as well. This was not intended.

In the years just before American entry into the First World War, the years, in other words, just before and after he began his own academic career, Mr. Frankfurter was sanguine. The Court, he thought, had responded in the past to "a period of luxuriant individualism," but this period of individualism and fear is over. Occasionally there is a relapse, but on the whole we have entered definitely upon an epoch in which Justice Holmes has been the most consistent and dominating force, and to which Justices Day and Hughes have been great contributing factors. [This was written in February 1916, just after Brandeis had been nominated.] It is the period of self-consciousness as to the true nature of the issues before the Court. It is the period of realization that . . . contemporary convictions of expediency as to property and contract must not be passed off as basic principles of right.[47]

This optimism derived from cases such as Muller v. Oregon,[48] and Noble State Bank v. Haskell.[49] It was short-lived. Certainly, as Mr. Frankfurter pointed out in 1915, there was a "radical difference in mental attitude"[50] between the opinion in the Lochner[51] case and that in Muller v. Oregon. But the difference, if it ever held sway, did so for a few short years only. Mr. Frankfurter liked to think that Theodore Roosevelt's "vigorous challenge of judicial abuses was mainly responsible for a temporary period of liberalism . . . however abhorrent the remedy of judicial recall appeared to both bar and bench." Roosevelt, as he himself "shrewdly observed," rather put the fear of God into the judges.[52] But by 1920, the fear of God was going out of them again. And in a few years Mr. Frankfurter was writing:

The "fear of God" very much needs to make itself felt in 1924. Let any disinterested student of constitutional law read the decision of the Supreme Court last spring invalidating legislation fixing a standard weight for a loaf of bread and deny that we have never had a more irresponsible period in the history of that court.[53]

Looking back in 1930, he wrote, stating the heart of his critique:

Since 1920 the Court has invalidated more legislation than in fifty years preceding. . . . Since 1921 the Court has held laws invalid in about 30 per cent of the cases under the due process clauses. . . . The crucial criticism of the Court is that it is putting constitutional authority behind the personal opinion of its members in disputed and difficult questions of social policy.[54]

The fierceness of Mr. Frankfurter's attack can be gauged, and its quality and point assessed, by a reading of his *New Republic* editorial on Truax v. Corrigan.[55] Arizona's first legislature after statehood, which Arizona achieved in 1912, faced up to the problem of how and whether and to what extent the law should deal with labor conflicts. And it decided to withdraw the extraordinary remedy of an injunction in cases of disputes between an employer and his employees concerning terms and conditions of employment unless violence was involved. In the absence of violence, the parties were remitted to ordinary suits for damages. Now this area of policy, "if anything can, affords peculiarly a field for the exercise of legislative discretion; if there can be any justification at all for having legislatures, a stronger case for determining the state's policy by the responsible judgment of its legislature can hardly be imagined." And now "the Supreme Court holds that Arizona has laid impious hands upon the Ark of the Covenant as enshrined in the Fourteenth Amendment." Here was a decision that immediately affected thirty million wage earners, and yet, Mr. Frankfurter surmised, to a layman the result "must appear as incredible as the process by which it is reached is mysterious. . . ." Moreover, the layman's bewilderment will not be "lessened by the fact that this appalling result is reached by the votes of five men as against the votes of four men." Mr. Frankfurter found this decision of the Supreme Court to be "fraught with more evil than any which it has rendered in a generation." Where did the Court get its result? Certainly not from the Fourteenth Amendment, which could be thought to state the beginning of the problem, if it stated anything of relevance, although for "Chief Justice Taft the beginning of the problem is the end." There was nothing in the Chief Justice's majority opinion but "jejune logomachy." "For all the regard that the Chief Justice of the United States pays to the facts of industrial life, he might as well have written this opinion as Chief Justice of the Fiji Islands." The labor injunction, with which Arizona chose to dispense, was a very recent invention as a judicial remedy. And yet "by 1921, the right to an injunction has become 'an immutable principle of liberty and justice,' world without end!" The Chief Justice "is a victim . . . of self-delusion."[56]

This, I think one may say, is hard-hitting criticism. No wonder Taft, who did not become Chief Justice of the United States in order to preside over the judiciary of the Fiji Islands, wrote privately in 1922 (to Pierce Butler, as it happens, who had just been nominated):

> I haven't seen what the *New Republic* has said, because I don't read that paper, but I have no doubt that it said everything that it ought not to say. Frankfurter is one of its contributors. It was one of the few papers of the country that attacked my nomination, and really a man whom it does not attack is of questionable reputation as to his loyalty and his sound constitutional views. . . .[57]

But there is more than polemical brilliance and the Thayerian thesis in this attack. There is also, perhaps somewhat hidden in it, another point, indicating the limits of context within which the critique is to be read, and indeed the limits and qualifications of the Thayerian thesis. The Justices themselves were, after all, in verbal agreement with Thayer's conception of the scope of the American doctrine of judicial review. "The Fourteenth Amendment, so the Supreme Court has told us again and again,"

Mr. Frankfurter wrote, "is not the arbiter of policy. Only 'immutable principles' are in its keeping." And then:

> Is it really possible for anyone living in the present day to insist that the restriction of the use of the injunction in labor cases is the denial of "a fundamental principle of liberty and justice which inheres in the very idea of free government and is the inalienable right of a citizen of such a government"?[58]

So the issue was not so much whether judges ought to feel free to read their views of policy into the Constitution, but rather which views of policy they ought to feel free to read in. Immutable principles there may be, all right, and nothing that Thayer wrote or that Mr. Frankfurter wrote denied that it is the function of judges in the name of the Constitution to enforce such principles as law, at least in the qualified sense in which the processes and judgments of the Supreme Court acting under the Constitution can be deemed law. Under the commerce clause, judgments of practical policy, prudential judgments, are tolerable, because they are indispensable, and although Mr. Frankfurter did not often emphasize this point, because ultimately they are not final judgments legitimating or cutting off government power altogether, but rather allocations of power between states and nation, and insofar as they apply to the states, not final also in the sense that Congress can revise them. But under the due process and equal protection clauses, judgments are in all senses final, to the extent that our society accepts finality from the Court. Such judgments cannot draw for justification on the same necessities of federalism, and they can be tolerable only if founded in sound "immutable principles." The premise, although often silent, of Thayer's thesis and of Mr. Frankfurter's critique was that no one in his right senses could honestly believe that the kind of picky revisions of garden-variety socio-economic legislation that the Court was engaging in was based on "immutable principles." No one with an adequate sense of the history of these issues and of the economic facts of life could so believe, and anyone who deluded himself into erecting immutable principles in this area was simply wrongheaded. The length of a workday, the size of a loaf of bread, the proper rate to be allowed a utility—these were not matters of principle, but everyday matters of legislative and executive policy.

Yet principles there are, and they are in the Court's keeping. Just before himself going on the bench, Mr. Frankfurter wrote of Cardozo:

> In the domain of economic affairs, the penumbral region where law and policy blend, Cardozo walked humbly. But when those ethical precepts which are embodied in the Bill of Rights were invoked, he responded with all the certitude of one whose most constant companion was reason and whose life was rooted in the moral law.[59]

In a more famous passage, Mr. Frankfurter wrote of Holmes:

> There is truth behind the familiar contrast between rights of property and rights of man. But certainly in some of its aspects property is a function of personality, and conversely the free range of the human spirit becomes shrivelled and constrained under economic dependence. . . . But the various interests of human personality are not of equal worth. There is a hierarchy of values. And so we shall find that some manifestations of the human spirit seemed to Mr. Justice Holmes so precious that in specific instances he found no justification for legislative restrictions, tolerant though he was of the legislative judgment. Thus he accorded to some claims the protection of the Constitution which he denied to others, although all claimed the shelter of the "liberty" which it protects.

The Justice deferred so abundantly to legislative judgment on economic policy because he was profoundly aware of the extent to which social arrangements are conditioned by time and circumstances, and of how fragile, in scientific proof, is the ultimate validity of a particular economic adjustment. He knew that there was no authoritative fund of social wisdom to be drawn upon for answers to the perplexities which vast new material resources had brought. . . .

[But] . . . Mr. Justice Holmes attributed very different legal significance to those liberties of the individual which history has attested as the indispensable conditions of a free society from that which he attached to liberties which derived merely from shifting economic arrangements. These enduring liberties of the subject, in the noble English phrase, were, so far as the national government is concerned, specifically enshrined in the Bill of Rights. But they have gradually found protection even against state action through a slow process of expansion of the liberties secured by the Fourteenth Amendment, after that clause, in the course of half a century, had established itself as the instrument for supervising the whole gamut of state legislation. Because these civil liberties were explicitly safeguarded in the Constitution, or conceived to be basic to any notion of the liberty guaranteed by the Fourteenth Amendment, Mr. Justice Holmes was far more ready to find legislative invasion in this field than in the area of debatable economic reform.[60]

The reader will have noted, and perhaps been startled to note, the emphasis on "specific" safeguards in the Bill of Rights. The explicitness that Mr. Frankfurter found was more historical than literal. He thought also that judicial construction of the constitutional prohibitions "intended to protect individual rights" gave rise "to relatively little difficulty."

These guaranties are based upon the history of a specific political grievance, or they embody a specific limitation of power in the formulation of governmental powers which came out of the

Philadelphia convention. . . . The definiteness of the terms of these specific provisions, the definiteness of their history, the definiteness of their aims, all combine to limit narrowly the scope of judicial review in the rare instances when their meaning is called into question. Only occasionally is doubt raised as to whether "a fact tried by a jury" has been "re-examined in any court of the United States" otherwise than "according to the rules of the common law" . . . or whether a crime is "infamous"; or whether the prohibition against "unreasonable searches and seizures" is violated. Here, in other words, is a part of constitutional law relatively easy of application because it allows comparatively meager play for individual judgment as to policy.[61]

And Mr. Frankfurter tended to assimilate the First Amendment to this analysis:

But the Constitution was also the product of great historic conflicts, and sought specifically to guard against the recurrence of historic grievances by preferring the risks of tolerance to the dangers of tyranny. Mr. Justice Holmes' dissenting opinion in the *Abrams*[62] case will live as long as the august majesty of English prose has power to thrill.[63]

These are not statements that particularly commend themselves to us today, especially as students of the Justice's later work, even though we continue to admire the dissent in Abrams.[64] Nor do these statements constitute an entirely coherent whole with the later work of the Justice, except with respect to the bill of attainder clause,[65] and in the area of federal application of the Fourth Amendment.[66] The explanation of these rather aberrant views—and I shall show that they were, indeed, aberrant in the full context of Mr. Frankfurter's writings of these years—is perhaps to be found in the remark that "only occasionally is doubt raised" about provisions safeguarding individual rights. And when doubt was in fact raised, however infrequently, it was most often in cases that we would today think of as relatively easy, or as not raising the constitutional issue in clear-cut fashion. Abrams itself is one illustration. Another is the Milwaukee *Leader*[67] case, which, as Mr. Frankfurter brilliantly demonstrated, was a delegation rather than a First Amendment case. (It is worth digressing here to point to one of the finest instances of Mr. Frankfurter's phrasemaking. The real basis of the majority's decision in the Milwaukee *Leader* case, Mr. Frankfurter contended, was that government ought to be competent to wage war against internal as well as external enemies. Hence, Postmaster General Burleson was allowed in effect to suppress a newspaper, despite the lack of explicit statutory authorization. " 'Government,' " Mr. Frankfurter remarked, "is a large abstraction for a little Burleson."[68]) The Bill of Rights was simply not in the forefront of constitutional litigation in these years, and it is no wonder that the problems that would later arise from application of its substantive provisions were not very clearly in focus. For once—and it is a rare occurrence in the body of these writings—Mr. Frankfurter was voicing abstract views, with little relation to actual controversies and their surrounding circumstances.

When he dealt with actual controversies, Mr. Frankfurter, in these years as later, used history to different ends, and took a different view of the conclusiveness for the present of findings about the past. History was part of what he was accustomed to call, as we shall see, the "scientific" study of law. He used it defensively (even as later in the bill of attainder cases[69]), for then as now purported history served as often as the purported clarity of the constitutional text to screen the judges' policy preferences and their tendency to canonize "the familiar into the eternal." In his famous article on "The Power to Regulate Contempts,"[70] with Landis, Mr. Frankfurter exploded the notion that the "judicial power" conferred by Article III of the Constitution necessarily must include a power to punish all manner of contempts without benefit of jury trial. He exposed without mercy the unfounded historical assumptions and the shabby scholarship of the government's brief in the Toledo Newspaper[71] case, on which Chief Justice White, with such pompous assurance, based the holding that a judge without a jury could punish a newspaper for being vigorously critical of his actions in a rate case. No doubt this decision illustrated for Mr. Frankfurter that, as he wrote elsewhere, even "in their interpretation of the guaranty of 'freedom of speech,' the decisions prove that the Supreme Court is not immune to temporary fears and passions."[72] It was to counter such temporary judicial fears and passions that he used historical research. He went on in the "Contempts" article similarly to explode a holding by the Seventh Circuit that a provision in the Clayton Act of 1914 for trying contempts to a jury was unconstitutional.[73] The sole basis for this holding turned out to be an oft-repeated historical error, propounded by Wilmot, C.J. in 1765, which was in fact the temporary product of Stuart politics. The Seventh Circuit's opinion, Mr. Frankfurter wrote,

> reads as though the court which rendered it was the impersonal conduit of the Constitution; that the Constitution poured its content of "judicial power" through the court. For all practical purposes, however, the court . . . "poured" Wilmot's judgment into the Constitution and then "poured" Wilmot's judgment out of the Constitution.[74]

The "Contempts" article is, however, perhaps not entirely in point for present purposes, since Mr. Frankfurter deemed the phrase "judicial power" in Article III, on which the issue there turned, to be one of the broad provisions similar to the due process and equal protection clauses, not one of the guaranties "based upon the history of a specific political grievance." Just what he was prepared to make of history with respect to one of the guaranties of this latter description is better illustrated by the equally famous paper, "Petty Federal Offenses and the Constitutional Guaranty of Trial by Jury,"[75] with Thomas G. Corcoran. The question was whether Congress could provide for the trial of petty federal offenses, under the Volstead Act and otherwise, without a jury. An adequate answer required for Mr. Frankfurter a "scientific" exploration of the historic genealogy of the jury guaranties of the Constitution, which he did place in the category of specific provisions embodying specific historical grievances or practices. He discovered what, on adequate historical research, the jury guaranties did not mean. They did not mean that every conceivable petty offense had to be tried to a jury. But he concluded also, and this is the crucial point for our purposes, that the historical genealogy "may not exclude acquired characteristics of meaning." While the Constitution "was written in 1787, it was not written for 1787. Its language . . . may spread beyond into fresh soil." And: "To what extent respect for continuity demands adherence merely to what was, involves the art of adjudication. . . ." And finally:

> The history of the common law does not solve the problem of judgment which it raises in demonstrating that the guaranty of a jury did not cover offenses which, because of their quality and their consequences, had a relatively minor place in the register of misconduct.

History saves neither Congress nor the Court "from the necessity for judgment in giving past history present application."[76] This attitude places matters in a different light, of course. It places matters where later the Justice found them. History must be treated with respect and with the scruple of the scholar. Most often it will be found to liberate judgment, but it cannot displace it. For, as the Justice said, concurring in Sweezy v. New Hampshire, "in the end, judgment cannot be escaped—the judgment of this Court."[77] The Court must speak for "the best traditions" and also "the deepest needs of the country."[78]

What further do these writings tell us about the proper function of the Court in the area of individual rights, where, plainly, Mr. Frankfurter thought the judicial function ought to be exercised? There emerges, very insistently—and here again is a striking element of continuity—an abhorrence of absolutes. The word "absolute," Mr. Frankfurter admonished, quoting Santayana, is "the most false and the most odious of words."[79] He attributed to Holmes the conviction "that our constitutional system rests upon tolerance and that its greatest enemy is the Absolute."[80] Holmes, he said, "did not erect even freedom of speech into a dogma of absolute validity nor enforce it to doctrinaire limits."[81] Nor did Brandeis.[82] Distrust of the absolute is a fundamental and pervasive attitude of mind, which Mr. Frankfurter illustrated as pithily as anywhere in a quite different context when urging that the Eighteenth Amendment be given a fair trial run:

> Like Mr. Franklin, I prefer a civilization with moderate drinking to the flatness of prohibition. But it is dangerous to identify one's personal preferences with the limits of Liberty. The opportunity to drink intoxicating liquors is not one of the Immutable Rights of Man.[83]

And so with Holmes, Mr. Frankfurter expounded, in this period as later, "the philosophy of differences of degree."[84] This is the philosophy that unites the celebrated article, "Hands Off the Investigations,"[85] with United States v. Rumely[86] and Sweezy v. New Hampshire[87] as well as with his votes in Barenblatt v. United States[88] and like cases.

A number of further elements fill out the line of continuity. One is the special attachment to procedural observances, and to what Mr. Frankfurter called "the integrity of the judicial process."[89] To this attachment, to the painstaking labor and utter fearlessness with which it was buttressed, and to the capacity for savage indignation[90] that is one of the splendors of Mr. Frankfurter's temperament, *The Case of Sacco and Vanzetti* is, of course, the chief monument. Mr. Frankfurter shared with Brandeis the conviction that "the history of liberty is to a large extent the history of procedural observances."[91] No doubt his view of the function of the Court in procedural cases was affected also by the realization that in such cases the Court's judgment does not foreclose the pursuit of substantive policy. Yet even the attachment to procedural observances was qualified by considerations of federalism and of the institutional competence of the Court, both kinds of considerations having important general application in Mr. Frankfurter's thought.

In discussing Powell v. Alabama,[92] which he called "a notable chapter in the history of liberty," Mr. Frankfurter was careful to observe that the Fourteenth Amendment "is not the basis of a uniform code of criminal procedure federally imposed." Further:

> In no sense is the Supreme Court a general tribunal for the correction of criminal errors, such as the Court of Criminal Appeal in England. On a continent peopled by 120,000,000 that would be an impossible task; in a federal system it would be a function debilitating to the responsibility of state and local agencies.[93]

And Mr. Frankfurter never suggested that the Sacco and Vanzetti case should have been reviewed by the Supreme Court. Mr. Frankfurter, to be sure, was not a "states' rights" man. Federalism had a deeper, more functional meaning for him. " 'States' rights' as a slogan," he remarked, "has the vitality of a low organism."[94] The conviction and imagination with which he preached and practiced his own brand of functional federalism may be sensed, among other places, in his article with Landis, "The Compact Clause of the Constitution."[95] Here is an exercise in creative federalism. Mr. Frankfurter recommended widespread use of the compact clause, and more particularly, regional arrangements to solve the electric power problem. "Control by the nation," he thought "would be ill-conceived and intrusive." Again, writing about the Federal Securities Act of 1933, of which he approved, and noting what it omitted, he said:

> I should regard it a matter of regret if the failure of the states to meet their responsibilities to each other, and to work out interstate relationships through devices other than national legislation, should make federal incorporation a necessity.[96]

The Supreme Court, he believed, could be the most destructive instrument "of undue centralization . . . because judicial nullification on grounds of constitutionality stops experimentation at its source, and bars increase to the fund of social knowledge by scientific tests of trial and error."[97]

This devotion to the creative possibilities of federalism, coupled with a subtle awareness of the impossibilities of overcentralization, operated as a qualification for Mr. Frankfurter over the full range of the Supreme Court's function, even in procedural matters. So did the not entirely unrelated order of considerations having to do with the institutional competence of the Court. The framers themselves had such considerations in mind, and they prescribed in Article III the basic limitation on the Court's function. The Court may give judgment only in actual cases. Like Brandeis, Mr. Frankfurter, in these years as later, favored rigorous adherence to the constitutional limita-

tion, and also strict regard for the gloss on that limitation which
has been developed in the jurisprudence of the Court:

> Every tendency to deal with constitutional questions abstractly,
> to formulate them in terms of barren legal questions, leads to
> dialectics, to sterile conclusions unrelated to actualities.[98]

> The Court is not the forum for a chivalrous or disinterested
> defense of the Constitution. Its business is with self-regarding,
> immediate, secular claims.[99]

And so the occasions of the Court's judgments had to be certain
rather particular ones.

Other, equally important limitations on the Court's function
are imposed by the nature of the institution and its process.
Here is a body of nine men, each charged with independent
responsibility for the full work load of the institution. These
nine men are required to reach a collective judgment on great
issues. The essential quality of their process, as contrasted with
the processes of the political institutions, is detached, rational,
"scientific" deliberation. The process must be manifested in
opinions which attempt to justify the result and to persuade
those to whom it proves initially unpalatable. It follows quite
plainly that only a restricted number of cases can benefit from
this process at each term of Court, and that if the number is too
high, a cost will be exacted in the quality of the process. One of
the chief tasks of the Court, therefore, is to choose carefully the
cases it will decide from among those that are offered. The
Court ought to take no cases that involve merely factual questions, no cases on inadequate records, no cases, in short, that in
one fashion or another waste the precious resources of this
unique institution. That splendid series of articles bearing the
title "Business of the Supreme Court at October Term ——," to
which I shall return presently, developed this theme term by

term,[100] until it was taken up by the Justice in opinions and dissents on the Court, virtually without a break. Mr. Frankfurter similarly argued for an attitude of wise economy in assigning business to the lower federal courts:

> One thing is surely clear—we make our law courts do more than they are capable of doing. That is not the least of reasons why they perform less competently what they alone can do.[101]

The federal courts had to be maintained as an expert judiciary, suited to the performance of "peculiar federal tasks."[102] Thus there was no contemporary excuse for the burdens imposed by the diversity jurisdiction.[103] These were not, it must be emphasized, the negative strictures of a sort of technician, an engineer of judicial institutions. The animating ideal behind these strictures was a most positive, and a passionate one. What was in play was, again, "the integrity of the judicial process," the process of deliberate, detached, rational judgment and of the educational exposition of judgment. This is a process that needs above all else adequate time. Behind these seemingly mechanical strictures or admonitions to elegance is the passion of the great dissent in Rosenberg v. United States.[104]

Finally, the possibilities of the judicial process as a force for the achievement of the good society are subject to an additional qualification, which is perhaps the sum of all the others. The Justice was to speak much and eloquently on this truly grand theme. Mr. Frankfurter put it most powerfully in these years in an unsigned *New Republic* editorial on Pierce v. Society of Sisters,[105] entitled "Can the Supreme Court Guarantee Toleration?"[106] Here was a decision Mr. Frankfurter, of course, welcomed: "Thus comes to an end the effort to regiment the mental life of Americans through coerced public school instruction." But there is a price paid "for these occasional services to liberalism." The same due process clause in which the Supreme Court finds warrant for so beneficial a judgment as this was the source also of the many decisions stifling socio-economic legislation. What is more important, how effective can such judgments as that in the Pierce case ultimately be? *Can* the Supreme Court ultimately guarantee toleration? What measure of "intrinsic promotion of the liberal spirit" results from "the Supreme Court's invalidation of illiberal legislation"? We must not forget that the Supreme Court legitimates by inescapable implication laws that it does not invalidate, and yet, of course, much that is not unconstitutional is unwise and illiberal. But the Court's reviewing function tends to focus attention on constitutionality, and tends to render constitutionality synonymous with propriety. "Such an attitude is a great enemy of liberalism." The "real battles of liberalism are not won in the Supreme Court."

> Only a persistent, positive translation of the liberal faith into the thoughts and acts of the community is the real reliance against the unabated temptation to straitjacket the human mind.

As the full context of these writings and the later work of the Justice amply demonstrate, this was no cry of nihilism, no attempt to deny the value of the Court's constitutional function in the area of human rights, no denial of the Court's potent educational faculties. It was a note of caution, sounded from the deep; an indication of limits.

Law, Mr. Frankfurter remarked when he had been teaching it for one year, is not a fixed science, since considerations of social advantage rarely permit quantitative determination. Yet: "This need not deter us from the scientific method; it all the more makes scientific treatment our soundest hope." Medicine, after all, is also only a science of probabilities. Like the medical schools, the law schools have to become "organized experiment stations."[107] The "scientific" study of law was Mr. Frankfurter's pursuit throughout his teaching career. The term "scientific" as applied to law has a quaint, overly sanguine, naïve sound for the present generation; it is not much in use just now among lawyers. But that is a matter of fashion. Mr. Frankfurter also knew well enough, as Holmes once remarked, that in one sense, the law "is not a science, but is essentially empirical."[108] But the word "scientific" did have a number of definite meanings for Mr. Frankfurter, and was a perfectly serviceable name for a path-breaking method, which, let it be quickly said, has absolutely nothing in common with current trends in behavioral studies.

The effort, wrote Holmes, "to reduce the concrete details of an existing system to the merely logical consequence of simple postulates is always in danger of becoming unscientific, and of leading to a misapprehension of the nature of the problem and the data."[109] The first task of science in the law is to displace "simple postulates." So Mr. Frankfurter, in his first scholarly effort, adduced the science of law against the conceptualisms of Lochner v. New York.[110] Proper scientific method must demonstrate to a court—as had Mr. Brandeis in Muller v. Oregon[111]—that in fact it is tenable to think that long hours of labor are a detriment to health; that, on the other hand, as a matter of historical truth, considerations of the public health are not, and have not been, the sole source of legislative power in the premises; and that the authority of the Lochner case had been shaken by learned articles and by changed circumstances since the date of decision. "If the Court, aided by the bar," Mr. Frankfurter believed, "has access to the facts and heeds them, the Constitution is flexible enough to respond to the demands of modern society."[112] The science of law, therefore, could bring the constitutional philosophy of James Bradley Thayer to fruition in the decisions of the Supreme Court.

The scientific method, then, founded the law in relevant social and economic facts. And it attacked assumptions of antiquity and other forms of historical beatitude, as, signally, in the articles on "Contempts" and on "Petty Federal Offenses," mentioned earlier. The question was put as follows in the paper on "Contempts":

> What then may Congress do [to regulate the power of a judge to punish for contempts]? It is futile to draw the answer from abstract speculation. The scope and qualities of a power [the regulatory power of Congress] which has been voluminously exercised since 1789 must be looked for in the cumulative proof of its exercise. What is the picture of congressional authority over the work of the inferior Federal courts, as revealed by an analysis of all the Acts of Congress dealing with these courts, from the first session of the First Congress down to the present session of the Sixty-eighth Congress? An adequate picture can be formed only by a detailed scrutiny of what Congress has done, as set forth in a mass of legislation covering one hundred and thirty-four years and scattered over the dreary pages of forty-two volumes of the statutes at large.[113]

In both these uses the word "science" was free of any delusion of precision. Science was to disprove, not to prove; it was to dispel that ignorance which consists of knowing many things that aren't so, not to lay a precise basis for judicial or legislative lawmaking. No one emphasized more continuously than did Mr. Frankfurter that lawmaking *is* empirical. Yet—empirical, but not necessarily ignorant, for a science of probabilities is also a science, and a little knowledge is better than none.

Thirdly, the scientific method meant close thinking on a set of materials that are cognate and relevant and can be controlled. In this sense the scientific method meant substituting the reality of case materials, used with the scruple of the craftsman, for slogans, formulas, maxims. Thus again in the "Contempts" article:

Differences due to differences in constitutional provisions, judicial history and State legislation make resort to State cases treacherous and unscientific.[114]

More generally, the method emphasized quantitative analysis, careful classification, and case studies that studied the whole case and not merely its reported decision. Altogether, the scientific method in Mr. Frankfurter's hands was a powerful, innovating tool. The present generation rather tends to take the method for granted, because it was formed by it. We were formed by it, but have we benefited quite as we might have? The task of administrative law, for example, Mr. Frankfurter wrote in 1927,

> is to know what is happening by objective demonstration of intensive scientific studies, instead of merely speculating, even wisely speculating. . . . Here, as in other branches of public law, only here probably more so, we must travel outside the covers of lawbooks to understand law.
>
> Only a physiological study of administrative law in action will disclose the processes, the practices, the determining factors. . . .[115]

Has this task been performed? Have we indeed even engaged in the "vertical" studies of judicial review of administrative orders that he recommended?[116] In the last three decades has any area of the law's concern been studied scientifically the way Frankfurter and Greene studied—explored and then demolished, as an obstruction to road building is demolished—the labor injunction?

The scientific method at the hands of Mr. Frankfurter resulted also in two other achievements, and these were the most brilliant and original. They are related, and they come together most strikingly in *The Business of the Supreme Court*. Quite unlike anyone else, Mr. Frankfurter sensed and conveyed—

sensed and conveyed as an artist, and solidly understood as a scientist—the forces, the movements, and the accidents of American history which are reflected in constitutional and other legal doctrines and in the institution of the federal judiciary, and which in turn were affected and sometimes deflected by those doctrines and that institution. Thayer, in a borrowed phrase, spoke of the law's "ennobling alliance" with history.[117] Mr. Frankfurter made of this alliance a continous, everyday connection—in a word, a marriage. It is impossible briefly to render the quality of Mr. Frankfurter's illumination of constitutional law through history and of history through law; it is impossible to render the quality of a marriage. The reader is directed to the superb lectures published as *The Commerce Clause Under Marshall, Taney and Waite*, and also to the entry on interstate commerce, mentioned earlier, in the Encyclopedia of Social Sciences. And he is directed, of course, to *The Business of the Supreme Court*. "The story of these momentous political and economic issues," Mr. Frankfurter wrote in the preface to that volume,

> lies concealed beneath the surface technicalities governing the jurisdiction of the Federal Courts. This book is an attempt to uncover these technicalities, and to fit the meaning of the successive Judiciary acts into the texture of American history.[118]

And so he did, in a hundred details, and also in the masterful sweep of such a chapter, for example, as the second, entitled "From the Civil War to the Circuit Courts of Appeal Act," which tells the story of post-Civil War nationalism perhaps as well as it needs to be told, mirrored in the expansion of federal jurisdiction.

Both *The Commerce Clause* and *The Business of the Supreme Court*, but particularly the latter and the serial articles of the same title that followed it, are not only studies in law and history, but also institutional studies. There were great scholars of the Constitution before Mr. Frankfurter, but he was the first scholar of the Supreme Court. The study he pursued was not constitutional law, but institutional law. Thus he founded a tradition of scholarship. He studied the sources, the volume, and the nature of the Court's business, over time and contemporaneously, and perceived anew the Court's role in American government. He studied the operations and methods, the administration and customs of the Court. He studied, with the meager materials available, but with insight and imagination, as in *The Commerce Clause*, the judges and their impact on one another, as well as the impact of the bar on the judges and their work. He counted such things as the percentages of certioraris granted, of affirmances and reversals, of cases disposed of *per curiam*, the number of dissents and concurrences, the number and provenance of FELA cases and admiralty cases and due process cases and common law cases; he had an eye to the quality of briefs and to the quality of lower court opinions, on which the Court was required to pass; he worried about time allowed for argument and about time for leisure during summer vacation, about the administrative duties of the Chief Justice, about time for opinion writing and time for dissents and time for drafting jurisdictional statutes and time for conference discussion. He knew and evaluated everything, counting it if it could at all be counted—and he understood the Court as no one ever had before him, as no single man has since. Thus he showed us newly and truly what is meant by our Constitution.

It remains to underline two aspects of this amazing body of work, which must surely have impressed themselves on the reader well before now. One is Mr. Frankfurter's style. Lucid, precise, polemical, and often harshly so, controlling strong passion without suppressing it—Max Lerner said in a review somewhere that it crackles, and it does. I have quoted much, and so its flavor should be evident, and I have occasionally called attention to the crackle of the phrase. For phrases, here is an almost random additional bushel. About a most extraordinary labor injunction obtained by Harry M. Daugherty from a complaisant Judge Wilkerson of the United States District Court in Chicago: "What's the Constitution between friends? —even though one of them happens to be the Attorney General of the United States and the other a federal judge?"[119] In 1936: "Alphabetical agencies will continue, or analphabetical agencies will take their place."[120] "People talk glibly about 'principles of government' as though there were a pharmacopoeia of politics and economics to which one could go for prescriptions."[121] Why I am for Smith: "Wise foreign relations require fundamentally not a body that has travelled, but a mind and spirit capable of travelling. . . ."[122] "Multiplying judges by no means multiplies justice."[123] "The mobility of words at the present time brings in its train what might be called immobility of reflection."[124]

Secondly, it must not escape re-emphasis that nothing in this body of writings is from the cloister. On the contrary, nothing about them is more striking than the utter engagement of these writings with the world's business. Many of the finest pieces of scholarship were directed at a burning issue of immediate import. The journalism, of course, was in the thick of the fight. This work is alive with its time, and for this reason, no doubt, all the more timeless.

Themes in United States Legal History

James Willard Hurst,
University of Wisconsin Law School

The study of United States legal history will come of age when its practitioners give as much effort to framing questions as to assembling answers.[1] A vital philosophy of law needs to work upon the full-dimensioned stuff of experience which legal historians can supply; if there is little reason to be satisfied with the contributions which jurisprudence has been making to the understanding of legal order in the past generation, the deficiencies reflect in part the thin flow of historical studies useful to philosophy. Because the historian's job preoccupies him with concrete particularities, he incurs occupational hazards which may rob his work of meaning. Immersed in detail, he may be diverted into the collectors' mania, and wind up an antiquarian. The passing days make him painfully aware how time-costly it is to uncover the full dimensions of events. Harassed by the calendar, he begrudges time taken from collecting data in order to shape and test the theoretical framework of his inquiries. So he is tempted into a naïve empiricism—using his research simply to document the unexamined assumptions and prejudices of common sense or tradition, or behaving as if he believed that meaning could be squeezed out of data by the sheer weight of their accumulation.

If research in legal history becomes more critical of its objectives and its methods, its greater sophistication will owe much to path-breaking work done in the 1920's and 1930's. A substantial part of that indebtedness will run to Felix Frankfurter. The debt will be owing both for motivations he stirred and insights he cultivated in the classroom and around the seminar table, and for examples he offered in a relatively limited but significant published output bearing on the relation of law to the growth of the United States. A great teacher has effect not by imparting information, but by generating the electricity of new insight and fresh curiosity. What Professor Frankfurter taught a generation of law students was a higher self-respect for themselves as men of law. To them he conveyed his conviction that there was no more challenging and exciting business in the world than the responsible, craftsmanlike handling of the power of the state—whether that power was invoked on behalf of private clients or in the name of the public. It was a point of view which had the greater impact because it ran head on into prejudices deep-seated in the late nineteenth and early twentieth centuries, which depreciated the importance and the moral worth of the legal order and those who worked in it, especially as compared with the importance of the market and the values of private self-seeking. "I do take law very seriously, deeply seriously, because fragile as reason is and limited as law is as the expression of the institutionalized medium of reason, that's all we have standing between us and the tyranny of mere will and the cruelty of unbridled, undisciplined feeling."[2]

The respect for the wise use of law which Professor Frankfurter transmitted to students invited closer study of legal history. It was primarily the time dimensions of legal operations which he saw as challenging men to responsible and skillful use of law. Sensitive awareness to these factors likewise put a distinctive stamp upon what he wrote. Professor Frankfurter and his co-author, James M. Landis, contributed a modern classic to the literature of our legal history in the monograph on *The Business of the Supreme Court*.[3] Here, and in other essays, the most exacting moral and operational issues in legal order are seen as fashioned by the cast which time gives to affairs—through the influence of trend and contingency, of succession and conjunction in events, and of the emergence of role and function out of the maturing of legal institutions. For "time is the decisive element in all phases of government, as in war."[4]

Change, Reason and Emotion

In an observation made by Mr. Justice William Johnson, able colleague of John Marshall, Professor Frankfurter found a basic text for studying the roles of law in the growth of this society. "The science of government," said Mr. Justice Johnson, "is the most abstruse of all sciences; if, indeed, that can be called a science, which has but few fixed principles, and practically consists in little more than the exercise of a sound discretion, applied to the exigencies of the state as they arise. It is the science of experiment."[5] This was an angle of vision like that which Professor Frankfurter found revealing in the philosophy of Mr. Justice Brandeis: "Problems, for him, are never solved. Civilization is a sequence of new tasks. Hence his insistence on the extreme difficulty of government and its dependence on sustained interest and effort, on the need for constant alertness to the fact that the introduction of new forces is accompanied by new difficulties. This, in turn, makes him mindful of the limited range of human foresight, and leads him to practice humility in attempting to preclude the freedom of action of those who are to follow."[6]

From this point of view, law's most important function in the United States has been to provide processes by which men might deal more effectively with tumultuous social change. Change was the dominant note in the country's history. Other institutions than law worked to help men experience life as growth—family and church in more intimate elements of personality, school and market in more impersonal adjustments of relations. But as social ties grew in complexity, and as this complexity created new centers of power and greater potentials for good or ill, prevailing opinion demanded closer attention to the good order of social relationships and to the kinds and locations of power. This trend in prevailing values responded not just to the greater complexity of our affairs, but to their increased scale and the higher stakes that went with bigness. "This element of size is perhaps the single most important fact about our government and its perplexities."[7] Thus the course of law in the life of the United States was marked by increased use of the state, and especially from the 1890's on "the entry of government into all the secular affairs of society."[8] Less and less could one draw sharp lines between law and the general life. "If the Thames is 'liquid history,' the Constitution of the United States is most significantly not a document but a stream of history. . . . Constitutional law, then, is history. But equally true is it that American history is constitutional law."[9]

In our tradition of constitutional (responsible) power, wielded through regular procedures designed to help get at facts and argument addressed to facts, legal process invited men to enlarge the application of reason to their affairs, and to discipline emotion by employing its energies in the service of ends and with means which reason could ratify. This was an exacting approach to creating social order through law, requiring "a new public temper, a fructifying atmosphere of good will and humility. Only thus shall we attain to an understanding of the task and its responsibility—the ardent and patient devotion of science to a common social purpose and a common faith. Only thus shall we still the unrest, through processes of law, and not by incantations of 'law and order.' "[10] Moreover, constitutional legal processes carried meaning deeper than the resolution of immediate conflicts. Through such processes men were impelled to examine and order the values to which they gave their loyalty. That the community could thus educate itself to more sensitive awareness of what it stood for and what it might stand for was a promise of constitutional legal order especially important to this society of bustling, worldly growth. Professor Frankfurter reminded us that in 1876, Huxley had posed the country a challenge: "Size," said Huxley, "is not grandeur, and territory does not make a nation. The great issue, about which hangs a true sublimity and the terror of overhanging fate is, What are you going to do with all these things?" As we pointed toward mid-twentieth century, Frankfurter found that "Fifty years of the most feverish preoccupation with material development in the world's history, with its accompaniment of appalling social and industrial problems, have made Huxley's prescient inquiry the most pervasive and exigent question in American politics. Not that politics alone should be expected to furnish relief; not even that political action can supply the chief forces for the making of a truly civilized commonwealth. But politics must be looked to for a good deal, not so much through the specific acts of government as in the ideals which it pursues and the spiritual atmosphere which it helps to generate."[11] What Frankfurter said of Herbert Croly was plainly as true of his own interest in the flow of affairs under law: "He had an avid interest in the shifting scenes of contemporary politics and in its fleeting personalities. But for him, politics floated in the stream of history and was significant only in so far as it fulfilled the possibilities of man's nature."[12]

This emphasis upon the moral and educational effects of a constitutional legal order suggests important corollary themes for the study of legal history. Let us consider three of these corollary themes:

(1) There has been subtle and elusive interplay between public opinion and the special traditions and practices of legal agencies in enforcing responsibility upon public and private power. Study of our constitutional tradition has focused too much on the logic of classic debates and of leading cases. The reality has been more complicated. To grasp the reality leads legal history into the history of ideas and sentiment, as also into the history of procedure and professional tradition. "[A]fter all, the Constitution is a *Constitution*, and not merely a detailed code of prophetic restrictions against the ineptitudes and inadequacies of legislators and administrators. Ultimate protection is to be found in the people themselves, their zeal for liberty, their respect for one another and for the common good—a truth so obviously accepted that its demands in practice are usually overlooked. But safeguards must also be institutionalized through machinery and processes. These safeguards largely depend on a highly professionalized civil service, an adequate technique of administrative application of legal standards, a flexible, appropriate and economical procedure (always remembering that 'in the development of our liberty insistence upon procedural regularity has been a large factor'), easy access to public scrutiny, and a constant play of criticism by an informed and spirited bar."[13]

(2) The enforcement of responsibility upon power holders involves large themes of our legal history. But this approach has

the defect of emphasizing the negative or restrictive aspects of a
legal order which has been characterized also by vigorous, positive use of law to shape key conditions of social life. A major
subject for the historian of law in the United States must be
the complex development of ideas and feeling in relation to
practice concerning such affirmative uses of law. Most controversial, and most clouded by inept philosophy and partisan po-
lemic, has been the use of law to give positive guidance to the
economy. "Our major domestic issues [have been] . . . phases
of a single central problem: namely, the interplay of enterprise
and government. Taxation, utility regulation, control of the
security markets, labor standards, housing, banking and finance,
all these current issues turn essentially on the relation of government to money-making and of money-making to the government.
This central problem was with us long before the New Deal
and will be long after it has passed into history. The controversies which it engenders have at bottom not been differences
over details, but as to essential attitudes toward the organic
nature of modern, large-scale, industrialized society, and ultimately turn on the conception of the relation of individuals one
to another in the circumstances of our society."[14]

(3) We have said that a prime function of this legal system
has been to help educate and energize men to cope with problems generated by social change. The ground of men's response
to change is their perception of the facts of their situation. Thus
an important corollary theme of legal history is the appraisal of
law's performance in sharpening perception of facts and their
relationships, preliminary to choosing values and contriving
means to effect values. This function of law has been neglected
in the study of legal history, though it is implicit in Mr. Justice
Johnson's emphasis upon law as "the science of experiment."
The penalty for inadequate perception of fact was the failure
of legal doctrine to fulfill social interest. "If facts are changing,

law cannot be static. So-called immutable principles must accommodate themselves to facts of life, for facts are stubborn and will not yield. In truth, what are now deemed immutable principles once, themselves, grew out of living conditions. Thus, the notion of unrestrained liberty of contract arose at a time when industrial conditions were shackled by restrictive legislation and the slogan of the hour was unrestricted industrial enterprise. The conditions of life have changed; the shibboleths remain. There is an increasing conviction of the need of collective responsibility and a demand of governmental intervention for fairer social adjustment."[15] The symbolic significance of Louis Brandeis' career at the bar was the originality with which he pursued this insight into the key role of law's fact-finding activity: "Mr. Brandeis would extend the domain of law . . . by absorbing the facts of life, just as Mansfield in his day absorbed the law merchant into the common law. This craving for authentic facts on which law alone can be founded leads him always to insist on establishing the machinery by which they can be ascertained."[16] This emphasis did not subordinate substance to technicality; the want of this emphasis spelled defects of substance in law's performance. "[T]he great men of law have always insisted that law must be sensitive to life."[17]

The Separation of Powers

If we give the term a broad definition, we may say that the separation of powers emerges from Felix Frankfurter's academic writing as a central concept about which to organize study of United States legal history. Interest in various facets of the separation of powers dominated the pattern of the two casebooks he co-authored—in the jurisdiction and procedure of the federal courts, and in administrative law—as well as of the monograph on *The Business of the Supreme Court* and the sketch of main currents of statute law and administrative regulation in *The Public and Its Government*.[18]

A good deal written about the separation of powers ends in sterile dogma or at best in ideas of narrow reach, depicting formal boundaries between legislative, executive, and judicial authority. But to Professor Frankfurter the separation of powers meant no sterile dogma. Rather, it spelled the growth of distinctive functions of legal agencies out of their interplay with living facts of community experience. To him the separation of powers could not be defined simply by formal boundaries. Form was not unimportant in distinguishing agency roles. However, the deeper significance of the separation of powers lay in different types of substantive contribution to public policy, appropriate to differences in equipment and procedures developed out of experience. Our separation of powers tradition included a restrictive element. The doctrine "embodies cautions against tyranny in government through undue concentration of power." But even in this narrower sense of the concept "as a principle of statesmanship, the practical demands of government preclude its doctrinaire application. . . . In a word, we are dealing with what Madison called a 'political maxim' and not a technical rule of law."[19] If one looked at the demands for action made upon law, it was the more important to study the distinctive functional capacities and limitations of different types of legal agencies and of different styles of declaring public policy. Law was called on to help men make positive adjustments to pressures of change derived from the social environment apart from the law. Legal processes could not respond to such challenges "while law maintains its Blackstonian essences."[20] Both authority and the limits of authority were most usefully defined by grasping the functional capacities and hazards characterizing different processes of making and implementing public policy. Vital separation of powers doctrine rested not on abstract concepts, but on realistic perception of time-tested legal functions and their interplay. "[T]he various organs of government are not mechanically set apart from each other."[21] To understand the separation of powers in such living terms was to help create "the process by which great activities of the government . . . are subdued by the reason appropriate to them."[22]

The legislature developed as the prime source for fresh response by law to the needs and tensions created by the general growth of this society. "Legislation is the most sensitive reflex of politics. It is the most responsive to public needs and public feelings, and largely determines the orbit within which the judiciary and the executive move."[23] Measured by the affirmative impact of law on the general life, the most important and the most continuingly controversial element in the legislative role was what the legislature did to affect allocation of economic resources, by taxing and spending. "Taxation has always been the most sensitive nerve of government. . . . To balance budgets, to pay for the cost of progressively civilized social standards, to safeguard the future and to divide these burdens with substantial fairness to the different interests in the community, strains to the utmost the ingenuity of statesmen."[24] Time showed only increase in the importance and complexity of the legislature's fiscal role, not only in provision of public services but in the implicit regulatory effects of taxes and public spending upon private activity. "The radiations of taxation have steadily extended the intrusion of government into economic affairs. . . . The enormous diversity in types of business activity, the nice calculations involved in making classifications at once fair and effective, the repercussions of different taxes upon diverse enterprises are among the most exigent but elusive riddles for those charged with governing."[25]

If taxing and spending legislation showed the widest front of living exchange between law and the life of the community, nonetheless regulatory legislation ran also in the main currents of the society. Statutory definition of standards and rules of conduct went on in pragmatic response to "evils at their points of pressure." Our history devolved upon the legislature the job of dealing at first hand with the full range of interests which sought legal recognition or protection. Thus, over a greater variety of concerns than fell to the lot of any other legal agency, the legislature had to make the law's first sifting and evaluation of facts of social relations. The work was often roughhewn; it reflected a good deal of trial and error; it was responsive to particular demands for action more often than to any broad plan or general concepts. The neat-minded could find a good deal of crudity in legislation. But in large measure the uneven growth of regulatory statute law was a functional reflection of the legislature's place on the moving frontier of public policy. "Legislation is essentially *ad hoc*. To expect uniformity in law where there is diversity in fact is to bar effective legislation. An extremely complicated society inevitably entails special treatment for distinctive social phenomena. If legislation is to deal with realities, it must address itself to important variations in the needs, opportunities and coercive power of the different elements in the state."[26]

The primacy of legislation in the growth of public policy was already well marked in our first years as a nation.[27] The substantial development of executive roles came later. Not until the twentieth century did the functions of executive and administrative offices take on major stature. Two trends stood out:

(1) The classic executive role was to implement general public policy in particular application. Yet this area of the separation of powers was persistently one of weakness in our legal history, in concept and organization and in performance. Although "the central problem of law . . . is enforcement," the

record showed us impatient or inattentive toward giving adequate time and resources to the development of executive processes.[28] Thus even when in form we devised special means to cope with difficult problems of implementing public policy, as in the regulation of public utilities, "the administration of public service laws [was] . . . nowhere 'at its best,' and almost everywhere . . . meager and ineffective."[29] And when public emotion was temporarily stirred by dramatic deficiencies in law enforcement, notably in the administration of criminal law, too often public opinion turned to a "jaunty optimism which hoped to manufacture resistances to and deterrents against crime in much the same mood and with much the same methods that are successful in manufacturing Ford parts."[30] The principal challenge which Professor Frankfurter posed to the legal historians in this aspect of the separation of powers was to understand the deep-seated, stubbornly persistent attitudes and habits of thought and action which starved the executive process proper of development appropriate to its responsibilities. "Especially true is it of the United States that alertness to administration is a very late stage in the art of government."[31]

(2) The most effective developments in executive and administrative roles were those which supplemented the legislative process.[32] On the national scene the Presidency came to have large importance as an agency for mustering and forming public opinion to supply sustaining energies for major lawmaking. The President held the opportunity to make himself "the most powerful teacher in the country."[33] In matters more specialized and demanding closer attention to detail, the growth of administrative legislation under powers delegated by the legislature was "perhaps the most striking contemporary tendency of the [twentieth-century] Anglo-American legal order."[34] The rise of this supplementary legislative function of the executive branch responded to urgent practical needs of the

legal order. At the same time, this enlargement of executive or administrative roles enhanced the dangers of arbitrary action, and so in new fashion penalized us for inattention to the structure and equipment of executive processes. "It is idle to feel either blind resentment against 'government by commission' or sterile longing for a golden past that never was. Profound new forces call for new social inventions, or fresh adaptations of old experience. . . . The vast changes wrought by industry during the nineteenth century inevitably gave rise to a steady extension of legal control over economic and social interests. At first, state intervention manifested itself largely through specific legislative directions, depending for enforcement generally upon the rigid, cumbersome and ineffective machinery of the criminal law. By the pressure of experience, legislative regulation of economic and social activities . . . turned to administrative instruments. Inevitably this . . . greatly widened the field of discretion and thus opened the door to its potential abuse, arbitrariness. In an acute form and along a wide range of action we [were] . . . confronted with new aspects of familiar conflicts in the law between rule and discretion."[35]

The historic place of the courts in our separation of powers may profitably be viewed with reference to the relations of judicial process to the needs of the legal order for legislation (generalization of public policy) and for execution (application of generalized public policy). This is to say that, with different emphasis and in different sequences of events, the history of judicial roles in the United States shows functional analogies to the history of the executive. Professor Frankfurter gave major attention to the specialized problems of the federal courts, and especially of the Supreme Court of the United States, relative to problems of federalism and of judicial review of the constitutionality of official action.[36] His preoccupations, otherwise, were with currents of public policy expressed chiefly in legislation and administration. Thus he offers the legal historian less guidance in dealing with the more everyday functions of courts—and especially of courts in the states—than regarding any other aspect of the separation of powers.

Within these limits we should note two points. (1) The most distinctive judicial responsibility in our system (and the function which has most durably remained special to the judiciary) has been to provide processes of decision substantially independent of the legislative and executive branches, to promote the fair (equal) and rational (orderly and evidence-based) application of general public policy in particular instances. One of the "basic conceptions" of Anglo-American law was "the role of the judiciary in safeguarding individual rights in the accomplishment of modern social purposes."[37] In an essay which not only related history but became a part of history, Professor Frankfurter paid tribute to this function of the courts, in *The Case of Sacco and Vanzetti.*[38] (2) Judges contributed to making standards and rules by which law regulated conduct. The judicial contributions were made not only in building common law, but also—and of increasing importance over the years in this country—by interpreting the language of constitutions and statutes. What gave a particular cast to judge-made generalization of public policy was that it went on within the limits of lawsuits. The confines of litigation created both elements of strength and of weakness in judicial lawmaking. Professor Frankfurter was inclined to emphasize the elements of strength in "the common law instinct for empiricism in deciding live, concrete, real adversary issues, sticking close to fact, avoiding abstraction and the enunciation of premature generalization."[39] We are entitled to take this praise of common-law processes with some reservations. Professor Frankfurter's interests did not lead him into any broad studies comparing the quality of common law with the law embodied in statutes and administrative rule making.

Yet implicit in his emphasis on the historic growth of the legislative and administrative roles was recognition that litigious lawmaking was seriously inadequate to the demands which the years made on this legal order. We sense that what Professor Frankfurter most prized in the common law approach to policy making was that it supplied cautionary analogies to guide our judges in their unique role as interpreters of constitutional limitations upon legislative and executive action. "[T]his healthy pragmatic instinct [taught by the common law tradition], this concentration on the complications of the present and not heedlessly borrowing trouble by seeking to discern the too dim image of the future, will be disdained only by those who have not adequately experienced the serious clash of forces so often embedded in the procedural interstices of constitutional litigation, or who do not appreciate to what extent the Supreme Court's prestige has been won through its self-denying ordinances."[40]

Craftsmanship and Content in Legal History

Separation of powers themes stand midway between two broader types of subjects toward which Professor Frankfurter urges the legal historian. On the one hand is study of the functions of law in the whole sweep of social change—the focus of the first subdivision of this essay. On the other hand is study of the particular performance of law in the context of particular times and situations. Legal history, that is, may be regarded both from the standpoint of law's relation to the history of social structure and processes in the United States, and from the standpoint of law's relation to the history of concrete problems in defining values, adjusting tensions, and serving needs at given junctures in the country's life.

History should teach sophistication in appraising the relative weight of impersonal events and trends on the one hand, and of men's contrivings on the other. Such sophistication is especially relevant to wise use of law. The organized polity is man's most potent invention apart from science for affecting the conditions of his life. There is wisdom, however, in recognizing that law works upon the margin of events. Such wisdom will help keep lawmakers close to living fact. "Events, not men, have been the most powerful molders of Anglo-American law. To the extent that men have molded events, the great propulsions to legal development have come not from lawyers but from those outside the law who have changed the face of society, of which law is largely the mirror. Watt and Stephenson were much more responsible for undermining the dominantly feudal legal system expounded by Blackstone, than Bentham and Brougham. Edison and Ford have loosed forces more transforming to the law than did David Dudley Field and Mr. Justice Holmes."[41] Moreover, other factors than technology set the social environment within which law operates. Thus "early in the investigation [of criminal law administration in a twentieth-century metropolis] it became plain that the system of criminal justice had some of its roots deep in the whole social and spiritual life of the city."[42] Though the vitality of a constitutional system rested on moral energy, moralizing was not a fruitful approach to analysis of legal order. So with the issues of criminal justice in the city: "The problem is more comprehensive and its elements more manifold than the good-man–bad-man explanation of political phenomena assumes. Personalities, of course, play their part, but a relatively small part. The task is that of diagnosing the causes of a system whose origins must be traced back to social, economic, and political conditions distant in time and different from the present, and whose consequences cannot be understood apart from the civic standards and economic preoccupations of today."[43] Historical perspective helped assign proper weight to the essential contributions which informed opinion and sustained operations must make for effective legal change. "So much of our 'reform' effort does not stay 'put' because the aim is to 'put things over.' The complexities of an industrial democracy cannot be solved by the psychology of advertising. The starting-point of reform is the education of the public to the necessity of a sustained interest. . . . [T]ime is a necessary element and continuity of effort indispensable."[44]

To recognize that law works upon marginal opportunities afforded by the total social situation is to recognize the importance of two collateral themes for legal history. The first of these corollaries which Professor Frankfurter emphasized is that substantial importance may reside in technical detail. This is true because so much of the public policy that counts is built up only by long-time accretion of specific instances along sustained lines of institutional action. "The history of liberty . . . cannot be dissociated from the history of procedural observances."[45] The impress of policy upon life was according to the way policy worked. Thus "the labor injunction derives significance from the mode by which it has operated. What is called procedure determines results."[46] Interpretation of a statute offered less obvious drama than judicial review of the constitutionality of the statute. But "again and again behind so-called questions of 'statutory construction' . . . lurk great issues of policy."[47] The development of the effective roles of legal agencies could be traced through their procedures. "[T]he history of the Supreme Court, as of the Common Law, derives meaning to no small degree from the cumulative details which define the scope of its business, and the forms and methods of performing it—the Court's procedure, in the comprehensive meaning of the term. Not merely in its work of technical adjudication inseparably related to the procedural rules and practices of the Court. The essentially political significance of the Supreme Court's share in the operations of the Union can hardly be overemphasized. The role of procedure in the evolution and activity of political institutions has been little heeded by political scientists. But, as Professor Wallace Notestein has ... demonstrated ... the formalities and modes of doing business, which we characterize as procedure, though lacking in dramatic manifestations, may, like the subtle creeping in of the tide, be a powerful force in the dynamic process of government."[48]

The second corollary to recognizing law's marginal effectiveness amid the total of social causes is to acknowledge the consequent importance of craftsmanship in the lawman's job. This was the aspect of the separation of powers which most interested Professor Frankfurter. He measured the quality of men and agencies of law by the skill with which they realized the special potentialities of their situations. So "Marshall's commerce clause decisions reflect both his awareness of the problems of statecraft cast into legal issues, and the tentative, experimental adjustments within the legal process whereby adjustments without are made."[49] The sureness of the craftsman might derive from a subtle and imaginative intelligence, as well as from a practical knowledge of operations. "[T]hough [Holmes] did not bring to the Court the experience of great affairs, not even Marshall exceeded him in judicial statesmanship. Other great judges have been guided by the wisdom distilled from an active life; Mr. Justice Holmes was led by the divination of the philosopher and the imagination of the poet."[50] But, as important as was the quality of exceptional men, the determinative craftsmanship was that of the ordinary officer acting under the discipline of his function. "Confidence in the competence of the Court has not been won by the presence of a rare man of genius. The explanation lies rather in the capacity of the Court to dispose adequately of the tasks committed to it"—within an organizational frame which respected human limitations, and under internal procedures developed out of experience as "indispensable to a seasoned, collective, judical judgment. . . ."[51]

The historian, then, should study the limits of effective legal action, and the corollary significance of techniques and craftsmanship. But ultimately he would want to study, also, the particular content of public policy declared and made more or less effective through law. The law contributed many threads to the richly diverse patterns of life in the United States. Professor Frankfurter emphasized two subject matter areas as of salient importance: the criteria for the organization and use of the public force itself, and the employment of law in the management of the economy.

Legal order in this country was distinctive especially because of the pervasive effects of the ideals of constitutionalism and of federalism. In this system political power was deemed legitimate "in so far as it fulfilled the possibilities of man's nature."[52] Because power must be responsible power, "our administrative law is inextricably bound up with constitutional law."[53] But responsibility was not simply a restrictive concept. Hence a major theme of the history of the constitutional ideal in this legal order was the development of positive conceptions of law's role. Law should be "not a system of artificial reason, but the application of ethical ideals, with freedom at the core."[54]

Woven closely into the affirmative and the restrictive aspects of the constitutional ideal were the special problems of a federal system. Given the turbulence of growth in a nation which came to continental scope, it was not strange that the constitutional history of the federal idea showed a "rhythm of emphasis now upon national power, now upon state power," developing from the years in which "Marshall could draw with large and bold strokes" to those in which "decisions . . . depend more and more on precise formulation of the issues imbedded in litigation, and on alertness regarding the exact scope of past decisions in the light of their present significance."[55] The dominant fact was the insistent pressure of interests and functions appropriate to an economy of ever extending reach and scale. "Just because modern economic forces work so strongly for centralization, there [proved to be] . . . no more challenging problems of statesmanship than to decide what tasks [should] . . . be assumed by the central government and by which instruments and methods it [should] . . . perform them."[56]

Professor Frankfurter had too keen a sense of the political elements in social growth to adopt any dogmatic economic interpretation of legal history. However, legal development was profoundly affected by the large role which the institution of the market played in this social order, and by the revolutionary changes which advances in science and technology brought to the organization of economic activity. "The essential problems of modern government involve the interplay of economic enterprise and government."[57]

Professor Frankfurter emphasized two currents of demands upon law, consequent upon major trends in the economy. Private economic power tended to become more concentrated. At the same time, the economy tended toward greater specialization of functions. Interdependence enhanced the influence of those who controlled strategic intersections in these more intricate patterns of economic relations. A principal legal reflection of these developments was the growth of regulation of transport, communication, and electric power facilities. "Urgent public needs prompted the legislation. Its rationale was public protection through governmental instrumentalities that should be capable of matching in power and in technical resources the

JAMES WILLARD HURST

power and resources of the public utilities."⁵⁸ Growth in the law
of public utilities, of labor relations, and of antitrust all reflected
new concern in the community with the balance of power and
its implications for the relative social and economic status of
individuals and groups. Older lines of distinction between matters of "public" and of "private" importance blurred. Prevailing
opinion responded to the more intricate organization of society
by insisting, in effect, that private as well as public power must
be brought within the constitutional ideal of responsibility.
"Government in industry, like unto political government, must
be worked out where power and responsibility are shared by all
those who are participants in industry as well as the dependent
'public.' The task is nothing less than devising constant processes
by which to achieve an orderly and fruitful way of life."⁵⁹

Problems of the balance of power generated the most prominent legal responses to economic change in the late nineteenth
and early twentieth centuries. Meanwhile, however, as recur-
rent depressions brought alarming social and economic disloca-
tion, other issues loomed larger, pertaining to the functional
health of the economy. Popular opinion finally rejected the
"shallow fatalism" which counseled that depressions must be
endured "like epidemics of old as part of the burden of life."
The community demanded that fiscal and regulatory powers of
law be mobilized to help limit disastrous swings of the business
cycle. "To realize that there is a new economic order and to
realize it passionately, not platonically, [became] . . . the central
equipment for modern statesmanship."⁶⁰ We did not take these
new directions as rapidly as experience would have dictated, or
without acute controversy. Indeed, in this aspect the history of
public policy making was such as to raise serious question
whether our legal processes were adequate to bring issues to
rational decision with sufficient despatch to meet the pace of
social change. "Surely the social historian of the United States

219

will on the whole judge the course of events since 1887 a great social waste, he will assess the relations between business and government as needless social friction. Needless waste and friction not because opposition to all legislation is not in itself a contributing factor, nor because the specific enactments should not have been opposed in detail and sometimes even been delayed in passage. The social waste has derived from the fact that obvious reforms, now recognized by all men, were unduly delayed, and that in the intransigent opposition to legislation as such, the democratic legislative process was deprived of the indispensable constructive criticism from those with special knowledge even though sometimes also with special interest."[61]

Once again experience thus should remind us that a vital legal order is not a product of procedural gadgetry or of genius in public office, but depends upon the sustaining force of a mature and responsible citizenry. "[D]emocracy must vindicate itself otherwise than through political action," for "political action is itself an aspect of mature education and co-operative living."[62] Nonetheless, the significant promise and hope of constitutional legal processes was that men learned by living within such a frame of order. Such a legal system had its most profound effects on life not by prohibiting and regulating, or taxing and spending, but by teaching. "In a democracy, politics is a process of popular education—the task of adjusting the conflicting interests of diverse groups in the community, and bending the hostility and suspicion and ignorance engendered by group interest to the reconciliation of a common interest and a common understanding."[63] To Felix Frankfurter the most profound significance of the legal history of the nation was what it mirrored of the development of the character of the nation.

Law and Politics

Archibald MacLeish, *Poet*

The convictions of a Justice of the Supreme Court, like the convictions of any other man, are the products of his experience. Mr. Frankfurter's experience of the kind of nation this nation is began with an immigrant's landing in New York in 1896. One thing he was certain of then, and has been certain of ever since, is the democracy of the country to which he came. What other men inherited and therefore took for granted he discovered for himself and therefore earned. There may have been other Justices of the Court who have held American democracy in as great respect as Mr. Frankfurter holds it: none has respected it more, or more earnestly resented its disrepute. What he said in April, 1938, he meant—"I can express with very limited adequacy the passionate devotion to this land that possesses millions of our people, born like myself under other skies, for the privilege this country has bestowed in allowing them to partake of its fellowship."

But American democracy, as he soon learned, had its problems also, and two months after his graduation from the Harvard Law School in 1906 he was dealing with one of the most pressing. That problem was the problem of the application of the laws, including the criminal laws, to the great property interests which had acquired a control not only of the national economy but of a considerable part of the national government as well. Theodore Roosevelt's attempt to bring within the law the "malefactors of great wealth" of lower Manhattan had enlisted the aid of Colonel Henry L. Stimson who took over the job of District Attorney for the Southern District of New York. Colonel Stimson had hired Felix Frankfurter as an assistant. And Felix Frankfurter spent the first five years of his career as a lawyer in the struggle to teach Big Business that it also owed obedience to the people's laws.

That experience was illuminating. The young lawyer who won the appeals in the Sugar Fraud cases was a young lawyer who had learned unforgettable things. But what followed was even more instructive. By a curious twist of history Felix Frankfurter was dropped, in 1911, into the center of one of the first American attempts at a regulation of industry not for police purposes only but for an affirmative, social end. Colonel Stimson was again the god in the machine. Colonel Stimson had become Secretary of War Stimson under Taft, and Felix Frankfurter had gone to Washington as Law Officer of the Bureau of Insular Affairs, and counsel to the Secretary in the exercise of his jurisdiction over rivers and harbors. It was in this last capacity that Mr. Frankfurter found himself again on the Government-Big Business front. President Taft had announced at the beginning of his administration that no permits were to be issued for the construction of dams on navigable streams without some *quid pro quo* to the government. That principle, once enunciated, produced in the logic of time the Federal Power Commission and the yardstick theories developed by the TVA. And Mr. Frankfurter, as counsel to the Secretary, was the guardian of the principle. Through the last two years of Mr. Taft's administration and the first year of Mr. Wilson's, Mr. Frankfurter was thus concerned with the conflict between democratic government and industrial imperialism at the point where that conflict was sharpest and most sharply felt.

But it was not merely his professional work which turned his mind in this period to the place of the law and of lawyers in the economic problems of a democratic society. It was also his friends. The two men who most influenced the thinking of Mr. Frankfurter at this time, and throughout his life, were Mr. Justice Brandeis, then a practicing lawyer in Boston, and Mr. Justice Holmes.

Mr. Justice Holmes was a man of the world, who was also a philosopher, who was incidentally a lawyer. The result was that he was a very great judge—so great a judge indeed that his quality as a man and as a mind was often hidden behind his judicial eminence. But his influence on his friends, which was itself one of the great forces of his time, was always the influence of a personality and a way of thinking. It was not in all cases— however heretical it may be to say so—a fortunate influence. The skepticism and the philosophic detachment which sat so easily with Mr. Justice Holmes himself, giving flavor and taste to his strong humanity as salt gives flavor and taste to fresh meat, had a caustic and pickling effect on lesser vitalities, so that many of the great Justice's disciples were left only with the skepticism and the detachment and without the human and believing force.

But with Mr. Frankfurter, and with others of equal exuberance of mind and of emotion, the influence of Mr. Justice Holmes was a sovereign prescription. For Mr. Justice Holmes saw the law, as few great jurists have ever seen it, in a decent relation to a world which contains also men and women and poetry and work and wars. He saw the pretensions of the law to final precision as skeptically as he saw the pretensions of philosophers to ultimate truth or the pretensions of politicians to disinterested service. And he, therefore, perceived and taught and said that the law—even the law of the Constitution—must make its own adjustments to its time. What he gave his fortunate friends was not a complete philosophy: it is more than doubtful that he had one. What he gave them, and Mr. Frankfurter among them, was an understanding of the relation of the law to life which made impossible a conception of the law as anything but a means to an end. To most great lawyers the law sooner or later become a substantive, a noun. To Mr. Justice Holmes it was always a verb having a predicate to follow.

The influence of Mr. Justice Brandeis was more immediate, more specific, more controlling, and perhaps less deep. To Mr. Justice Brandeis also the law was a means to social ends, but a specific means to specific social ends. Though no philosopher in the humanistic sense, Mr. Justice Brandeis held more precise philosophic beliefs than Mr. Justice Holmes and his trace in Mr. Frankfurter's thinking is easier to follow. He is directly responsible, for example, for an early interest in scientific management and the Taylor Society which Mr. Frankfurter developed before the War. He is directly responsible, also, for Mr. Frankfurter's concern with labor legislation after Mr. Frankfurter's appointment to the faculty of the Harvard Law School in 1914 and thus indirectly responsible for Mr. Frankfurter's war-time career first on the President's Mediation Commission and eventually as Chairman of the War Labor Policies Board. And echoes of his views about the evils of industrial "bigness" and the advantages of Federalism may be caught in much of what Mr. Frankfurter has since written.

But Mr. Justice Brandeis's principal contribution to the shaping of Mr. Frankfurter's mind was his development, in association with Mr. Frankfurter and Miss Josephine Goldmark, of a new technique for the argument of cases involving social and economic issues—a technique which was to have radical effects not only on the pleading of such cases but on the attitude toward them of the profession and even of the general public. It was Mr. Brandeis's view that appellate briefs in cases involving social and economic legislation should argue not only the principles of law involved, but the factual background of relevant social and economic considerations which had influenced the legislature. The statute, in other words, should be looked at, not through the cracks in the constitutional fence, but out in the open lot where its place in a total social organization of people actually alive in an actual world might be seen. The Oregon ten-hour law was thus presented in a Brandeis-Frankfurter-Goldmark brief in the case of *Bunting* v. *Oregon* and Mr. Frankfurter, after the appointment of Mr. Brandeis to the Bench, successfully argued that brief in the Supreme Court. From that time forward, in subsequent magazine articles as well as in subsequent briefs, Mr. Frankfurter's thinking was deeply affected by the implications of this method. In a 1916 article in the *New Republic*, of which magazine he was a contributing editor from the beginning, he cites with approval Mr. Brandeis's remark to the Chicago Bar Association that he hoped to be able to extend the domain of law by absorbing into it the facts of life, as Lord Mansfield, in his day, extended the common law by absorbing into it the law merchant.

The influence of these two greatest of modern judges, Holmes and Brandeis is to be seen in Mr. Frankfurter's reluctance to accept for himself any of the definable political positions of his time; a matter of vivid concern to many of his friends upon the Left. Writing in 1937 (*A Rigid Outlook in a Dynamic World*), Mr. Frankfurter expresses his conviction that dogmatic positions and universal theories must yield to fact. ". . . In the resistance to these practical, empiric, *ad hoc* interventions of organized society by doctrines which either have become obsolete or only partially valid because qualified by counter-doctrines, we find the clue not only to the history of the last fifty years but to the tensions of the future. Once there is adequate recognition of the intrinsic complexity of the problems that confront us and the extremely limited range of issues that can be settled out of hand by invoking general formulas, however hallowed, the whole mental climate in which these problems are thought out and worked out will be changed. For then it will become manifest that the science of government is really the most difficult of all the arts, that it is, in the language of one of the great Justices of the Supreme Court, uttered more than a hundred years ago, 'the science of experiment.'" Those who believe that there is very little time for democratic experiment left and that blundering action is preferable to advised inaction may object to so detached a view. They must admit, however, that it is the natural child of the philosophic skepticism of Holmes and of Brandeis's passion for the facts.

But if Mr. Frankfurter's masters taught him to bring his laboratory methods into politics they also taught him to take his political conscience into the laboratory. In 1914, after three years of Washington, Mr. Frankfurter was called to the Harvard Law School as a member of the faculty. The Harvard Law School, in 1914, was what it had long been, the greatest school of law and one of the greatest educational institutions in the country. It made young men who had never used their minds before use their minds until they forgot to eat and sleep. But even the Harvard Law School had its failings, the chief of which was its attitude toward "the law." "The law" at Harvard at that time was an intellectual pattern which young men, armed with a dialectical tool called the Socratic Method, were expected to excavate, like some beautiful and buried city which needed only digging to be known. The relating of cases to their occasions or of legal principles to their human effects was not encouraged. There was no nonsense about justice in the Harvard Law School of the years before the War.

To this school Mr. Frankfurter came as a young man of thirty-two with ten years of public service and many evenings of exciting talk in the back of his mind. The law to him was a very different thing from the law as it appeared to many of his older colleagues. "I look forward," he quotes Holmes as saying, "to a time when the part played by history in the explanation of dogma shall be very small and instead of ingenious research we shall spend our energy on a study of the ends sought to be attained and the reasons for desiring them." What concerned Mr. Frankfurter from the beginning of his teaching was the study of "the ends sought to be attained and the reasons for desiring them." The law to him was not a buried antique city lying perfect underground, but a means by which the city of the future might perhaps be built.

That there were differences of opinion between Mr. Frankfurter and his older colleagues will surprise no one. Neither should it be surprising that the bright young men who were adept at sapping and mining in the traditional manner should find Mr. Frankfurter frivolous. Passionate golfers and chess players take the same attitude toward those who ask them why they play. But what *is* perhaps surprising is the fact that Mr. Frankfurter was able to survive that opposition and eventually to leave an ineffaceable mark not only on the instruction of the School but on the lives of many of the best men who attended it. For years—long before the New Deal—he was diverting to a brief experience of public service men who, in the old days, would have sniffed at anything but a warm berth in a big New York office. The Federal Trade Commission, the Interstate Commerce Commission, the chambers of Justices of the Court, and the many federal bureaus and commissions of the War, were peppered with Harvard Law School men. Most went back to private practice. A few stayed. But all had formed a different picture of the law. From the days of the War on there were fewer graduates of the Harvard Law School who could look forward complacently to a lifetime spent in a down-town law office with the hope perhaps of rising to the presidency of a bank.

Mr. Frankfurter's own experience of the relation of law to the life of his time did not end with his appointment to the School. In 1917 he left Cambridge for a Washington week-end with Secretary of War Newton D. Baker, which lasted for two years.

Mr. Frankfurter's previous experience of the adaptation of the law to social necessities had familiarized him with two aspects of the struggle of government to control Big Business. Now he was to see the legal implications of the struggle of labor to gain economic freedom. First as Secretary and Counsel to the President's Mediation Commission, investigating labor difficulties, and later as Chairman of the War Labor Policies Board, framing a labor policy for the country as a whole, Mr. Frankfurter had extraordinary opportunities to study the American labor situation at first hand and in national terms.

What he there observed influenced his actions over the next ten years and gave him the intellectual preoccupations which, more than anything else, have determined the public estimate of his character. The Labor issue, in the years of the Great War and the years immediately following, was not so much an economic issue or a social issue as an issue involving fundamental questions of civil rights. Mr. Frankfurter's War Labor Policies Board worked out collective bargaining standards which were extremely useful to the farmers of the NIRA and the Wagner Act. But it was Mr. Frankfurter's experience on the President's Mediation Commission which most deeply influenced his thinking. His service on that Commission took him to California to study and report on the Mooney Case, and to Bisbee, Arizona, to inquire into the deportation by vigilantes of a thousand IWW miners who were marooned without adequate food or water in a desert town. Having seen industrial terrorism at first hand, it was natural that he should take action when Attorney-General Palmer began his Red Raids in the Boston Area in 1919, and natural that he should take part in the formation of the American Civil Liberties Union which shortly followed. Having committed himself thus to the defense of civil rights, it was natural also that he should join forces with those who attempted to save Sacco and Vanzetti from legal lynching in the capital of Massachusetts.

Notes

Felix Frankfurter at Oxford, *Isaiah Berlin*

1. I have said nothing here of Marion Frankfurter. This is a deliberate omission: her distinction in every respect is too great to be treated in what would inevitably have been a marginal manner. That she deserves a full-length portrait to herself, none of those who have been admitted to her friendship would, I think, deny. I have proceeded on the principle that a blank is better than an unworthy sketch.
2. He died in 1963.

To Gather Meaning Not from Reading the Constitution, but from Reading Life, *Francis Biddle*

1. Frankfurter, Law and Politics 30 (1939).
2. Holmes, Laski Letters 89 (1953).
3. *Ibid.*, 98.
4. *Ibid.*, 218.
5. *Ibid.*, 333.
6. *Ibid.*, 1121.
7. *Ibid.*, 210.
8. *Ibid.*, 211, n. 2.
9. *Ibid.*, 999.

10. *Ibid.,* XV.
11. *Ibid.,* 997.
12. *Ibid.,* 1226.
13. Wallace Mendelson, Justices Black and Frankfurter, Conflict in the Court 14 (1961).
14. *Id., passim.*
15. Mr. Justice Holmes and the Supreme Court 7 (1938).
16. *Ibid.,* 3.
17. *Ibid.,* 9.
18. Felix Frankfurter Reminisces, *supra* 245.
19. *Ibid.,* 248.
20. Law and Politics, *supra* 248.

A Fifty Year Friendship, *Edmund Morris Morgan*

1. James Barr Ames, Dean, Harvard Law School, 1895–1909.
2. John Chipman Gray, Professor of Law, Harvard Law School.

Felix, *Herbert B. Ehrmann*

1. When Mr. Ehrmann was invited to contribute a chapter to the *Festschrift* in honor of Justice Frankfurter, he was already at work on an autobiography. It was therefore agreed that his contribution would be a personal narrative which might later be published as part of such a volume.

Mr. Justice Frankfurter, *Paul A. Freund*

1. Holmes employed a different metaphor: "When you get the dragon out of his cave on to the plain and in the daylight, you can count his teeth and claws, and see just what is his strength. But to get him out is only the first step. The next is either to kill him, or to tame him and make him a useful animal." The Path of the Law, in Collected Legal Papers 167, 187 (1920).
2. Frankfurter and Corcoran, *Petty Federal Offenses and the Con-*

stitutional Guaranty of Trial by Jury, 39 HARV. L. REV. 917 (1926).

3. Frankfurter and Landis, *Power of Congress Over Procedure in Criminal Contempts in "Inferior" Federal Courts—A Study in Separation of Powers*, 37 HARV. L. REV. 1010 (1924). See Michaelson v. United States, 266 U.S. 42 (1924), decided four months after the publication of the article.

4. Frankfurter and Corcoran, *op. cit., supra* n. 2, at 981.

5. *Chief Justices I Have Known*, 39 VA. L. REV. 883, 902 (1953), reprinted in Of Law and Men, 111, 134 (1956).

6. *Introduction* to Sheldon and Eleanor Glueck, One Thousand Juvenile Delinquents viii (1934).

7. McNabb v. United States, 318 U.S. 332 (1943).

8. Sibbach v. Wilson and Co., 312 U.S. 1, 16 (1941) (dissent).

9. Harris v. United States, 331 U.S. 145, 155, 157 (1947) (dissent).

10. *Id.*, at 163.

11. Rochin v. California, 342 U.S. 165, 168–170 (1952).

12. Caritativo v. California, 357 U.S. 549, 550 (1958) (dissent); Solesbee v. Balkcom, 339 U.S. 9, 14 (1950) (dissent).

13. Of Law and Men 77, 81 (1956).

14. Heikkila v. Barber, 345 U.S. 229, 237 (1953) (dissent).

15. Joint Anti-Fascist Refuge Committee v. McGrath, 341 U.S. 123, 149, 171–172 (1951) (concurring).

16. Keifer & Keifer v. RFC, 306 U.S. 381 (1939); Larson v. Domestic and Foreign Commerce Corp., 337 U.S. 682, 705 (1949) (dissent).

17. Butler v. Michigan, 352 U.S. 380 (1957).

18. Sweezy v. New Hampshire, 354 U.S. 234, 255 (1957) (concurring).

19. Bridges v. California, 314 U.S. 252, 279 (1941) (dissent).

20. Toynbee, *Two Kinds of Extremism*, OBSERVER, p. 20, c. 5–6 (Feb. 8, 1959).

21. Francis v. Resweber, 329 U.S. 459, 466 (1947) (concurring).

22. Article on Holmes in 21 Dictionary of American Biography 417, 424 (1944), reprinted in Of Law and Men 158, 175 (1956). See also Frankfurter, Mr. Justice Holmes and the Constitution 51 (1938).

23. Santayana, Reason in Science, in The Life of Reason 401–402 (rev. ed., 1955).

24. Acton, A Lecture on the Study of History 73 (1905).

25. Larson v. Domestic and Foreign Commerce Corp., 337 U.S. 682, 705–706 (1949) (dissent).

Applied Politics and the Science of Law: Writings of the Harvard Period, *Alexander M. Bickel*

1. 107 OUTLOOK 55, 70G (May 9, 1914).
2. Felix Frankfurter Reminisces 165–168 (Phillips ed., 1960).
3. Law and Politics—Occasional Papers of Felix Frankfurter, 1913–1938, pp. 48, 52 (Prichard and MacLeish eds. Capricorn ed., 1962).
4. 2 Howe, Justice Oliver Wendell Holmes 282 (1963).
5. L and P 3–9.
6. 40 A.B.A. Rep. 365, 372 (1915).
7. P. 315.
8. N.H.B.A. Pro. 73, 76 (1932–1933).
9. *Book Review*, 32 COLUM. L. REV. 920, 921 (1932).
10. 36 School and Society 110 (July 23, 1932).
11. Brandeis to Laski, Aug. 8, 1925. Library of Yale Law School.
12. Brandeis to Laski, Nov. 29, 1929. Library of Yale Law School.
13. Also in Universal Library paperback edition, 1962.
14. A second, very handsome edition was published in 1961 by Belknap Press of Harvard.
15. *Hours of Labor and Realism in Constitutional Law*, 29 HARV. L. REV. 353 (1916); *Constitutional Opinions of Justice Holmes*, 29 HARV. L. REV. 683 (1916); *Twenty Years of Mr. Justice Holmes' Constitutional Opinions*, 36 HARV. L. REV. 909 (1923); (with James M. Landis) *Power of Congress Over Procedure in Criminal Contempts in "Inferior" Federal Courts*, 37 HARV. L. REV. 1010 (1924); *Note to Advisory Opinions of National and International Courts*, 37 HARV. L. REV. 1002 (1924); (with Thomas G. Corcoran) *Petty Federal Offenses and the Constitutional Guaranty of Trial by Jury*, 39 HARV. L. REV. 917 (1926); *Mr. Justice Holmes and the Constitution*, 41 HARV. L. REV. 121 (1927); (with James M. Landis) *The Supreme Court Under the Judiciary Act of 1925*, 42 HARV. L. REV. 1 (1928); (with James M. Landis) *Business of the Supreme Court at Oct. Term, 1928*, 43 HARV. L. REV. 33 (1929); (with James M. Landis) *Business of the Supreme Court at Oct. Term, 1929*, 44 HARV. L. REV. 1 (1930); (with James M. Landis) *Business of the Supreme Court at Oct. Term, 1930*, 45 HARV. L. REV. 271 (1931); *Early Writings of O. W. Holmes, Jr.*, 44 HARV. L. REV. 717 (1931); (with

NOTES

James M. Landis) *Business of the Supreme Court at Oct. Term, 1931,* 46 HARV. L. REV. 226 (1932); (with Henry M. Hart, Jr.) *Business of the Supreme Court at Oct. Term, 1932,* 47 HARV. L. REV. 245 (1933); (with Henry M. Hart, Jr.) *Business of the Supreme Court at Oct. Term, 1933,* 48 HARV. L. REV. 238 (1934); *Mr. Justice Holmes,* 48 HARV. L. REV. 1279 (1935); (with Henry M. Hart, Jr.) *Business of the Supreme Court at Oct. Term, 1934,* 49 HARV. L. REV. 68 (1935); (with Adrian S. Fisher) *Business of the Supreme Court at the Oct. Terms, 1935 and 1936,* 51 HARV. L. REV. 577 (1938); *Mr. Justice Cardozo and Public Law,* 52 HARV. L. REV. 440 (1939).
16. (With James M. Landis) *The Compact Clause of the Constitution: A Study in Interstate Adjustments,* 34 YALE L.J. 685 (1925); *Distribution of Judicial Power Between the Courts of the United States and the Courts of the States,* 13 CORN. L.Q. 499 (1928); *Rationalization in Industry and the Labor Problem,* 13 Proceedings of Acad. of Pol. Sci. 171–177 (1928–1930); (with Nathan Greene) *Congressional Power Over the Labor Injunction,* 31 COLUM. L. REV. 385 (1931); *A Note on Diversity Jurisdiction—In Reply to Professor Yntema,* 79 U. PA. L. REV. 1097 (1931).
17. *Advisory Opinions (National),* 1 Enc. Soc. Sci. 475 (1930); (with Paul A. Freund) *Interstate Commerce* (United States), 8 Enc. Soc. Sci. 220 (1932); (with Nathan Greene) *Labor Injunction,* 8 Enc. Soc. Sci. 653 (1932); (with Henry M. Hart, Jr.) *Rate Regulation,* 13 Enc. Soc. Sci. 104 (1934); *Supreme Court, United States,* 14 Enc. Soc. Sci. 474 (1934).
18. *The Law School and the Public Service,* 17 HARV. ALUMNI BUL. 115 (Nov. 11, 1914); *The Law and the Law Schools,* 40 A.B.A. Rep. 365 (1915); *A National Policy for Enforcement of Prohibition,* 109 Annals Am. Acad. 193 (Sept. 1923); *Book Review,* 39 YALE L.J. 304 (1929); *Book Review,* 77 U. PA. L. REV. 436 (1929); *Book Review,* 16 A.B.A.J. 251 (1930); *Book Review,* 16 VA. L. REV. 743 (1930); *Book Review,* 39 J. POL. ECON. 401 (1931); *Book Review,* 32 COLUM. L. REV. 920 (1932); *Reconstruction and the Law,* N.H.B.A. Pro. 73 (1932–1933); *A Distinctively American Contribution,* 23 AM. LAB. LEG. REV. 169 (1933); *Introduction to A Symposium on Administrative Law,* 18 IOWA L. REV. 129 (1933); *Introduction* to Glueck, One Thousand Juvenile Delinquents (1934); *Foreward* to Jennings, *Courts and Administrative Law—The Experience of English Housing Legislation,* 49 HARV. L. REV. 426

FELIX FRANKFURTER—*A Tribute*

(1936); *Question of a Minimum Wage Law for American Industry*, 15 CONG. DIGEST 271 (Nov. 1936); *Summation of the Conference* [Cinc. Conf. on Functions and Procedure of Admin. Tribunals], 24 A.B.A.J. 282 (1938); *Foreword* to *A Discussion of Current Developments in Administrative Law*, 47 YALE L.J. 515 (1938); *Mr. Justice Cardozo*, 24 A.B.A.J. 638 (1938).

19. See *supra* n. 3. Like the preceding bibliographies, the following list of items not included in L and P is as complete as I could make it—or rather get it made and remade by a number of students. I harbor no illusions that perfection has been attained.

The Conservation of the New Federal Standards, 41 SURVEY 291 (Dec. 7, 1918); *French Policy and Peace in Europe*, 24 NEW REPUBLIC 138 (Oct. 6, 1920); *The President's Industrial Conference*, 22 NEW REPUBLIC 179 (Apr. 7, 1920); *Haiti and Intervention*, 25 NEW REPUBLIC 71 (Dec. 15, 1920); *Reply to Protest from the Clothing Manufacturers' Association*, 25 NEW REPUBLIC 202 (Jan. 12, 1921); *Mr. Lansing's Book*, 26 NEW REPUBLIC 198 (Apr. 13, 1921); *The Mooney Case*, 29 NEW REPUBLIC 215 (Jan. 18, 1922); *The Coronado Case*, 31 NEW REPUBLIC 328 (Aug. 16, 1922); *What Has Prohibition Done to America?*, 32 NEW REPUBLIC 305 (Nov. 15, 1922); *Joining the League*, 116 NATION 571 (May 16, 1923); *The Enforcement of Prohibition*, 33 NEW REPUBLIC 149 (Jan. 3, 1923); *Hands Off the Investigations*, 38 NEW REPUBLIC 329 (May 21, 1924); (with James M. Landis) *Bankers and the Conspiracy Law*, 41 NEW REPUBLIC 218 (Jan. 21, 1925); *Changing Men's Minds*, New York *World*, ed. section, p. 1, Feb. 8, 1925; *The Federal Courts*, 58 NEW REPUBLIC 273 (Apr. 24, 1929); *The United States Supreme Court Molding the Constitution*, 32 CURR. HIST. 235 (May 1930); *The Supreme Court and the Public*, 83 FORUM 329 (June 1930); *The Palestine Situation Restated*, 9 FOREIGN AFFAIRS 409 (Apr. 1931); *The Federal Securities Act*, 8 FORTUNE 53 (Aug. 1933); *October Days*, 3 TODAY 5 (Mar. 9, 1935); *A Rigid Outlook in a Dynamic World*, 27 SURVEY GRAPHIC 5 (Jan. 1938).

I have omitted Letters to the Editor from this list, and I do not, of course, remotely claim to possess a full or even a passable collection of these. Perhaps two letters printed in the Boston *Herald* within a week in 1924 will give some indication of range and flavor: One (Oct. 4, 1924, p. 8) was entitled "From a La Follette Supporter"; the other (Oct. 9, 1924, p. 14), no doubt trying hard to be less offensive, was headed "Bar Association as a Country Club."

20. L and P 113, 117.
21. L and P 48.
22. *Interstate Commerce, United States*, 8 Enc. Soc. Sci. 220 (1932).
23. *Supreme Court, United States*, 14 Enc. Soc. Sci. 474, 480 (1934).
24. (With Henry M. Hart, Jr.) *Business of the Supreme Court at Oct. Term, 1933*, 48 HARV. L. REV. 238, 280 (1934).
25. *The United States Supreme Court Molding the Constitution*, 32 CURR. HIST. 235, 240 (May 1930).
26. L and P 113.
27. The Commerce Clause Under Marshall, Taney and Waite 47 (1937).
28. L and P 119.
29. *Book Review*, 32 COLUM. L. REV. 920 (1932).
30. L and P 41, 47.
31. (With Henry M. Hart, Jr.) *Rate Regulation*, 13 Enc. Soc. Sci. 104, 108 (1934).
32. L and P 37, 39.
33. L and P 37, 40.
34. *Constitutional Opinions of Justice Holmes*, 29 HARV. L. REV. 683 (1916).
35. *The Supreme Court and the Public*, 83 FORUM 329, 334, 331 (June 1930).
36. L and P 48, 52.
37. L and P 10, 11–12.
38. L and P 10, 12.
39. *E.g., The Supreme Court and the Public*, 83 FORUM 329, 332 (June 1930).
40. *Interstate Commerce (United States)*, 8 Enc. Soc. Sci. 220, 226 (1932).
41. 12 How. 298 (1851).
42. *Interstate Commerce (United States)*, 8 Enc. Soc. Sci. 220, 222 (1932).
43. *The Supreme Court and the Public*, 83 FORUM 329, 332 (June 1930).
44. *Interstate Commerce (United States)*, 8 Enc. Soc. Sci. 220, 224–225 (1932); see Brown, *The Open Economy: Justice Frankfurter and the Position of the Judiciary*, 67 YALE L.J. 219 (1957).
45. L and P 10, 16.
46. L and P 113, 117.
47. L and P 108, 109.

48. 208 U.S. 412 (1908).
49. 219 U.S. 104 (1911).
50. *The Law and the Law Schools*, 40 A.B.A. Rep. 365, 367 (1915).
51. Lochner v. New York 198 U.S. 45 (1905).
52. L and P 10, 15.
53. *Ibid.*
54. *The United States Supreme Court Molding the Constitution*, 32 CURR. HIST. 235, 239–240 (May 1930).
55. 257 U.S. 312 (1921).
56. L and P 41–47.
57. Taft to Butler, Dec. 12, 1922. W. H. Taft Papers, Library of Congress.
58. L and P 41, 45.
59. L and P 88, 96–97.
60. Mr. Justice Holmes and the Supreme Court 74–76 (2nd ed., 1961).
61. L and P 10, 12.
62. Abrams v. United States, 250 U.S. 616, 624 (1919).
63. *Twenty Years of Mr. Justice Holmes' Constitutional Opinions*, 36 HARV. L. REV. 909, 923 (1923).
64. See, *e.g.*, Levy, Legacy of Suppression (1960).
65. See, *e.g.*, United States v. Lovett, 328 U.S. 303, 318 (1946).
66. Compare, *e.g.*, Harris v. United States, 331 U.S. 145, 155 (1947), with Frank v. Maryland, 359 U.S. 360 (1959).
67. Milwaukee Pub. Co. v. Burleson, 255 U.S. 407 (1921).
68. L and P 129, 133.
69. See *supra* n. 65.
70. *Power of Congress Over Procedure in Criminal Contempts in "Inferior" Federal Courts*, 37 HARV. L. REV. 1010 (1924).
71. Toledo Newspaper Co. v. United States, 247 U.S. 402 (1918).
72. *The Supreme Court and the Public*, 83 FORUM 329, 332 (June 1930).
73. Michaelson v. United States, 291 Fed. 940 (7th Cir., 1923), *rev'd*, 266 U.S. 42 (1924).
74. *Power of Congress Over Procedure in Criminal Contempts in "Inferior" Federal Courts*, 37 HARV. L. REV. 1010, 1049 (1924).
75. 39 HARV. L. REV. 917 (1926).
76. 39 HARV. L. REV. 917, 921, 922, 981, 982.
77. 354 U.S. 234, 255, 267 (1957).

78. L and P 129, 134.
79. *Constitutional Opinions of Justice Holmes*, 29 HARV. L. REV. 683, 699 (1916).
80. L and P 80, 86.
81. Mr. Justice Holmes and the Supreme Court 76 (2nd ed., 1961).
82. L and P 113, 122.
83. *What Has Prohibition Done to America?*, 32 NEW REPUBLIC 305 (Nov. 15, 1922).
84. *Constitutional Opinions of Justice Holmes*, 29 HARV. L. REV. 683, 688 (1916).
85. 38 NEW REPUBLIC 329 (May 21, 1924).
86. 345 U.S. 41 (1953).
87. *Supra* n. 77.
88. 360 U.S. 109 (1959).
89. L and P 189, 193.
90. Swift has sailed into his rest;
     Savage indignation there
     Cannot lacerate his breast.
     Imitate him if you dare,
     World-besotted traveler; he
     Served human liberty.
     YEATS, *Collected Poems* 277 (1950).
91. The Public and Its Government 60 (1930); see also L and P 189, 194.
92. 287 U.S. 45 (1932).
93. L and P 189, 192, 194.
94. (With Nathan Greene) *Congressional Power Over the Labor Injunction*, 31 COLUM. L. REV. 385, 390 (1931).
95. 34 YALE L.J. 685, 708 (1925).
96. *The Federal Securities Act*, 8 FORTUNE 53, 55 (Aug. 1933).
97. The Public and Its Government 50 (1930).
98. *Advisory Opinions (National)*, 1 Enc. Soc. Sci. 475, 478 (1930).
99. (With Adrian S. Fisher) *The Business of the Supreme Court at the Oct. Terms, 1935 and 1936*, 51 HARV. L. REV. 577, 623 (1938).
100. They include a full-fledged massive attack on the FELA jurisdiction, 46 HARV. L. REV. 226, 240 *et seq.* (1932).
101. *Book Review*, 32 COLUM. L. REV. 920, 922 (1932).
102. *The Federal Courts*, 58 NEW REPUBLIC 273, 274 (Apr. 24, 1929).

103. *Distribution of Judicial Power Between United States and State Courts*, 13 CORN. L.Q. 499 (1928).

104. 346 U.S. 273, 301 (1953).

105. 268 U.S. 510 (1925).

106. L and P 195–197.

107. *The Law and the Law Schools*, 40 A.B.A. Rep. 365, 371 (1915).

108. 2 Howe, Justice Oliver Wendell Holmes 63 (1963).

109. *Id.*, at 157.

110. *Supra* n. 51.

111. *Supra* n. 48.

112. *Reconstruction and the Law*, N.H.B.A. Pro. 73, 81 (1932–1933).

113. (With James M. Landis) *Power of Congress Over Procedure in Criminal Contempts in "Inferior" Federal Courts*, 37 HARV. L. REV. 1010, 1018 (1924).

114. *Id.*, at 1010, n. 3.

115. L and P 231, 237.

116. *Id.*, at 236.

117. See Freund, Sutherland, Howe and Brown, Constitutional Law —Cases and Other Problems v (1st ed., 1954).

118. P. vii.

119. L and P 220.

120. *Id.*, at 241.

121. *Id.*, at 246.

122. *Id.*, at 328.

123. *The Enforcement of Prohibition*, 33 NEW REPUBLIC 149, 150 (Jan. 3, 1923).

124. The Public and Its Government 34 (1930).

Themes in United States Legal History,
James Willard Hurst

1. *Cf.* Frankfurter, *Book Review*, 45 HARV. L. REV. 1433 (1932).

2. Felix Frankfurter Reminisces 189 (Harlan B. Phillips ed., 1960). See also Frankfurter, *The Young Men Go to Washington*, 14 FORTUNE 61 (1936), reprinted in Law and Politics: Occasional Pa-

pers of Felix Frankfurter, 1913–1938, 238, 240 (MacLeish and Prichard eds., 1939).

3. Frankfurter and Landis, The Business of the Supreme Court (1927).

4. Frankfurter, *Supreme Court, United States,* in 14 Enc. Soc. Sci. 474, 476 (1934), reprinted in Law and Politics 21, 25 (1939). *Cf.* Frankfurter, Introduction to Criminal Justice in Cleveland, ix (1922).

5. Quoted in Frankfurter, *The Young Men Go to Washington,* 14 FORTUNE 61, 63 (1936), reprinted in Law and Politics 238, 246 (1939); and in Frankfurter, *The Shape of Things to Come,* 27 SURVEY GRAPHIC 5, 6 (1938), reprinted in Law and Politics 345, 352 (1939). See Also Frankfurter, The Public and Its Government 49 (1930). The observation by Johnson, J., will be found in his opinion for the Court in Anderson v. Dunn, 6 Wheat. 204, 226 (U.S. 1821).

6. Frankfurter, *Mr. Justice Brandeis and the Constitution,* 45 HARV. L. REV. 33, 105 (1931), reprinted in Mr. Justice Brandeis 47, 124 (Frankfurter ed., 1932), and in Law and Politics 113, 126 (1939).

7. Frankfurter, The Public and Its Government 8 (1930).

8. *Id.,* 23.

9. Frankfurter, The Commerce Clause Under Marshall, Taney and Waite 2 (1937).

10. Frankfurter, *Law and Order,* 9 YALE REV. 225, 236 (1920), reprinted in Law and Politics 211, 217 (1939).

11. Frankfurter, *Why I Shall Vote for La Follette,* 40 NEW REPUBLIC 199 (1924), reprinted in Law and Politics 314 (1939).

12. Frankfurter, *Herbert Croly and American Political Opinion,* 63 NEW REPUBLIC 247 (1930), reprinted in Law and Politics 305, 307 (1939).

13. Frankfurter, *The Task of Administrative Law,* 75 U. PA. L. REV. 614, 618 (1927), reprinted in Law and Politics 231, 235 (1939).

14. Frankfurter, *The Shape of Things to Come,* 27 SURVEY GRAPHIC 5, 6 (1938), reprinted in Law and Politics 345, 347 (1939).

15. Frankfurter, *The Zeitgeist and the Judiciary,* 29 THE SURVEY 542, 543 (1913), reprinted in Law and Politics 3, 6 (1939).

16. Frankfurter, *Brandeis,* 6 NEW REPUBLIC 4, 5 (1916), reprinted in Law and Politics 108, 110 (1939).

17. Frankfurter, *Mr. Justice Brandeis and the Constitution,* 45 HARV.

L. Rev. 33, 37 (1931), reprinted in Mr. Justice Brandeis 47, 52 (Frankfurter ed., 1932), and in Law and Politics 113, 116 (1939).

18. Frankfurter and Landis, The Business of the Supreme Court (1927); Frankfurter, The Public and Its Government (1930); Frankfurter and Katz, Cases and Other Authorities on Federal Jurisdiction and Procedure (1931); Frankfurter and Davison, Cases and Other Materials on Administrative Law (1932).

19. Frankfurter, The Public and Its Government 77 (1930).

20. Frankfurter, *Foreword* to *A Symposium on Administrative Law,* 47 Yale L. J. 515 (1938).

21. Frankfurter and Landis, The Business of the Supreme Court 86 (1927).

22. Frankfurter, *Introduction* to *A Symposium on Administrative Law Based Upon Legal Writings 1931–1933,* 18 Ia. L. Rev. 129, 130 (1933).

23. Frankfurter, The Public and Its Government 10 (1930).

24. Frankfurter, *Mr. Justice Brandeis and the Constitution,* 45 Harv. L. Rev. 33, 41 (1931), reprinted in Mr. Justice Brandeis 47, 56 (Frankfurter ed., 1932); and in Law and Politics 117–118 (1939).

25. Frankfurter, *Mr. Justice Cardozo and Public Law,* 52 Harv. L. Rev. 440, 446 (1939), reprinted in Law and Politics 88, 92–93 (1939).

26. Frankfurter, *Mr. Justice Brandeis and the Constitution,* 45 Harv. L. Rev. 33, 50, reprinted in Mr. Justice Brandeis 47, 65 (Frankfurter ed., 1932), and in Law and Politics 118–119 (1939).

27. Frankfurter, The Public and Its Government 10–31 (1930).

28. *Id.,* 72.

29. *Id.,* 113.

30. Frankfurter and Corcoran, *Petty Federal Offenses and the Constitutional Guaranty of Trial by Jury,* 39 Harv. L. Rev. 917, 919 (1926).

31. Frankfurter and Landis, The Business of the Supreme Court 217 (1927).

32. Frankfurter, *Foreword* to Jennings, *Courts and Administrative Law,* 49 Harv. L. Rev. 426 (1936); and *Foreword* to *A Symposium on Administrative Law,* 47 Yale L.J. 515, 518a (1938).

33. Frankfurter, *Why I Am for Smith,* 56 New Republic 292, 293 (1928), reprinted in Law and Politics 320, 321 (1939).

34. Frankfurter, *The Task of Administrative Law,* 75 U. Pa. L. Rev. 614 (1927), reprinted in Law and Politics 231 (1939).

35. *Id.*, 617, and Law and Politics 234 (1939).
36. Frankfurter and Landis, The Business of the Supreme Court 217 (1927); Frankfurter, *Distribution of Judicial Power Between United States and State Courts*, 13 CORN. L.Q. 499, 506 (1928); Frankfurter, The Public and Its Government 8, 29, 48–49 (1930).
37. Frankfurter, *Foreword* to Jennings, *Courts and Administrative Law*, 49 HARV. L. REV. 426, 428 (1936).
38. Frankfurter, The Case of Sacco and Vanzetti (1927).
39. Frankfurter and Hart, *The Business of the Supreme Court at Oct. Term, 1934*, 49 HARV. L. REV. 68, 98 (1935).
40. *Ibid.*
41. Frankfurter, *Foreword* to *A Symposium on Administrative Law*, 47 YALE L.J. 515 (1938).
42. Frankfurter, *Introduction* to Criminal Justice in Cleveland, vi (1922).
43. *Id.*, vii.
44. *Id.*, ix.
45. Frankfurter, *The Supreme Court Writes a Chapter on Man's Rights*, New York *Times*, Nov. 13, 1932, Sec. 2, 1:8, 2:1, reprinted in Law and Politics 189, 194 (1939).
46. Frankfurter and Greene, *The Labor Injunction*, 8 Enc. Soc. Sci. 653, 654 (1932), reprinted in Law and Politics 222, 223 (1939). Compare, by the same authors, The Labor Injunction 49, 65, 76–77, 200, 202 (1930).
47. Frankfurter, *Press Censorship by Judicial Construction*, 26 NEW REPUBLIC 123, 125 (1921), reprinted in Law and Politics 129, 133 (1939).
48. Frankfurter and Landis, The Business of the Supreme Court vi (1927); *cf. id.*, 2.
49. Frankfurter, The Commerce Clause Under Marshall, Taney and Waite 22 (1937). Compare the criticisms of Waite, C.J., for his "total want of style," *id.*, 76, 79, 102.
50. Frankfurter, Mr. Justice Holmes and the Supreme Court 24–25 (1938).
51. Frankfurter, *Supreme Court, United States*, in 14 Enc. Soc. Sci. 474, 481 (1934), reprinted in Law and Politics 21, 31, 32 (1939).
52. Frankfurter, *Herbert Croly and American Political Opinion*, 63 NEW REPUBLIC 247 (1930), reprinted in Law and Politics 305, 307 (1939).
53. Frankfurter, *The Task of Administrative Law*, 75 U. PA. L.

Rev. 614, 618 (1927), reprinted in Law and Politics 231, 235 (1939).
54. From the dedication to Mr. Justice Brandeis, in Frankfurter and Greene, The Labor Injunction (1930).
55. Frankfurter, *Mr. Justice Cardozo and Public Law*, 52 Harv. L. Rev. 440, 465 (1939), reprinted in Law and Politics 88, 99 (1939); and *Mr. Justice Brandeis and the Constitution*, 45 Harv. L. Rev. 33, 78–79, reprinted in Mr. Justice Brandeis 47, 96 (Frankfurter ed., 1932), and Law and Politics, 113, 120 (1939).
56. Frankfurter, *Distribution of Judicial Power Between United States and State Courts*, 13 Corn. L.Q. 499, 506 (1928).
57. Frankfurter, The Public and Its Government 2 (1930). Compare Frankfurter, *The Shape of Things to Come*, 27 Survey Graphic 5, 6 (1938), reprinted in Law and Politics 345, 347 (1939).
58. Frankfurter, The Public and Its Government 85 (1930).
59. Frankfurter, *Law and Order*, 9 Yale Rev. 225, 233 (1920), reprinted in Law and Politics 211, 215 (1939).
60. Frankfurter, *What We Confront in American Life*, 22 Survey Graphic 133, 134 (1933), reprinted in Law and Politics 334, 335, 336 (1939).
61. Frankfurter, *The Shape of Things to Come*, 27 Survey Graphic 5, 7 (1938), reprinted in Law and Politics 345, 350–351 (1939).
62. Frankfurter, *Herbert Croly and American Political Opinion*, 63 New Republic 247 (1930), reprinted in Law and Politics 305, 308 (1939).
63. Frankfurter, *Why I Am for Smith*, 56 New Republic 292, 293 (1928), reprinted in Law and Politics 320, 324 (1939).